Endorsements

Without a doubt, Barbara De Simon has written a treasure with this book, and released a tremendous gift to us as she clarifies the absoluteness of God's healing love both from a biblical perspective as well from her personal experiences of walking out the reality of healing and restoration in her own life.

I am excited, along with her (as she writes in her Foreword), about "how your life will change as you apply the strategies in this book. So, without delay, let's discover how we can get into the flow of God's mercy, power, and grace over EVERY aspect of our being—spirit, soul, and body, and not miss a thing God has for us in this life."

Simply put, if we take them seriously, Barbara's insights on eliminating blockages will prove to be invaluable in maturing us as people of the Kingdom.

Mary Audrey Raycroft
Teaching Pastor, Catch the Fire, Toronto, Ontario
Author, Itinerant Speaker and Founder of Releasers of Life Equipping Ministry

I know and respect Barbara De Simon. She has published several books I have written and has been a valuable help to me. Barbara is stirred by the love and compassion of Jesus. She wants others to see Jesus as active in their lives as He has been in hers. *Position Yourself for Healing* is born out of her love for God, gratefulness for what He has done for her, and compassion for those who need His touch.

A powerful truth is highlighted through the Gospels and the book of Acts. Love and compassion are the hinge upon which the door of miracles hang. When Jesus and His followers saw people in distress, their compassion stirred them to partner with the Father in doing what He was doing and speaking what He was speaking. Such compassion, mixed with faith, led to outstanding healings: the blind received their sight, the deaf heard, the lame walked, the woman bent over by a spirit of infirmity immediately felt her spine straighten. Another woman had spent years and all her money on physicians without getting better. Jesus' love and compassion stirred faith and she received healing. Simon Peter's mother-in-law was healed so quickly she got up and prepared a meal for her guests. Lepers were cleansed, a boy was delivered of a deaf and mute spirit, and the man with a legion of demons, who no one had been able to help was set free. Miracles abound on the hinge of compassion!

It is the love and compassion of Jesus that stirs Barbara to minister to the sick, release freedom to captives, and bind up the wounds of the broken hearted. It is compassion that moved her to write this book and make it available to those who want to do what Jesus did, and even greater things than these, because He has gone to the Father.

On occasion, Jesus and His followers were so moved by compassion for mourners, they raised their dead to life—a mother's son, Dorcas whose friends gathered in her house and mourned her passing, and Mary and Martha's brother, Lazarus. The shortest verse of the Bible simply says, "Jesus wept" (John 11:36). Perhaps He wept not only from the grief He shared with Mary and Martha, but because He was calling Lazarus back to this world, knowing Lazarus would face persecution from the religious and would die again. I wonder if Jesus reflected on how He personally left the splendour of heaven when He entered this sin-sick world. Lazarus, like Jesus, was persecuted by those who

ENDORSEMENTS

had a form of religion but tried to squelch the power thereof. It is rumored that Lazarus never smiled again after being raised from the dead.

As I opened my computer and scanned *Position Yourself for Healing*, I yearned to have the book in my hands so I could take notes and highlight things we will incorporate in our ministry of healing and deliverance. The first part of the book gives a necessary foundation for receiving and/or ministering healing. Part II, *Eliminating Blockages*, reveals powerful truths to help those seeking healing and those ministering healing so they can remove every obstacle hindering the healing they seek. I wholeheartedly recommend Barbara De Simon and her newest book!

Dr. Douglas Carr
www.dcfreedomministry.com

Barbara's book, *Position Yourself for Healing*, fully demonstrates God's desire and grace upon our lives to take us into healing and wholeness. Regardless of the difficult situations of life we have been through, God is able to take every intended curse and turn it into a wonderful blessing. This book will help you to find the place to hope again, even in the midst of any negative situation. Read, enjoy, and receive the healing power of the Lord in your life that leads into victory and freedom.

Faith Marie Baczko, Author, Speaker, and President
Headstone Ministries

POSITION *Yourself* for HEALING

Finding the Sweet Spot Where
Healing Becomes Reality

BARBARA DE SIMON

© 2022 by Barbara De Simon

Published in Windsor, Ontario, Canada, by ROOTED Publishing (www.rootedpublishing.com).

All rights reserved. This book is protected by the copyright laws of the United States of America. No part of this publication may be reproduced, stored in a retrieval system, or transmitted in any form or by any means—electronic, mechanical, photocopy, recording or any other—except for brief quotations, without prior permission of the author.

This book is not intended as a substitute for the medical advice of physicians, registered counsellors, therapists or any other professional. The reader alone is responsible to seek the help of a professional when needed, at their discretion.

Scripture quotations identified NIV® are from the New International Version®. Copyright © 1973, 1978, 1984, 2011 by Biblica, Inc. ™ Used by permission. All rights reserved worldwide.

Scripture quotations identified NKJV are from the New King James Version®. Copyright © 1982 by Thomas Nelson, Inc. Used by permission. All rights reserved.

Scripture quotations marked NASB are from the New American Standard Bible. Copyright © 1960, 1962, 1963, 1968, 1971, 1972, 1973, 1975, 1977 by the Lockman foundation. Used by permission.

Scripture quotations marked NLT are taken from the Holy Bible, New Living Translation, copyright 1996, 2004.

Scripture quotations marked AMP are taken from The AMPLIFIED Bible, Copyright © 1954, 1958, 1962, 1964, 1965, 1987, 2015 by The Lockman Foundation. All rights reserved. Used by permission. (www.Lockman.org)

Cover design by ROOTED Publishing

ISBN: 978-1-7774720-5-4

POSTION
Yourself
FOR
HEALING

DEDICATION

It is with a grateful heart that I dedicate this book to my late parents, Ella May and Victor Faulkner. I honor you and thank you for who you were—always doing the best you knew how. Thank you for teaching me Who my Heavenly Father was and still is; it has been the bedrock of my life and has enabled me to stand firm and never waver in the truth that God is love and God is good. Praise to His name! The Lord is ALWAYS for me, not against me. His will and purposes are always for my benefit. Thank you, mom and dad. Rest in peace with Jesus.

TABLE OF CONTENTS

Author's Foreword... xiii
Introduction... xix
1. Passover... 1
2. Out of the Box... 9
3. Going Back to Go Forward... 23
4. Foundations... 33
5. Authority... 57
6. Praise and Worship... 81
7. Living by the Spirit... 89
8. The Lord's Supper... 105

PART II ~ ELIMINATING BLOCKAGES

Blockages... 113
The Religious Spirit or Mindset... 122
Anger and Forgiveness... 132
Idolatry... 148
Iniquity... 160
Words and Power... 175
Body Perspective... 186
Repressed Emotions... 194
Injustice... 200
Shame and Self-Hate/Rejection... 203
The Orphan Spirit or Mindset... 207
False Religions and Secret Societies... 217
Final Thoughts... 228
Appendix A ~ Roadmap to Healing Digestive Issues... 231
Appendix B ~ Healing Scriptures... 244
About the Author... 245
Bibliography... 247

Author's Foreword

I can't think of any better way to begin this labour of love than with the following scripture:

> "If I could speak all the languages of earth and of angels, but didn't love others, I would only be a noisy gong or a clanging cymbal. If I had the gift of prophecy, and if I understood all of God's secret plans and possessed all knowledge, and if I had such faith that I could move mountains, but didn't love others, I would be nothing. If I gave everything I have to the poor and even sacrificed my body, I could boast about it; but if I didn't love others, I would have gained nothing. Love is patient and kind. Love is not jealous or boastful or proud or rude. It does not demand its own way. It is not irritable, and it keeps no record of being wronged. It does not rejoice about injustice but rejoices whenever the truth wins out. Love never gives up, never loses faith, is always hopeful, and endures through every circumstance. Prophecy and speaking in unknown languages and special knowledge will become useless. But love will last forever! Now our knowledge is partial and incomplete, and even the gift of prophecy reveals only part of the whole picture! But when the time of perfection comes, these partial things will become useless. When I was a child, I spoke and thought and reasoned as a child. But when I grew up, I put away childish things. Now we see things imperfectly, like puzzling reflections in a mirror, but then we will see everything with perfect clarity. All that I know now is partial and incomplete, but then I will know everything completely, just as God now knows me

completely. Three things will last forever—faith, hope, and love—and the greatest of these is love" (1 Corinthians 13 NLT).

This says it all, doesn't it? Although we are able to prophecy and speak in tongues, it is only in part AND although they are both valuable, it is more important to love—to begin with love, to love through, and to end with love being at the forefront of our mind and heart. With love being the goal, let us put childish things away and grow up in the Lord and in His truth, accepting His revelation according to the Holy Spirit.

In these days of confusion and tolerance, it is crucial to know what love is and what it is not. In the world, love seems to require the acceptance of ALL things and ALL behaviors and has an expectation of agreement from everyone, on every matter. If I don't agree with someone, it is seen as hate. But this is not a biblical understanding of love. Although love is patient, kind, and does not dishonor others, it also rejoices with the truth and will protect others no matter the cost.

If I saw that a person was about to cross the street in front of a speeding car, I would intervene. I would stop them! Obviously, it wouldn't be love for me to just stand by as they get hit by a car! On a lighter note, if a woman is about to exit a public restroom with toilet paper stuck to the bottom of her shoe, I stop her and tell her! Even if it's a stranger. It might embarrass her FOR A MOMENT, but it's much better than the ongoing humiliation she would suffer if I ignored it.

In the same way, if I experience breakthrough in my life and the Lord reveals a key that others can also use, it is not love for me to keep it to myself. And if the Lord puts a word on my heart that could bring healing to someone, I'm going to share it, gently, for redemptive purposes, even if there is a possibility it won't be received; my ego or feelings are of no consequence when it comes to someone else's wellbeing. I would rather speak and be rejected than not speak at all.

Ephesians 4:11-16 tells us that Christ has given the church, apostles, prophets, evangelists, pastors, and teachers to equip God's people to do the work of the Kingdom and to build up the body of Christ until we ALL come into unity of the faith and of the knowledge of Jesus, being made perfect, growing up into the fullness of Christ. This is accomplished by speaking the truth in love, NOT by speaking easy words, comfortable words or words that tickle the ears, but TRUTH IN LOVE. Truth can be hard to hear, but love speaks it anyway. Love is not always ooey, gooey, dripping with sentiment, but can be tough at times, necessary, but also life giving and redemptive. Speaking "in love" isn't about the tone of our voice, it is about having love in our heart for the person we are speaking with (thank you to Dr. Bernardine Daniels for that nugget of truth).

So often when a person speaks truth, it can come from a place of annoyance or judgement, but this is when we need to be silent. It is not for us to speak truth when our heart is not right. Only when our heart is full of love for an individual should we speak; only then are our words seasoned the right way, in the power of God and able to bring about transformation.

All the challenges addressed in this book I have had to work through myself, with God. I am no stranger to adversity in various forms and I am still a work in progress, but I am submitted to the One Who redeems it all—who makes beautiful, NEW things out of broken pieces. I don't write this book because I'm perfect or have all the answers; I write this book because God has put a love for people in my heart and a passion to see the fullness of Christ's resurrection power made manifest in my life and the lives of others.

Having said that, here's your first tough love truth: As true followers and disciples of Christ, when we don't experience ALL

Christ died to give us (complete salvation including the healing of our soul and body), the deficit is not on God's end. The deficit is on our end, *possibly* in our life, *perhaps* in our heart, or our mind, but DEFINITELY at minimum, in this world. When that happens, we must CONTEND for what is rightfully ours. How we contend is the subject matter of this book.

Have you ever just tolerated something like a minor physical or emotional issue that just kind of wore you down, until finally, one day, you rose up and said, "enough is enough?" I have.

I felt like Eeyore from Winnie the Pooh—always with a dark cloud over my head, never really feeling successful and always sensing unfortunate events coming my way. I knew these feelings were not in line with who I was as a daughter of God, and I had prayed and dealt with what I knew was tied to it, but finally one day, as this gloom persisted, I kind of snapped (in a good way). I finally decided I wasn't going to tolerate it anymore and I allowed myself to express the deep exasperation I felt about it, in prayer.

With this familiar darkness hovering, I began to make my way to the clinic for blood work. Again, I was getting blood drawn for a cholesterol test and I wasn't happy about it. The doctor just wouldn't let up. I had no other markers for potential heart problems. My blood pressure was fine. I didn't smoke. But I was in my fifties and my family history was riddled with red flags. So, there I was again. All the numbers indicated high cholesterol despite what I did with my diet and exercise, and I was fed up with the doctor's pressure to take medication.

As I drove, I prayed with fervour. I prayed LOUDLY, fully persuaded of my words and in full agreement with them. First, I praised God for Who He is, and I declared the finished work of Christ on my behalf. I declared who I am in Jesus, and I let the devil know his time was up. I COMMANDED all curses to be broken and all familiar spirits to leave me alone, in Jesus' name.

AUTHOR'S FOREWORD

I got my sword out and I fought the good fight with the truth, clearing the atmosphere around me. . . What happened next changed me. What happened next shifted my entire life; the presence of the Lord God Almighty fell in my car like I've never experienced before.

I pulled over to park by the curb as the Glory of God fell and hung in the air, thick like honey. I was grateful the Lord waited until I was almost parked as I literally became afraid to move. I was frozen. Hands out, head bowed, hot tears leaking from my eyes, my mouth whispering prayers in a heavenly language, taking Him in. Loving Him. Loving Him, loving me. Completely overtaken by His goodness and kind of in shock as I had never experienced His presence with such intensity. It turns out, when we take a bold stand for Jesus—for all He died to give us—for righteousness and for ourselves to live in God's fullness, heaven manifests in the here and now and we're never the same. From that day forward, I never felt that dark cloud looming over me again. All praise and glory to our saviour and best friend, Jesus.

So, I begin "Position Yourself for Healing" in a posture of love and in "the love of Christ" before you, and I encourage you to reject any and all false guilt and condemnation that might want to come against you as you read (it is not coming from me or my words). There is NO condemnation in my heart or my intent with this book, only love, encouragement, and exhortation to enter into a FULL gospel according to the scriptures and God's heart for you. There's work to do in this world. Every disciple of Jesus has a purpose for God, and we must be well enough, emotionally and physically, to fulfill it.

In a world where evil exists and lives, we MUST CONTEND for heaven to manifest in our midst and in our body. It is not an easy road. It is a road of standing and then standing some more, just as Ephesians 6:10-18 outlines, as we submit to God and resist evil. Our battle is not against flesh and blood but against evil rulers and unseen powers in the earthly realm and atmosphere. We don't fight for victory, we fight FROM victory, enforcing the truth and the reality of it, in our lives.

I'm excited about how your life will change as you apply the strategies in this book. So, without further delay, let's discover how we can get into the flow of God's mercy, power, and grace over EVERY aspect of our being, spirit, soul, and body, and not miss a thing God has for us in this life. Let's take a deep dive together!

Introduction

It's a confusing time. Currently, as I write this, it's early in the year 2022, and we've been in a pandemic for two full years. Many have sadly lost loved ones. Many have prayed their hearts out for healing for their loved ones but did not see what they had hoped for. If you've lost a loved one, I'm so very sorry; you have suffered a great injustice. In addition to losing your loved one, you were likely separated from them in their last days, and this should not have been. I pray for the comfort of Holy Spirit to surround you and for new strength to come back into your heart.

I believe in faith that even right now, God is causing evil agendas to be exposed, undone, and overturned and that soon, the leadership of Canada and the United States will return to the Lord and righteousness, becoming strong witnesses to the rest of the world. Until then, let us seek the Lord, be strengthened, and healed so we are ready and equipped to fulfill our assignment on the earth, bringing in the greatest harvest of souls ever known. It is imperative now, as never before, for God's people to rise up and overcome the maladies trying to confine them.

In addition to what we've endured over the last two years, humanity continues to contend with MANY other health conditions that threaten to hold us hostage and sometimes cut the number of our days short. Praying for and experiencing healing of these things for ourselves and others has been elusive; sometimes we have won and sometimes we have lost. I have been on both sides of the contention; I have prayed for myself and been healed, AND I have prayed for myself and NOT been healed... YET. I have prayed for others and seen healing. I have also prayed for others and not seen healing—at least how I had hoped. I had that experience just a few days ago and am finding myself fighting off discouragement to remain in truth.

If you're an intercessor, someone who is drawn to come alongside others to pray and declare the truth of God's Word on their behalf, perhaps you have also been tempted to feel disappointed, but let me just say this: praying for someone else is a whole lot different than praying for yourself. Why? I think several reasons but one that has stuck with me is, simply put, we KNOW what WE want, but we don't always know what others want—not REALLY anyway. Sometimes (now don't shoot the messenger), WE want healing for someone else MORE than they want it for themselves. SOMETIMES this affects outcomes, but nothing is black and white here. We want our loved one healed because we don't want them to leave us, but it is possible that once our loved one gets a glimpse of heaven, they would rather cross over and remain there, rather than be in this world a minute longer. The perspective of the one who is considering the possibility of finally being home with Jesus IS a lot different than the perspective of the one about to lose their loved one. For the one crossing over, being home with Jesus is the greatest healing possible.

There is a reason why Jesus asked the man at the Pool of Bethesda, "Do you *want* to get well?" (John 5:6b NIV, emphasis mine). Sometimes people don't want to be healed here on earth—perhaps because they're weary of this fallen world or a difficult life, or because they just really love Jesus, and heaven is so inviting. Other times, unfortunately, people can even have a strange sense of heroism or martyrdom in enduring illness and dying early. And even other times people have become accustomed to their maladies, and their maladies have become part of who they are. Regardless of the reasons, we will not experience healing here on earth if we first do not desire it—no matter who is praying for us.

INTRODUCTION

Of course, a lack of desire is not the only reason for not seeing the miracle we want in others; there could be other reasons, but we don't always know what they are. God's ways are higher than ours and there are some things we won't understand until we get to heaven. This beautiful relationship we have with God requires faith and trust in Him, believing that in ALL things, God works for the good of those who love Him. What the enemy intends to use to harm, God takes in His hands and says, "NO! She (he) is mine! I will redeem it. I will comfort and restore her (his) heart."

Even though there are still mysteries with God, I do believe, going into the year 2022, we are on the cusp of the greatest outpouring of revelation and glory we have ever seen. The veil between heaven and earth is getting thinner and we will "see" and understand more about the Kingdom of God than we ever have before. Throughout 2022 and 2023, many mysteries will be unveiled, and greater breakthrough will be had by many.

Healing. The whole topic is a bit messy. There can be a whole lot of emotion tied up in it, which makes me just want to avoid the conversation all together because I don't want to offend, but the Lord is not letting me. My heart is compelled by love to reach out to you and every reader, with encouragement, truth, tools, and strategies on living your best life under the protection of Christ, free from chronic illness, disease and strife which comes directly from the evil one. Hopefully you will see and receive that love, throughout these pages.

If there is something you can do or pray that will alleviate your own suffering, don't you want to know what it is? Are you surprised by that possibility? Are you thinking, *but isn't my healing all up to God?* If you thought that, you're not alone, but here's the answer: It's actually not. We participate with God in partnership to bring about our own healing and HOW we participate is the topic of this entire book. So, I implore you, keep reading. Push past your inclination to be offended. Push past your religious rebuttals and allow Holy Spirit to whisper to you; you could find a key that will unlock the healing and divine health you've been looking for.

Welcome to "Position Yourself for Healing." I pray this book delivers revelation so powerful, it ushers in a whole new victory and breakthrough in your life and causes you to remain and abide in TRUE life abundant, just as Jesus promised in John 10:10.[1]

Pull up a chair friend; the table is being set. The Cook in the kitchen has been marinating these words for years and Holy Spirit is all about serving them up to you in such a way that you can and will receive them. Be healed in Jesus' name!

---

[1] "The thief does not come except to steal, and to kill, and to destroy. I have come that they may have life, and that they may have it more abundantly" (John 10:10 NKJV).

Chapter 1

PASSOVER

This book has been on my heart for many years, ever since I re-released my first book, *Barren No More* in 2016. It has taken me five years to finally get these first words down on paper (or on my computer to be exact), not because it's not important, but because it is. It is extremely important. It is vital to many in this hour so they can experience the victory they need, here and now. Many are called to extraordinary assignments but won't be able to achieve them without healing in their mind and body. There has been much resistance in the spirit to me writing this book; even now, there are five other things trying to distract me, but I resolve now, to do as the Lord has called.

My book, *Barren No More*, is a book that contains twenty-one steps to inner healing and deliverance but was written for women/couples going through infertility struggles or a delay in childbearing. In it, I give my testimony of healing and breakthrough in bearing children which had much more to do with heart and emotional issues than physical issues, but as we know, the body's health will follow the health of the soul (inner man/heart) so it's possible my body had an issue, I just never had it diagnosed. (See additional resources: The Deepest Well by Dr. Nadine Burke Harris and Scared Sick by Robin Karr-Morse and Meredith S. Wiley.) For biblical references supporting this truth see Proverbs 14:30, Proverbs 15:13, Proverbs 17:22, Proverbs 18:14, Proverbs 4:23, and Proverbs 23:7.

Today, two days post Easter Sunday (Resurrection Day) and Passover 2021, a year when Easter and Passover coincide perfectly, seems like a great time to begin writing this book for two reasons: Passover and Easter coinciding is a wonderful picture of the Jewish and Christian faiths coming together AND Passover illustrates for us God's heart for healing and deliverance in a powerful way.

Passover is one of the Jewish feasts that God commanded the Israelites to celebrate each year. It's a time of remembrance—a time to recall and honor the first Passover—God's great act of deliverance on behalf of Israel's ancestors who were oppressed, enslaved, and held captive in Egypt. Passover is also a strategic time for us, believers on and in Jesus, to remember and honor Who God really is on our behalf—to bring to the forefront of our mind the desire of God's heart for all His children to be free, walking in deliverance, divine health, and healing.

After generations of enslavement, the God-ordained time of Israel's deliverance had come. God called Moses to stand in His place and become the deliverer for Israel as he stood before the Glory of God in a bush on fire—yet unconsumed. After some convincing, Moses headed to Egypt to fulfill his mission, but for a time, God hardened Pharoah's heart so that he would not allow the Israelites to leave. Pharoah relentlessly refused to let the Israelites go, lasting through 10 plagues, until his own eldest son was taken. Every first-born son and cattle among Egypt perished and became a sign of God's judgement against the Egyptians (Exodus 4-12) for their mistreatment of God's people.

In a great foreshadowing of Jesus' mandate, the Lord provided a way out and a great deliverance for His people through the blood of a spotless lamb applied to the door frames of Israel's homes. The spirit of death which visited every household that fateful night, passed over those who had dipped the hyssop branch and created a blood barrier—a blood streaked, blood dripping down, entryway.

The blood marked their homes. The blood sealed their doors shut to the spirit of death just as now, the blood of Jesus, our spotless Lamb and our Heavenly Father's first-born Son, seals our doors shut to death as well. Indeed, the blood of Jesus still works, completely delivering us from early and eternal death, WHEN WE APPLY IT, to every part of our lives.

For Israel's deliverance to occur, God's people needed a prophet to hear God's voice and specific direction on how to proceed; they needed God's Word in that hour, not their own good ideas or soulish musings. They needed Moses, who was able to communicate with God, face to face, and who was willing to be obedient to God's call on His life. We too need to hear God's voice to know His heart and direction for our own healing and deliverance.

After 430 years, God's hand moved and the time of Israel's oppression in Egypt came to an end. Amidst the details of their mass exodus, the heart of our God and Healer is revealed. Not only were the Israelites set free from slavery—back-breaking work and mistreatment, they were also enabled to plunder Egypt causing them to leave with articles of clothing and objects made of silver and gold. The fear of God fell on the Egyptians and whatever the Israelites asked for, they were willing to give. After the first-born of all the Egyptians died, they must have been very eager to see the Israelites go! Additionally, God promised to keep the Israelites in good health as they submitted to His ways:

> "There the Lord issued a ruling and instruction for them and put them to the test, He said, 'If you listen carefully to the LORD your God and do what is right in his eyes, if you pay attention to his commands and keep all his decrees, I will not bring on you any of the diseases I brought on the Egyptians, for I am the LORD, who heals you" (Exodus 15:25b–26 NIV).

Through forty years in the wilderness, the Israelites' clothes did not wear out and their feet did not swell (Deut. 8:4 NIV). The Lord God fed them with Manna from heaven and met all their needs. It was God's heart to take care of His children in every way, from the top of their heads to the tip of their toes. Unfortunately, the Israelites rebelled against God and yes, God allowed them to feel the consequences of their disobedience, but His heart was and is always for restoration, deliverance, and healing. We see it all throughout the Exodus story.

God wants us to intersect His Glory, His healing stream, so we can be well and healed in every way. God wants us to hear His direction and instruction and heed His Word to experience the manifestation of ALL Jesus died to give us. God has done His part; He has accomplished all He needed to, to heal us completely. Jesus hung on the cross and with His last breath said, "It is finished." Jesus' job of destroying the works of the devil, atoning for our sin, bearing away our sickness and disease, restoring us to the Father, graciously granting to us His health and righteousness was finished and DONE.[2] He needed to do nothing more. The power of sin and death and *everything tied to it*—sickness, weakness and disease was broken; these things no longer have any hold on us (born-again lovers and followers of

---

[2] Colossians 2:13-15, 1 John 3:5&8, 2 Cor. 5:21, 1 Peter 2:24

Jesus), and no longer have any authority in our lives. Romans 8:1-2 says:

> "Therefore, there is now no condemnation for those who are in Christ Jesus, because through Christ Jesus the law of the Spirit who gives life has set you free from the law of sin and death" (NIV).

This verse tells us we are no longer bound to the law which caused us to live in sin, to be dead to God and to remain in a perpetual state of dying, but we have been set free and are now bound to a different law—the law of the Spirit Who gives life. Now, we are empowered to live holy and righteous[3] as we continually receive renewing life from the Spirit, bringing about healing in every aspect of our being. Romans 8:11 says:

> "The Spirit of God, who raised Jesus from the dead, lives in you. And just as God raised Christ Jesus from the dead, he will give life to your mortal bodies by this same Spirit living within you" (NLT).

This is the absolute truth, however, living it and experiencing it takes our surrender and our participation. We are called to put to death the misdeeds of the flesh and live by the Spirit: "For if you live according to the flesh, you will die; but **IF** <u>by the Spirit</u> YOU put to death the misdeeds of the body, you will LIVE" (Romans 8:13 NIV, emphasis mine). "You will live" indicates life abundant, not just a beating heart, but emphatically living true life, actively with FULL vigour and health.[4]

Jesus makes ALL things new (Rev. 21:5), but this is *mostly* a process in our lives and not an instantaneous event at our re-birth. When we are born-again, we are re-born *immediately* in spirit, in fact God's Spirit comes to dwell within us, but our soul

---

[3] "By his divine power, God has given us everything we need for living a godly life" (2 Peter 1:3 NLT).

[4] https://www.blueletterbible.org/lexicon/g2198/kjv/tr/0-1/

and body are not *immediately* regenerated or healed; our soul and body are healed over time *as we submit* to the Lord and invite Holy Spirit to OVERTAKE every aspect of our being. Perhaps a person's re-birth experience is so powerful that their soul is transformed in great measure at the same time, but we can't assume it happens that way for everyone. Our complete transformation is a work of Holy Spirit, and the Lord will re-new us according to His purposes and in His time as we submit to Him.

It is a glorious thing to be renewed by the Lord. As we are willing to allow it, by being in the Spirit and willfully submitting our soul and body to the Spirit, God will encounter us, touch our wounded places, and heal our emotions. He may even give you direction on things to change in the natural to bring about healing in your body. He may instantaneously heal your body, or He may heal you over time as you submit to His direction. Your body may heal simply as a wonderful side effect of having your mind, emotions and heart healed. Either way, Jesus is interested in healing EVERY part of you, including your broken heart, weary soul and your weakened or sick body—after all, He did create EACH part of you with perfect intentions and He wants to see each part of you come back to that same wholeness.

Just as God COMPLETELY liberated the Israelites from ALL oppression connected to Egypt, so He has provided for our COMPLETE liberation from our Egypt, including freedom from sin, sickness, disease, and death (unto hell) through Jesus Christ. Jesus stepped into our world with all its chaos, oppression, and sin, and allowed the weight of all our pain, suffering, illness, disease, and death to fall on Him. Anything we could possibly suffer in this world He suffered and took it upon Himself.[5] Despite the crushing weight of it all, He emerged victorious

---

[5] "This High Priest of ours understands our weaknesses, for he faced all of the same testings we do, yet he did not sin" (Hebrews 4:15 NLT).

offering new life to all who are willing to partake. We can enter in, to that same new life with Christ when we completely surrender our lives to Him and give Him control, dying to ourselves, our wants, our will, and our desires.

If you're asking, "If Jesus took death upon Himself, why are we still experiencing it?" first, I would say, we're not; we aren't experiencing death. Disciples of Christ don't experience death; we experience transition—from one reality to another. We will never taste death which is hell. Even though our flesh and blood—our earthly *tent* shuts down and ceases to function, our inner man, *who we really are*, goes from this world straight to heaven, with Christ, where we will immediately be present with Him in our heavenly body. I am not suggesting that in this world we will never die; our earthly bodies are temporal and will pass away. In this world we are subject to time, so our bodies age, but it is the will of God for us to age gracefully and fulfill the days He has ordained for us on this earth.

Laying hold of these truths and believing them with all our heart is our first step to seeing it manifest in our lives. If we're unsure, we will miss out. Consider James 1:5-8:

> "But if any of you lacks wisdom, let him ask of God, who gives to all generously and without reproach, and it will be given to him. But he must ask in faith WITHOUT ANY DOUBTING, for the one who doubts is like the surf of the sea, driven and tossed by the wind. For that person ought not to expect that he will receive anything from the Lord, being a double-minded man, unstable in all his ways" (NASB, emphasis added).

These verses speak about asking the Lord for wisdom but can be applied to asking the Lord for anything. Asking in faith looks like being FULLY persuaded that you will receive what you ask for; it is believing WITHOUT even a hint of doubt. Doubt and faith do

NOT mix; in fact, doubt nullifies faith. Jesus said in Matthew 21:21-22:

"I tell you the truth, if you have faith AND DON'T DOUBT, you can do things like this and much more. You can even say to this mountain, 'May you be lifted up and thrown into the sea,' and it will happen. You can pray for anything, and if you have faith, you will receive it" (NLT, emphasis added).

So many people believe God CAN heal but they aren't convinced He's willing. Unfortunately, this is enough doubt to cause us to be double-minded, not receiving anything from the Lord. God's Word is clear. We have already been healed by His stripes[6] (the wounds inflicted on Jesus' body), but we MUST *completely* believe it to experience it.

In Matthew 8, a man with leprosy came to Jesus worshipping Him and saying, "Lord, if You are willing, You can make me clean" (Matthew 8:2 NKJV), and Jesus said, "I AM WILLING; be cleansed" (Matthew 8:3 NKJV, emphasis added). The Spirit of Jesus is MORE than willing to heal YOU too, my friend; He is no respecter of persons. In fact, Jesus has already done it. Believe it. KNOW IT, and it will manifest.

Passover was not just for the Israelites. Passover is also for us, the Gentiles, and followers of Jesus Christ; Jesus is our Passover lamb, and His blood still works on our behalf as we apply it to our life, our soul, our body, and every point of entry. Dip the hyssop branch in the blood friend; apply it to the gateways of your life. Plead the blood—declare your innocence in Christ and watch as healing comes like a wave of refreshment and renewal, crashing through your pain, grief, illness, and everything trying to hold you back. Believe it; put your faith behind it and you will see it.

---

[6] "—by whose stripes you were healed" (1 Peter 2:24 NKJV).

Chapter 2

OUT OF THE BOX

The healing power of God shows up in unlikely places—amidst a crowd *imparted* to an inconspicuous woman who had been bleeding for 12 straight years (Mark 5:25-34); a meeting between Jesus and a Greek woman as she fell at His feet, believing in faith that all her daughter needed were crumbs from His table (Mark 7:24-30); a cobblestone street in Israel as Healing Evangelist Todd White ministered to a man who was Muslim,[7] and even a small fishing cottage in northern Ontario as my pre-Christian father successfully positioned himself in the love and mercy of God.

There my father sat on the couch in that cottage—Bible open. Me, young, impressionable, maybe 7 years old or so, taking it all in. I don't remember anything else from that trip, except for the horror of that massive fishing hook jammed right into my father's thumb, straight clear through to the other side,

---

[7] Darren Wilson, *Father of Lights* (WP Films), DVD.

sticking out front to back. Eyes wide, I wasn't sure how he would ever survive such a thing, but after a few days on that couch, praying and reading, he calmly removed that hook from his own thumb, without incident. Perhaps you don't think that's a big deal, but to me, it was a miracle.

    I wonder if you're catching my point. Did you notice? Jesus healed many BEFORE His crucifixion and resurrection. A woman was healed simply by touching Jesus' garment without His prior knowledge or consent, as power was drawn out of Him by her desperation, expectation, and faith—or simply put, the cry of her heart. Jesus healed the daughter of a *Greek* woman after He very outwardly stated He had come first and primarily for the Jews; she could have taken offense, but she chose to remain humble and faithful, shifting the compassion of God in her favor. The healing power of God worked for a Muslim man, and my father who didn't yet believe in the divinity of our risen Christ.[8]

    For years I was under the false thinking that one must first be a follower of Christ to be healed. This simply is not true; being a Christian is not a pre-requisite for healing. In the Bible, Jesus healed many who were not yet His followers. In fact, healing was used as a demonstration to many, for the truth of Jesus' identity and the love of God. Holy Spirit will still do this today. Romans 5:8 says, "But God demonstrates His own love toward us, in that while we were still sinners, Christ died for us" (NKJV). While we were still sinning, still rejecting Him, Christ gave us His all—everything, including healing and His very life. Romans 5:8 could very well say, *while we were still sinners, Christ made healing available to us,* as it is prophesied in Isaiah 53:5 and re-iterated in 1 Peter 2:24, ". . .by His wounds you have been healed" (NIV). While we were still sinners, Christ took the scourging in His own body, so we could be healed in ours.

---

[8] "For in Christ all the fullness of the Deity lives in bodily form..." (Colossians 2:9 NIV).

Healing is indeed part of the redemption package Jesus died, rose again, and ascended for. Jesus Christ is our Saviour, Healer, and Deliverer, providing for us complete restoration of spirit, soul, and body. Just in case you're not convinced, here's Isaiah 53:4, "Surely He has borne our GRIEFS and carried our SORROWS; yet we esteemed Him stricken, smitten by God, and afflicted" (NKJV). The word "griefs" in this verse is translated from a Hebrew word which more accurately means *sickness*.[9] The word "sorrows" is translated from a Hebrew word which more accurately means *pain*.[10] Also, Psalm 103:2-5 makes it clear:

> "Bless the Lord, O my soul, And forget none of His benefits; Who pardons all your iniquities, Who heals all your diseases; Who redeems your life from the pit, Who crowns you with lovingkindness and compassion; Who satisfies your years with good things, So that your youth is renewed like the eagle" (NASB).

Second Corinthians 5:19 says that God reconciles us to Himself through Christ and in the process does *not count our sins against us*. Jesus, as demonstrated with the woman caught in adultery (John 8:1-11), does not condemn us, but sets us free through His love, compassion, and healing.[11] It's the kindness of God that leads us to repentance,[12] not a pointing finger, judgement, or anger. Neither should we hold anyone's sin against them nor look down on them, but we are to love people and be like Jesus to them regardless of their beliefs and/or actions. The mercy of God, healing, forgiveness, reconciliation, and eternal life are available to all to accept as His gift. The Lord

---

[9] Strong's Lexicon: https://biblehub.com/lexicon/isaiah/53-4.htm
[10] Strong's Lexicon: https://biblehub.com/lexicon/isaiah/53-4.htm
[11] "For God did not send His Son into the world to condemn the world, but that the world through Him might be saved" (John 3:17 NKJV).
[12] "...not knowing that the goodness of God leads you to repentance" (Romans 2:4 NKJV)?

in His kindness woos us to Himself, through Holy Spirit, longing and waiting for us to turn to Him—finally surrendering our lives to His Lordship in repentance.

> "The Lord isn't really being slow about his promise, as some people think. No, he is being patient for your sake. He does not want anyone to be destroyed, but wants everyone to repent" (2 Peter 3:9 NLT).

Although throughout these pages I present keys on how to co-operate with God to access healing for yourself, I am in no way saying, "you must jump through all these hoops" to be healed. God is sovereign and He, in His mercy, can cause His love and healing to break through to whomever He chooses, whenever He chooses. Perhaps the love of God will suddenly cause a miracle to happen in your body as you sleep in your bed. Perhaps healing will manifest when you least expect it, however if it doesn't, the keys found in this book may help you access it.

There is a river flowing from the throne of God, full of His healing oil and it falls from heaven to earth like a waterfall. Positioning yourself under that waterfall and in that river is vital and may require an adjustment of some sort—a heart shift, an attitude change, a fresh surrender, a deeper surrender, a look up or a bow down, a new stirring of faith through study and worship, perhaps even a bold declaration that will break oppression and perhaps shift the very trajectory of your life. Only God knows our best move, but He is more than willing, in fact, He is eager to tell us what that is. All we need to do is listen AND HEAR what the Spirit is saying with a humble heart.

The healing power of God has shown up in my own life numerous times, but most recently, quietly in my bedroom as I pled the blood of Jesus over my digestive system, all the way from the top to the bottom, as per the Lord's instruction. For roughly 6 years, I have suffered with severe indigestion, regurgitation, and acid reflux daily. I juggled different diet changes, medications and strategies trying to alleviate the problem, gaining only VERY short-term relief.

A few weeks ago, as I drove home from church, praying for a friend, the Lord downloaded a word of knowledge. I saw in my mind's eye a young boy, crouched and cowering in a corner, afraid and trying to protect himself from the rage spewing against him and I heard in my spirit the word, *terror*. As the pictures were coming, I also understood that terror had taken up residence in that young boy's digestive tract and the Lord said to me, "Plead the blood of Jesus over his digestive tract to heal the damage it has caused."

After I received the word, I resolved to connect with my friend as soon as I could, but I also realized that that same word also applied to me. Just last year, I met with a friend and pastor, Dr. Douglas Carr,[13] for a deliverance appointment, and he identified a spirit of terror in me that had come through abuse. He dealt with it, and I was delivered, so I knew that part was taken care of, but we didn't connect the dots to digestive issues. So, when I recently received the direction from God, I believed Him, and I prayed, pleading the blood of Jesus over every part of my digestive system, declaring the healing power of the blood over any damage caused by the spirit of terror, seeing in my mind's eye the coating of my esophagus, stomach, and intestines with that precious red flow.

I felt the shift immediately. I went through a few days of physical cleansing but was free from indigestion and reflux almost immediately. Now, months later, I am still free from chronic digestive upset. Praise God! The same miracle could

---

[13] Dr. Carr's website is www.dcfreedomministry.com where his resources can be purchased, and upcoming seminars are posted.

happen for anyone willing to exercise their free-will to be delivered from terror and whatever may have opened the door to it (abuse, watching horror movies, or any event or circumstance that caused severe fear). A roadmap to help you is presented in Appendix A. As I contemplated my healing afterward, I realized that I hadn't even "asked" God to heal me as typically we might, and the Lord said to me, "You don't need to; healing is already yours. Just take it."

Healing flowed quite easily in the New Testament. Lepers were touched and made clean. Even some, including Lazarus, were raised from the dead. The Bible says that ALL *who came to Jesus* were healed. Consider the following passages:

> "So the news about Him spread throughout all Syria; and they brought to Him ALL who were sick, those suffering with various diseases and pains, those under the power of demons, and epileptics, paralytics; and He healed them" (Matt. 4:24 AMP, emphasis added).

> "When evening came, they brought to Him many who were under the power of demons; and He cast out the *evil* spirits with a word, and restored to health ALL who were sick [exhibiting His authority as Messiah]," (Matt. 8:16 AMP, emphasis added).

> "Being aware of this, Jesus left there. Many followed Him, and He healed ALL of them [who were sick]," (Matt. 12:15 AMP, emphasis added).

> "And when the men of that place recognized Him, they sent *word* throughout all the surrounding district and brought to Him ALL who were sick; and they begged Him to let them merely touch the fringe

of His robe; and ALL who touched it were perfectly restored" (Matt. 14:35-36 AMP, emphasis added).

We see the word "all" several times in these verses. But does that mean that everyone who was ill was healed? No, it doesn't. It does NOT mean that every sick person was healed, but it does mean Jesus healed all *who came to Him—all who were hungry for it and all who sought Him out.* He never turned anyone away or said, "Oh sorry, you're going to have to stick this one out. Father is trying to teach you something." No. Never. He had compassion on everyone that came to Him. Jesus said in John 10:10, "The thief comes only to steal and kill and destroy; I have come that they may have life, and have it to the full" (NIV). Unfortunately, not everyone believed in the miracles He was doing. Not everyone was willing to put faith in Him. Not everyone could receive nor wanted to and not everyone was open to the truth of Who Jesus was.

Jesus healed a paralyzed man at the pool of Bethesda and His question to the man was, "Do you want to get well" (John 5:6b, NIV)? Seems like a silly question, but apparently it needed to be asked. Why? Perhaps he was used to his condition and wasn't completely motivated to live differently—perhaps he didn't like change—or perhaps Jesus was just trying to stir his faith and expectation. Many others were there by the pool paralyzed, unable to move, but Jesus didn't heal them nor did any of them seek Him for healing. It seems the Father sent Jesus to the pool for the one—the one man who was a Jew perhaps or the one who was chosen by God to play a part in His great story of redemption in that moment.

In addition, there was a time and place where Jesus *couldn't* heal. That place was His hometown of Nazareth. It wasn't that Jesus didn't *want* to heal in that place, he *couldn't*. Have you ever heard of Jesus not being *able* to do something? It seems heretical, doesn't it. What was it that seemed to make the power of God impotent in that place? According to Matthew 13:57, the people took OFFENSE at Jesus. They could not believe that Jesus, the carpenter, the boy that grew up in their own town, could do such things.

> "...And they were [deeply] offended by Him [and their disapproval blinded them to the fact that He was anointed by God as the Messiah]. Jesus said to them, "A prophet is not without honor (respect) except in his hometown and among his relatives and in his own household. And he COULD NOT do a miracle there at all [because of their unbelief] except that He laid His hands on a FEW sick people and healed them" (Mark 6:3-5 AMP, emphasis mine).

What did they struggle to have faith in? Or more accurately, Who? They had no trouble having faith in God; they doubted Jesus. They doubted that such miracles could come through, in their perception, JUST a man, and additionally the hands of someone they *thought* they knew. They had already made their minds up about who Jesus was and He wasn't the One sent by God to be their Messiah. In their eyes, He was not the Son of God. He was just one of the runny-nosed kids from the neighborhood who grew up and came back spouting lofty words, full of pride. They were stuck in their minds on their own fleshly opinions and not able to see the truth.

Many times, Jesus revealed that faith and belief made healing possible. He said, "Your faith has made you well" (Luke 17:19 NIV), "Daughter, your faith has healed you" (Mark 5:34 NIV), "Go,' said Jesus [to Bartimaeus], 'your faith has healed you" (Mark 10:52a NIV, brackets mine), "Go! Let it be done just as you believed it would" (Matthew 8:13 NIV), and "According to your faith let it be done to you" (Matthew 9:29 NIV). Faith is the currency of heaven; it will give you access to all heaven offers, however, faith must be joined with action and not mixed with doubt.

Faith is not only believing that God can
but KNOWING that God WILL.

How does healing come? We can't *physically* see Jesus, track Him down and ask Him to heal us like they did in the Bible, so how does Jesus heal us now? He heals us through the Holy Spirit, which is in fact the same way He healed those in the Bible. The healing power Jesus possessed *while on the earth* was the power of the Holy Spirit in and on Him.

Jesus' ministry began after His baptism in the Jordan and after His time of testing in the wilderness. Through this time, the Holy Spirit came upon Jesus and remained, filling Him, clothing Him, and empowering Him for ministry on earth. Yes, Jesus Christ is God and always has been God (John 1:1-3), but the scriptures are clear that Jesus willingly set His own divinity aside while on earth.

When Jesus was here, He functioned like that of a man only; Jesus did not heal in His own power, but in the power of Holy Spirit. We get this understanding from the following passages. First, Jesus' baptism from Luke 3:21-22:

> "One day when the crowds were being baptized, Jesus himself was baptized. As he was praying, the heavens opened, and the Holy Spirit, in bodily form, descended on him like a dove. And a voice from heaven said, "You are my dearly loved Son, and you bring me great joy" (NLT).

Then right after, in Luke 4:1&2:

> "Then Jesus, FULL OF THE HOLY SPIRIT, returned from the Jordan River. He was led by the Spirit in the wilderness, where he was tempted by the devil for forty days" (NLT, emphasis added).

After His time of testing in the wilderness, the Bible says in Luke 4:14:

> "Then Jesus returned IN THE POWER OF THE SPIRIT to Galilee, and news of Him went out through all the surrounding region" (NKJV, emphasis mine).

Jesus was baptized, FILLED with Holy Spirit, and then EMPOWERED by Holy Spirit after His time of temptation. In John 17:5 just prior to His crucifixion, Jesus prayed, "And now, Father, glorify me in your presence with the glory I had with you before the world began" (NIV). Philippians 2:5-8 gives us a great summary:

> "In your relationships with one another, have the same mindset as Christ Jesus: Who, being in very nature God, did not consider equality with God something to be used to his own advantage; rather, <u>he made himself nothing by taking the very nature of a servant, being made in human likeness</u>. And being found in appearance as a man, <u>he humbled himself</u> by becoming obedient to death—even death on a cross" (NIV, emphasis added)!

Holy Spirit is the Spirit of God and the presence of God on the earth; He is the One that connects us to Heaven. In John 16:7, Jesus says, "But very truly I tell you, it is for your good that I am going away. Unless I go away, the Advocate [Holy Spirit] will not come to you; but if I go, I will send him to you" (NIV, brackets mine). It is better for us to have the Holy Spirit Who is Spirit and accessible everywhere, unlike Jesus Who existed on earth as a limited physical person. Holy Spirit even lives inside us; He's that close!

"But the Advocate, the Holy Spirit, whom the Father will send in my name, will teach you all things and will remind you of everything I have said to you" (John 14:26 NIV). "And if the Spirit of him who raised Jesus from the dead is living in you, he who raised Christ from the dead will also give life to your mortal bodies because of his Spirit who lives in you" (Romans 8:11 NIV). God's power to heal already lives in your body, so if you haven't been healed yet, ask Father God to give you more of His Spirit. Ask Him to fill you continually!

Have you ever tried to top up your gas tank in your car when it was already full? No, neither have I. That would be dumb; gas would spill all over the ground! Our gas tanks were designed to only hold so much. Have you ever over-filled your coffee cup? Absolutely. It's important to get as much goodness in the cup as possible! Right? The problem is though, if you don't drink it black, you may need to dump a bit out to get cream in it. What am I getting at? Well, just as a gas tank and a coffee mug can only hold so much, it's possible we also have a maximum capacity. Perhaps if we want more of Holy Spirit living inside us, we may have to first release some other things to create space for Him to occupy. Something to think about.

Is it possible to be healed in a church service, conference, or revival meeting? Is it possible to be healed as a healing evangelist or pastor lays hands on you and prays? Is it possible to be healed as the elders of the church anoint you with oil and pray the prayer of faith? Is it possible to be healed when you respond to an altar call and receive prayer from a lay minister? Yes, yes, yes, and yes! All of it, YES! Absolutely, many healings have taken place in these situations and circumstances. I have received great emotional healing by responding to altar calls at different churches as well as engaging with the Spirit during worship. Indeed, I would say if you're in need of healing, make it a priority to get to special services and church gatherings as much as you can. However, just as these scenarios can bring healing, so it is just as possible for you to be healed in your own home as you seek the Lord in your own private space and time, within your very own intimate relationship with Christ. Now that is good news!

The love, goodness and power of God is not confined to church buildings, nor is it kept for the spiritual elite, those who you thought were more spiritual or holy than you or those who hold an office or have a title. Healing is not a one-time action of God nor something He does; healing is Who He is. It is part of His character and nature; when you encounter the presence of God, you also encounter healing power.

How can you experience and encounter God's healing power right at home? Well, if you're asking that question, you've picked up the right book! Packed within the next two hundred or so pages, you will receive incredible insight on how to put yourself right smack dab in the middle of the very goodness of God pouring out from His heart to you, which, without a doubt includes the healing of your spirit, soul, and body.

Never doubt that the power of God heals; all we need to do is get into position to receive. Remember the woman with the issue of blood from Mark 5:24-34? She had been bleeding for 12 straight years! She would have been anemic and so very weak, but despite that, she roused herself and ventured out from her home—her safe place—and into a crowd to find Jesus. She just KNEW if she could only touch the tassel of His garment, she would be healed.

In that day, she was seen as "unclean," and no one would have wanted to be near her. She would have been ostracized and rejected, probably living on the outskirts of town. It took great effort and fortitude for her to find Jesus. She pressed through a crowd, pressed through her own insecurities, pushed beyond the opinions of others as well as religious and social boundaries; she was not supposed to be there, but she went anyway. She did not let the expectations of others limit her. She was bold and desperate, so she went after her healing.

Only after relentlessly pursuing Jesus despite the obstacles in front of her, being in His presence and touching the edge of His garment, her bleeding stopped, and she was made whole. Her position to receive healing was out of her comfort zone, past all she thought she knew, past everything she had been taught in the synagogue. Her position for being healed was at the feet of Jesus. Have you ever wondered how she got through the crowd? Surely if someone had seen her, there would have been a riot. No, she got through the crowd undetected and unseen—maybe even on her hands and knees, crawling and scraping her way past everyone.

What about you beloved? Do you want to be healed? Are you willing to do whatever it takes to receive? Healing does not very often come when we are passive, nor does it come when we aren't willing to get "up close and personal" with the Father and/or Spirit of God. As believers, we are invited into an intimate relationship with God—to get "up close and personal," but relationships go both ways and relationships must be nurtured to be maintained and developed. In every relationship, we have a responsibility to do our part. Getting close with God takes a push through the natural realm, our flesh and carnality, false boundaries and sometimes our comfort zone to touch heaven—to enter into the sound and manifestation of healing.

Have you ever thought about what heaven is like? Revelation 21:4 says, "and He will wipe away every tear from their eyes; and there will no longer be any death; there will no longer be any mourning, or crying, or pain; the first things have passed away" (NASB). If there's no death, mourning, crying or pain in heaven, I think it's safe to say there's no sickness, illness, disease, virus, infection, condition, malformity, disfunction, disability, exceptionality, weakness, or infirmity AT ALL. And

Jesus instructed us to call the Kingdom of God into the earth realm and to declare God's perfect will which is in heaven to be done right here on earth as we pray: "Your kingdom come. Your will be done, On earth as it is in heaven" (Matthew 6:10 NASB). If Jesus told us to pray it, it must be possible! It IS possible to experience God's perfect heavenly will right now. Jesus didn't tell us to ASK for it; He told us to declare it. "Your will be done, on earth as it is in heaven," is not a question. It's a statement! It is a statement and declaration made in faith.

Are you ready to believe with everything in you that it is indeed God's will for you to be healed? Are you ready to press through? Are you ready to go beyond yourself, beyond your own understanding and beyond your natural state into the supernatural? If so, let's dive into deep waters and unpack more truth from Holy Spirit.

Chapter 3

GOING BACK TO GO FORWARD

Have you ever been confused about God and His heart for humanity based on the differences between the Old and New Testament? Have you ever felt like God may be schizophrenic—appearing mean and aggressive in the Old, then suddenly soft and forgiving in the New? What's the deal? What happened to God? Did He change or perhaps attend anger management class? All kidding aside, it may help us to understand healing if we understand God and where sickness began in the first place.

I recently had a newly born-again friend struggling with her health ask me questions about whether God caused her to be sick to punish her for the years she wandered away from Him. I have a feeling she's not alone in this, so let's nip this misunderstanding in the bud before we embark on any further study.

First, it's important to point out that there is a huge difference in how God's people were able to relate to God and experience Him in the Old Testament and the New. In the Old Testament, people experienced a lot of judgement from God because of their sin, but in the New Testament, God forged a new covenant of grace with them and us through Jesus because He wanted His mercy and love to win. Thankfully, when we are surrendered to Christ and living our lives "in Christ" or "in the Spirit," Jesus fulfills the requirements of the law (all the commandments to be righteous) on our behalf. Even in the Old Testament, God wanted to be merciful; He wanted to bless His people and have a love relationship with them but couldn't because of their weaknesses and inability to be holy before Him.

God embodies perfectly in His character absolute love, holiness, and righteousness; He always does what's right and good. There is not one ounce of bad or evil in Him. If we think that God is bad in any way, we are misunderstanding Him. Yes, there are times in the Old Testament when we see the judgement of God causing people to be ill and die, but it is not because God is evil and wants to hurt people. These instances come out of another attribute of His character which is linked to righteousness and that is His need for justice. While God is fully and completely love, He is also fully and completely just. He simply cannot let injustice and sin go; if He did, He would not be a good Judge. There must be a consequence for sin. Romans 6:23 says, the wages of sin is death.

Before Jesus and His new covenant of grace, God gave the people His instructions on how to come into His love and blessing. He gave them the 10 commandments and He gave them the "law" on what to do and not to do. God gave Israel ALL His instructions outlined in detail, a lot of which is found in the book of Deuteronomy. Over and over, you will see that the Lord says, "IF YOU DO THIS... THEN IT WILL GO WELL WITH YOU" (see

Deuteronomy 28:1-14 as an example). He also clearly warns the people of what will happen if they don't obey Him (see Deuteronomy 28:15-68). Again, not because He is mean, but because He is a holy God and must be a good and righteous Judge. Second Chronicles 7:13-14 is a great example:

> "When I shut up the heavens so that there is no rain, or command locusts to devour the land or send a plague among my people, if my people, who are called by my name, will humble themselves and pray and seek my face and turn from their wicked ways, then I will hear from heaven, and I will forgive their sin and will heal their land" (NIV).

God wanted to be merciful so He tells the people how they can access healing: humble yourself, pray, seek God's face, and turn from wicked ways (repent).

When people had trouble in the Old Testament, it was a consequence to their actions, rather than a mean vengeful God acting out against them. He told Adam and Eve, eat from all the trees of the garden except for one, for if you do, you will die. God simply told them, "This is how it is. If you eat of this tree, you will die" (paraphrased).

God created the heavens and the earth. He set up and put into motion all the laws of nature AND all the spiritual laws, like sowing and reaping, that would affect all the people of the earth. God knew that if Adam and Eve ate from the tree of the knowledge of good and evil, their understanding would be opened to evil, and they would know things they were not created to know nor could handle, so He warned them. Unfortunately, Adam and Eve were deceived by the snake in the garden, and they doubted what God told them. They chose to believe the lie of the enemy—that God was withholding something good from them—and they reaped the consequences of their disobedience to God. They died, spiritually, just as God told them they would, and that same "fall" became the doorway through which all sickness and disease would come. (Note: Dying spiritually means you become dead to and separated from God.)

Even in the Old Testament, God desired relationship with His people. God walked in the garden with Adam and Eve but because of their disobedience, God had to banish them from the garden and was forced to strip them of privileges and blessing. It wasn't what God wanted, but something He had to do because He is holy, a righteous Judge, and because He knew how best to protect Adam and Eve; God knew that if He allowed Adam and Eve to remain in the Garden, they would partake of the Tree of Life in their fallen state and remain "fallen" forever (Gen. 3-22-23). Unfortunately, all throughout the Old Testament we see the same disobedience to God that Adam and Eve began; we see a pattern of dishonor, idol worship and not following God's laws and ordinances.

If a parent warns their child, "Don't touch the stove or you will be burned," and the child touches the stove, do we blame the parent for the child's inevitable suffering? Do we think, *what a mean parent*? No. The parent warned the child and did everything in his/her power to lead the child so they wouldn't suffer, but the child used his/her own free-will and made a bad choice. Now the child suffers with a nasty burn to no fault of the parent. But, to illustrate for you the heart of God in this example, let's imagine for a moment that the child who is burned acknowledges his/her disobedience and repents. The earthly parent has no ability to ease the child's suffering beyond natural remedies, but because God is above all natural laws, His mercy can provide relief. If a disobedient child humbles himself/herself, prays, seeks the Lord with all his/her heart, and turns away from sin, God in His mercy, love and compassion could and very likely would, ease the pain of that burn and cause that burn to heal at a supernatural rate, far faster than it would have in the natural. This is God. This is how God's heart responds to humility, and repentance (a turning away from sin and a willing change of mind, heart, and attitude). You might even say, humility and repentance UNLOCKS the healing power of God that is available to all who believe.

God's heart has always been for His people, always preferring to be compassionate and merciful, to the point that He was willing to sacrifice His very own Son (Who was willing to submit to His Father's will). God in His timing, implemented His plan of salvation, making a way for mankind to live at peace with Him and experience complete freedom from sin and its affects. God made a way to, in effect, cancel the "fall" (the original sin of Adam and Eve) and empower us to live holy in Jesus through the Spirit.

In the OT, they were instructed to slaughter animals for the remission of sin. In the NT, Jesus became the last and ultimate sacrifice for sin. His blood paid the price for the sin of the whole world making it no longer necessary to kill anything else. Jesus was that ultimate sacrifice on our behalf because He was a man, yet he was sinless, and perfect; He had no sin of His own, making Him capable to carry the sin of others.

We used to be slaves to sin. We see it all through the OT; people could not be righteous on their own. Now, God has given us Jesus, Who has taken all our sin away and paid the price to fulfill the justice of God. God's justice has been met through the death of Jesus which means He no longer has to impute His justice on us. Jesus fulfills all the requirements of the law on our behalf. His righteousness has become our righteousness. We stand before God the Father forgiven and righteous, not because of anything we've done but because of what Jesus has done on our behalf. Once we accept that gift, we have the responsibility to live out that righteousness as the Spirit enables us. Philippians 2:12-13 says:

> "Therefore, my dear friends, as you have always obeyed—not only in my presence, but now much more in my absence—continue to work out your salvation with fear and trembling, for it is God who works in you to will and to act in order to fulfill his good purpose" (NIV).

God has also given us His Spirit to live inside us and He gives us the empowerment and ability to choose not to sin (2 Peter 1:3). But even when we slip up, God forgives us when we confess to Him. When our hearts are right, meaning we have given our heart to Christ, we love the Lord God with all our heart, and it is truly our hearts desire to be His child and to please Him, we stand in the mercy of God, which means we do NOT get what we deserve and the grace of God, which means we get what we don't deserve. Now that God's justice has been met through Jesus, He is free to express His love and compassion to us as He has always wanted. We are truly free to be His children and for Him to be our God and our most gracious Heavenly Father.

Have you ever heard the term double jeopardy? There is a clause in the 5th Amendment to the Constitution of the United States called the Double Jeopardy Clause. It prohibits anyone from being prosecuted (doing time or paying the price) twice for the same crime.[14] Well, Jesus paid the price for our crime/sin. The wages of sin is death and Jesus has already died that death on our behalf. Double jeopardy is not allowed. Our sin does not need to be paid for twice! Whatever we have confessed and received forgiveness for, is under the blood of Jesus and we no longer need to suffer consequences for that sin. If the accuser (the devil) is still accusing you of something you've already

---

[14] https://www.law.cornell.edu/wex/double_jeopardy

confessed and ceased, tell him to get lost, in Jesus' name. The devil is a liar and a deceiver. Confession and repentance activate God's forgiveness and pays your debt in full.

The thinking that God is punishing us for our past by putting sickness and disease on us can come from a misunderstanding of the Old Testament and the character of God, but also from an old worldly mindset that has not yet been renewed by the Word. Those who have not yet surrendered their lives to God are still experiencing consequences of sin, but those who God has called to be His, who have surrendered all, are now welcomed to live in the reality of His mercy, grace, and healing. However, it takes a renewing of our mind and prayer to experience it. Mercy and grace can be very foreign to us as we have spent many years living in the world doing things as the world does, trying to earn our way. Our minds must be renewed, out of a worldly mindset into a heavenly one. We must have a revelation of God's mercy and grace and shed our old way of thinking to experience it.

Sometimes, the renewing of our mind takes time. We may not fully grasp all God has done for us nor understand every benefit that is ours (Psalm 103). Unfortunately, this lack of revelation can hold us in a pattern of worldly thinking giving curses and illness an opportunity to continue to operate in our lives. It is therefore very important to renew our mind by reading the New Testament, asking God for understanding and revelation and BELIEVING the Word above all else, even when we don't yet see the manifestation of it. Romans 12:2, "And do not be conformed to this world, but be transformed by the renewing of your mind, that you may prove what *is* that good and acceptable and perfect will of God" (NKJV).

Some of the churches in the New Testament struggled to remain in the truth of the revelation of the Gospel; they seemed to keep sliding back to old thinking and old ways. But the apostles encouraged them to not be deceived again nor return to a yoke of slavery in their minds (Galatians 5:1). In other words, the churches were admonished to not go back to the law but remain in faith and the new covenant. The apostles warned them that if they went back to the old way of thinking, trying to be righteous on their own, they would come under the curse of the law once again. To reiterate, here's Romans 12:2 again but in the New Living Translation: "Don't copy the behavior and customs of this world, but let God transform you into a new person by changing the way you think. Then you will learn to know God's will for you, which is good and pleasing and perfect" (NLT).

It can be even more difficult for some. Some have been taught their whole lives, sometimes by strict, parenting methods, disappointments, and difficulties in life, that they will be punished harshly for bad behavior. Some have been trained by trauma and may have learned some of the following distorted beliefs:

- No one gets anything for free.
- "Get out of jail free" cards don't exist.
- Nothing will ever be handed to them on a "silver platter."
- There's no special treatment.
- Everything must be earned.
- Life is not fair.
- They don't measure up.
- They must look after themselves because no one else will.

Indeed, life in this world has been immensely difficult for some. Open arms, acceptance, and unconditional love can be COMPLETELY foreign, and some can't seem to wrap their minds around it at all. It takes a revelation from God and cataclysmic shift in their thinking to see it and accept it to be true *for themselves*. The good news is that God wants that for everyone—even you, possibly more than you want it. So, hang in there! Revelation of His goodness will come as you are obedient to reading and studying God's Word. The Word will break through, and strongholds of old thinking patterns will be broken by the power of the Spirit as we submit to and CHOOSE to BELIEVE His Word.

Allow me to share with you a few passages from Proverbs that speak about wisdom, understanding and God's (your Father's) instruction. Notice how according to these passages, your Father's Words and instruction will bring long life, protection, prosperity, and divine health to your body:

"My son, if you accept my words and store up my commands within you, turning your ear to wisdom and applying your heart to understanding—indeed, if you call out for insight and cry aloud for understanding, and if you look for it as for silver and search for it as for hidden treasure, then you will understand the fear of the LORD and find the knowledge of God. For the LORD gives wisdom; from his mouth come knowledge and understanding. He holds success in store for the upright, he is a shield to those whose walk is blameless, for he guards the course of the just and protects the way of his faithful ones" (Proverbs 2:1-8 NIV).

"My son, do not forget my teaching, but keep my commands in your heart, for they will prolong your life many years and bring you peace and prosperity. Let love and faithfulness never leave you; bind them around your neck, write them on the tablet of your heart. Then you will win favor and a good name in the sight of God and man. Trust in the LORD with all your heart and lean not on your own understanding; in all your ways submit to him, and he will make your paths straight. Do not be wise in your own eyes; fear the LORD and shun evil. This will bring health to your body and nourishment to your bones" (Proverbs 3:1-8 NIV).

"My child, listen to me and do as I say, and you will have a long, good life. I will teach you wisdom's ways and lead you in straight paths. When you walk, you won't be held back; when you run, you won't stumble. Take hold of my instructions; don't let them go. Guard them, for they are the key to life" (Proverbs 4:10-13 NLT).

"My child, pay attention to what I say. Listen carefully to my words. Don't lose sight of them. Let them penetrate deep into your heart, for they bring life to those who find them, and healing to their whole body" (Proverbs 4:20-22 NLT).

Friends, you can't get any plainer than that. All of God's instruction, His wisdom, knowledge and understanding is for our well-being and good. One of the best things we can do is "take" God's Word everyday by reading it over ourselves, just like we would take medicine. God's Word is healing to our body, mind, will and emotions. You can find a list of healing scriptures in Appendix B. Read them over yourself repeatedly and believe them with all your heart.

Chapter 4

FOUNDATIONS

We all know that building on a firm foundation is vital to the stability and integrity of any structure. In fact, a home that is not built on a firm foundation would not be inhabitable very long and possibly even dangerous to live in. Jesus uses this analogy in Matthew 7:24-27 as He teaches on the importance of obedience to His Word:

> "Anyone who listens to my teaching and follows it is wise, like a person who builds a house on solid rock. Though the rain comes in torrents and the floodwaters rise and the winds beat against that house, it won't collapse because it is built on bedrock. But anyone who hears my teaching and doesn't obey it is foolish, like a person who builds a house on sand. When the rains and floods come and the winds beat against that house, it will collapse with a mighty crash" (Matthew 7:24-27 NLT).

Jesus and our relationship with Him is our firm foundation for abundant life. There are three elements that are needed to establish that relationship and to keep it strong so we can receive healing. They are, an *authentic* transformation of the heart resulting in salvation, a filling and baptism in the Holy Spirit, and being able to hear and to follow the voice of the Lord in obedience.

To recap just a little before getting into our foundation in Christ, I want to establish again that it is quite possible for healing to suddenly manifest for someone who is not yet a believer in Jesus, especially when a minister is used by God to intercede (stand between/represent) and *demonstrate* God's love as he/she shares the Word/Gospel. God in His goodness sometimes just suddenly gives someone who's wayward, a TASTE of His mercy, with the purpose of showing them Who He truly is. This happened MANY times in the Bible (one example is in Acts 3:2-8) and is described by the scripture found in Mark 16:20 by the words, "the LORD worked with them (the New Testament apostles) and confirmed his word by the signs that accompanied it" (NIV, brackets mine).

Street healings happen with current-day healing evangelists like Todd White, and many others who are serving in obscurity every day; they share Jesus on the streets in their every day lives and God backs them up with words of knowledge, words of wisdom and miraculous healings. A pre-believer can very often receive healing like this because they are open, child-like, and soft-hearted. If they are not though, Holy Spirit can instantly soften their heart with one word of knowledge through the mouth of the evangelist. One supernatural Word spoken right to the heart can suddenly open a person's eyes to the reality and truth of God and His love for them, bringing revelation and healing to many issues.

A believer CAN suddenly receive healing in their body anytime anywhere as well, but it doesn't happen because God suddenly makes a choice to heal them or decides in that moment to have mercy on them; this would imply that there was a moment prior when God was withholding mercy and healing, which does not line up with scripture. Psalm 84:11 says, "For the LORD God is our sun and our shield. He gives us grace and glory. The LORD will withhold no good thing from those who do what is right" (NLT). Additionally, Romans 8:32, "He who did not spare his own Son, but gave him up for us all—how will he not also, along with him, graciously give us all things" (NIV)? The ONLY thing God would withhold from us would be things that we're not ready for but healing certainly doesn't fit in that category; God is a good, good Father with wisdom beyond us.

As I said earlier, God has already made the choice to invite ALL who trust in Him to be healed. God's mercy has been made complete for the believer and it has already been imputed to them in fullness. A believer is suddenly healed usually because they have boldly and persistently reached out in faith to grab it or something they've done, believed, or prayed in repentance has suddenly positioned them in AGREEMENT with God, causing everything demonic to flee and healing to manifest. An area where they were out of alignment or out of agreement with prior, was put into its rightful place.

It CAN (not always) be difficult for Christians to receive healing and I believe there are three reasons for that. First, once we accept the gift of salvation, we have a responsibility to be obedient to Christ[15] which sometimes is overlooked; some believers think they can take advantage of grace and not submit

---

[15]"Jesus replied, 'Anyone who loves me will obey my teaching. My Father will love them, and we will come to them and make our home with them" (John 14:23 NIV).

to the Spirit, nor grow in holiness. Disobedience, therefore, becomes a barrier to their healing.

The second and third reasons have to do with growing up in mainline denominational churches in North America; many have done a dis-service to their people in two ways. First, local churches in many main-line denominations have not taught on healing. They have not taught on the heart of God for our complete restoration. They have not taught inner healing and deliverance, nor have they taught on the need for it or its benefits. They have not taught a complete Gospel. They have also not taught their people to hear God's voice,[16] nor how to apprehend the presence of God. They HAVE taught how to get a ticket to heaven (fire insurance), some have thrown scripture around like a club, they've taught a list of rules and spiritual disciplines, but they have failed miserably on teaching Spirit-led faith, holiness, and discipleship. In fact, what most mainline churches have taught is religion, which has in part developed groups of Pharisees who are, experts at pointing fingers and blame-shifting, arrogant, self-righteous, and judgemental—NOT at all like Christ, not spiritual, and certainly not expectant of anything miraculous. Attempting to minister to someone on the streets who has been "churched" can be like running head-long into a brick wall; often they can be completely unbelieving in the things of the Spirit and even offended by your ministry. It is wise for street ministers to be sensitive to the Spirit's leading and only minister to those the Spirit leads them to. Most of the time (there's always exceptions) it's better to let "churched" believers seek healing for themselves IF they want it and believe for it. They can do this by seeking the Lord, reading the Word, praying, going to healing services and/or a Healing Rooms ministry, and of course using the keys presented in this book.

---

[16] "My sheep hear My voice, and I know them, and they follow Me" (John 10:27 NKJV).

A lot of what I have learned over my thirty-three years of Spirit-led faith, I have learned from, small-group experiences with Spirit-led facilitators, and privately in my own walk with Holy Spirit. It has also been confirmed by recent church leaders in my life who hear God, are free from religion, and on fire for the Lord. We should not be surprised at how the Holy Spirit, the Spirit of truth, speaks to us, making known to us the deep truths of God's Word, as well as giving us direction and a heads-up on what is coming. Remember, Jesus said in John 16:12-14:

> *"I have much more to say to you, more than you can now bear.* But when he, the Spirit of truth, comes, he will guide you into ALL the truth. He will not speak on his own; he will speak only what he hears, and he will tell you what is yet to come. He will glorify me because it is from me that he will receive what he will make known to you" (NIV, emphasis added).

Hearing Holy Spirit speak to us is NOT adding truth to the Bible as some religious people would accuse us of, but it is simply being in RELATIONSHIP with a LIVING God who has a voice and still loves to communicate with us now. Of course, God is not schizophrenic. He does not change in character, so He never speaks anything to us that contradicts His heart or written Word.

Secondly, the church in many main-line denominations have also done a dis-service to people by teaching that a simple prayer recited somehow leads to salvation. The traditional "pray after me" scenario has led some people to an experience where they have given their mental ascent to the Gospel but have not given their heart in love to Jesus. They have not had a revelation of Who Jesus is nor of His love for them which has led some people to think they are saved when *perhaps* they really aren't. Remember, Jesus is coming back for a BRIDE. He is not coming back for JUST friends or JUST servants, nor those that simply believe in Him; He is coming back for a BRIDE who is madly in

LOVE with Him. So, as a quick evaluation of your own heart, do you LOVE Jesus? Are you in love with Him? Jesus said in John 14:21, "Those who accept my commandments and obey them are the ones who love me. And because they love me, my Father will love them. And I will love them and reveal myself to each of them" (NLT).

A true salvation experience begins with a revelation of one's need, a revelation of one's own sin and brokenness. It continues with a revelation from Holy Spirit of Jesus and His sacrifice for us, then a revelation of the goodness and kindness of God which then causes a person to fall in love with Jesus and on their knees in repentance.[17] A true salvation experience is a change of heart *and* mind causing someone to stop and turn around, changing direction. It causes a person who is unknowingly headed for a cliff, to adjust their course so they turn around and head back to the arms of God. And it's this call back to God, back to love, that instigates and perpetuates a change in desires, through the Spirit, which leads to a change in behavior. Holiness is NOT an act of the human will. It is NOT striving and pulling up your bootstraps, trying to do better. It is a change of heart and transformation of the soul initiated and perpetuated by Holy Spirit, as we yield to Him.

Let's be real about our walk with God, Christian. Are you really a *follower* of Christ? Have you really SURRENDERED your life, every bit of it, even your will, to Jesus? A Christian is a follower of Christ which means they watch what Jesus does, and by the empowering of Holy Spirit, they imitate Him. They think how Christ thinks. They say what Christ says. They are "little Christs." They may not do it perfectly yet, but their desire is to get there. They are grieved by their sin and how they fall short, and they live a life of repentance when they do. They LOVE Jesus

---

[17] "... the goodness of God leads you to repentance" (Romans 2:4b NKJV)?

with all their heart; they don't just believe in Him (even the devil believes in Him). Born-again believers LOVE Him. They sacrifice for Him; they give things up to DO His Word. They live a life of service, and they are obedient to Christ. They long to be with Him.

Love for, trust in, and surrender to Jesus is a huge part of the foundation that we must have to experience relationship and intimacy with God—to encounter His presence, and to receive healing. Don't settle for less my friend. Seek Holy Spirit and ask Him to bring you ALL the way in. SURRENDER your life afresh today. I pray Holy Spirit captures your heart through these words; it is NOT His desire for you or anyone else to perish[18] nor to live one more day without His DISCERNABLE, abiding presence.

In addition to an authentic conversion and full surrender to the work and Word of Christ, a second experience as outlined in the New Testament called the baptism of the Holy Spirit[19] is crucial for a firm foundation, for numerous reasons. Being baptized in the Holy Spirit will cause your spiritual senses to awaken, giving you the potential to discern in the Spirit. As you exercise your spiritual senses, they will develop, and you will gain wisdom and understanding from God's perspective being able to "distinguish between what is morally good and what is evil" (Hebrews 5:14b AMP). You will read your Bible and get it. You will grow in your ability to recognize God's voice and discern His presence. And you will be empowered to overcome temptation and any other nonsense the devil throws at you.

---

[18] "In the same way, it is not my heavenly Father's will that even one of these little ones should perish" (Matthew 18:14 NLT).

[19] "I baptize with water those who repent of their sins and turn to God. But someone is coming soon who is greater than I am—so much greater that I'm not worthy even to be his slave and carry his sandals. He will baptize you with the Holy Spirit and with fire" (Matthew 3:11 NLT).

As you yield to Holy Spirit, you will experience a deeper prayer life; you will hear Holy Spirit direct you on how to pray and what to pray, so you are praying God's heart and not your own soulish desires. As you continue to yield, you can even begin to experience a new prayer language which is private and intimate between you and God. Best of all, you will begin to feel the love of God like never before and you will go from a Christian life that is just theory to a wonderful life of EXPERIENCING God. God will come alive to you! This is the beauty of being baptized in the Holy Spirit and it pains me to know so many Christians miss out because their church or denomination chooses to ignore it.

What does it mean to be "baptized" in the Holy Spirit? I would suggest to you that it means being fully immersed in, saturated by, inside and out, surrendered to, yielded to, and/or given over to. It is a state in which we give control over to Him.

This I think is the sticking point for some people; they see giving control over to the Spirit as not having control over themselves. This is utter nonsense; it's not one or the other. God never overrides our free will. We always have the choice to yield or not to yield in any given moment. God is good. God has our BEST interest at heart. He is a gentleman. He never forces Himself on us and He never FORCES us to do anything we don't want to do. He may gently nudge us out of our comfort zones, and want us to obey, but the final choice is always ours. He knows our heart completely. It really comes down to trust. Do we trust God enough to give His Spirit the reigns of our life? If not, there is likely a heart issue standing in the way which, will also end up standing in the way of our healing.

John the Baptist said in Matthew 3:11, "I indeed baptize you with water unto repentance, but He who is coming after me is mightier than I, whose sandals I am not worthy to carry. He will baptize you with the Holy Spirit and fire" (NKJV). We know from this passage that Jesus is the One to baptize us with the Holy

Spirit. It is worthy to note also that the Holy Spirit was imparted to the disciples twice—once with an emphasis on internal awakening and once with an emphasis on external equipping and empowerment. BAPTISM of the Holy Spirit causes one to not only be filled but to "wear" the Holy Spirit on the outside, equipped with Godly fire (passion) and power. The two instances of the disciples receiving the Holy Spirit are as follows:

1. John 20:19-22. After Jesus' resurrection, Jesus appeared to his disciples showing them his pierced hands and side. He commissioned them and BREATHED on them saying, "Receive the Holy Spirit." Jesus breathed on them with the intent of imparting the Holy Spirit to them internally. As Jesus breathed out, they breathed IN what Jesus released—the Holy Spirit. This impartation represents what happens for believers at their salvation experience.

2. Acts 1:5. The second instance of impartation happened at Pentecost and represents the BAPTISM of the Holy Spirit. Jesus gave the apostles instruction to remain in Jerusalem and wait for the "gift" His Father promised: "For John baptized with water, but in a few days you will be BAPTIZED with the Holy Spirit" (Acts 1:5 NIV, emphasis mine). The apostles waited in Jerusalem for Holy Spirit to come, as they were instructed. In due time, Holy Spirit came spontaneously just as Jesus said He would: "Suddenly a sound like the blowing of a violent wind came from heaven and filled the whole house where they were sitting. They saw what seemed to be tongues of fire that separated and came to rest on each of them. All of them were filled with the Holy Spirit and began to speak in other tongues as the Spirit enabled them" (Acts 2:2-4 NIV).

The baptism of the Holy Spirit can happen spontaneously as you believe, surrender, open your heart to Him, and ask to be filled and empowered. It can happen as you read these words right now or as an anointed leader imparts the Spirit to you by the laying on of hands, or as you listen to the Word being preached at church, in your car and even at home.

We see Jesus being spontaneously baptized in the Holy Spirit right after His water baptism in Matthew 3:16, "After his baptism, as Jesus came up out of the water, the heavens were opened and he saw the Spirit of God descending like a dove and settling on him" (NLT). We see new believers being baptized in Holy Spirit spontaneously as they listen to Peter share the Gospel in Acts 10:44 and we see others being baptized in Holy Spirit with the laying on of hands in Acts 8:17 and Acts 19:6.

Holy Spirit is not just for certain denominations. He is for everyone, and we need Him to connect to God. God is Spirit and in order to worship God, we must worship in Spirit.[20] If we want to approach the throne of grace in our time of need, we can only do so in Spirit.[21] Obviously, the throne of God is not in the natural, it is in the spiritual realm. If we want to receive healing, we must also do so in Spirit. Partnering with the Holy Spirit is not an option, if we want to function as a Christian who is alive, aware, walking in the things of God, hearing His voice, and receiving healing.

Robert Boyd Munger has written a very well-known devotional booklet called, *My Heart: Christ's Home*. You may have heard of it. This devotional introduces readers to what it means to surrender every aspect of their lives to the control of Christ by comparing our heart to a home. I've actually not read

---

[20] "God is Spirit, so those who worship him must worship in spirit and in truth" (John 4:24 NLT).

[21] "So let us come boldly to the throne of our gracious God. There we will receive his mercy, and we will find grace to help us when we need it most" (Hebrews 4:16 NLT).

it in its entirety, but I love the idea. Using this comparison, imagine that salvation (repenting, believing, confessing, and surrendering), is like inviting Christ into our home, through the front door. The front door is the entrance way, and the Lord has come in. He has brought life and light back into our home, but where does he reside? Does he just stay in the foyer or is he welcomed into *every* room? Is he restricted to the formal living room where things are in order or is he free to roam—to open closets and cupboards and look under the bed? Is he treated like a guest or like he belongs there? Is he treated like part of the family or is he treated properly—like he's the head of the house—like he's in charge?

Perhaps Jesus is honored well, given access to every room, and received as the authority figure in the home, but what about the Holy Spirit? The Holy Spirit is not synonymous with Jesus; they are two separate members of the Godhead with different assignments, functions, and roles in our lives. Do we invite the Holy Spirit in and honor him the same way we honor Christ?

Here's what I fear happens in denominations that don't believe in the *baptism* of the Holy Spirit: we open the door, and the Holy Spirit comes in, but then we immediately stuff him into the front hall closet, not permitting him to move, fill the house nor do any of what He desires to do—such as heal, comfort, transform and communicate truth.

Unfortunately, some Christians don't trust the supernatural demonstrations of God through the Holy Spirit as it can feel strange, and we can't understand it with our natural minds. It can offend our flesh, but we must allow our minds and our experience to be governed by the Spirit, not the flesh. Romans 8:6-8 says,

> "The mind governed by the flesh is death, but the mind governed by the Spirit is life and peace. The mind governed by the flesh is hostile to God; it does not

submit to God's law, nor can it do so. Those who are in the realm of the flesh cannot please God."

Friends, to experience the supernatural love of God, we are going to have to be willing to experience his supernatural Spirit. We should not be afraid to let the Holy Spirit do what He wants to do. He wants to bless us outrageously and heal us on the inside. I have had some of the most profound, amazing healing experiences flat on my back, on the floor, completely overtaken by the power of God, as the Holy Spirit ministered to me through visions on the screen of my imagination. He has taken me back to some very painful and traumatic experiences and brought me through them again amidst his presence, completely changing my memory of them. The only reason it was possible for God to do this for me was because I was willing to submit to him—I was willing to give Holy Spirit control.

If you've been fearful or prideful or not honoring of Holy Spirit, repent and ask God to forgive you, then open your heart to receive and simply ask God for His gift of the Spirit. Don't be shy. Jesus tells us in Luke 11 to ask for the Holy Spirit and to keep asking:

> "And so I tell you, keep on asking, and you will receive what you ask for. Keep on seeking, and you will find. Keep on knocking, and the door will be opened to you. For everyone who asks, receives. Everyone who seeks, finds. And to everyone who knocks, the door will be opened. You fathers—if your children ask for a fish, do you give them a snake instead? Of if they ask for an egg, do you give them a scorpion? Of course not! So if you sinful people know how to give good gifts to your children, how much more will your heavenly Father give the Holy Spirit to those who ask him" (Luke 11:9-13 NLT).

We can even ask again and again. In fact, I would encourage every believer to continually ask for more of the Holy Spirit; you will find that as you serve the Lord pouring out to others, you will need to be replenished with His power and presence.

Hearing the voice of God is the third element of our relationship, which is vital for our foundation. How can we have a relationship with anyone without hearing their voice and being able to talk with them? Jesus declares in the parable of the sheep in John 10 that He is the gate, and He is the good Shepherd who sacrifices His life for the sheep. He also says His sheep know His voice and follow it:

> "I tell you the truth, anyone who sneaks over the wall of a sheepfold, rather than going through the gate, must surely be a thief and a robber! But the one who enters through the gate is the shepherd of the sheep. The gatekeeper opens the gate for him, and the sheep recognize his voice and come to him. He calls his own sheep by name and leads them out. After he has gathered his own flock, he walks ahead of them, and they follow him because they know his voice. They won't follow a stranger; they will run from him because they don't know his voice. . . I am the good shepherd; I know my own sheep, and they know me, just as my Father knows me and I know the Father. So I sacrifice my life for the sheep. I have other sheep too, that are not in this sheepfold. I must bring them also. They will listen to my voice, and there will be one flock with one shepherd" (John 10:1-5, 14-16 NLT).

We absolutely have the ability through the Spirit to recognize the voice of Jesus our Lord and to be directed by Him. We hear His voice in different ways, but *primarily* through reading His written Word, the Bible.

Have you ever noticed that as you read the Bible, occasionally a certain passage, verse, phrase, or word will jump out at you or be highlighted—a portion of what you are reading penetrates your heart with power and reverberates in your inner being? This is an indication that God is bringing that portion of His Word to your attention and is SPEAKING it to you in that moment. You may not be able to identify what's happening, but if you pay close attention, you may notice that it feels like a vibration in your spirit. This is because God's voice is adding sound to the written Words you are reading. The written Word becomes the spoken Word. At this moment, His Word comes alive with power, changing and healing as it defies natural laws, exposing what needs to be exposed, cutting, and dividing what is soulish from what is spirit. Hebrews 4 puts it this way:

> "For the word of God is alive and powerful. It is sharper than the sharpest two-edged sword, cutting between soul and spirit, between joint and marrow. It exposes our innermost thoughts and desires. Nothing in all creation is hidden from God. Everything is naked and exposed before his eyes, and he is the one to whom we are accountable" (Hebrews 4:12-13 NLT).

Of course, the whole of the written Word is God's Word and is alive, but it is the portion that God wants you to hear in the moment that will pierce you when you need it. And you will just know in your spirit, *there's power on that Word FOR ME right now and I need to receive it, BELIEVE IT, and step into it, to experience the benefits flowing from it.*

Did you know that God created the world simply by speaking? He didn't have to hire an architect, or contractor to build anything. He didn't need any raw materials. He simply spoke and it was. "And God said, 'Let there be light'; and there was light" (Genesis 1:3 AMP). The sound of His voice creates. The sound of His voice establishes exactly what He says.

It's incredible what I noticed just the other day, in Matthew 14:22-32. Let me share it with you. Jesus sent His disciples out in the boat ahead of Him while He dismissed the crowd that had been listening to Him speak. Later, shortly before dawn Jesus went out to them, walking on the water. Initially the disciples were afraid and thought He was a ghost, but Jesus called out to them, calming their fear.

Peter, the zealous bold one, said to Jesus, "Lord, if it's really you, *tell me to come to you*, walking on the water" (Matthew 14:28 NLT, emphasis added). "'Yes, come.' Jesus said. So, Peter went over the side of the boat and walked on the water toward Jesus" (Matthew 14:29 NLT). I never thought of this too much before, but Peter asked Jesus to command him to come out on the water BEFORE he attempted it. He waited for the Word from Jesus. Why? Why not just get out of the boat and go? Well, Peter understood that he needed the Word of the Lord before he could experience supernatural things that defy earthly laws. Peter doesn't take anything for granted nor presumes anything and neither should we. The Word of the Lord creates, empowers, releases, and overcomes every earthly limitation. Therefore, we need to read healing scriptures over ourselves; something we read is going to catch the breath of God, cut through our issue and bring healing.

Seeking the Lord in the secret place is vital to hearing Him speak a Word of healing. When I say "secret place" I mean in a private place and way, so you and the Lord can be together intimately to share your hearts together. Don't just make time to pray quickly in the morning as you dress or drive the car or perhaps when you're doing chores. Seek the Lord INTENTIONALLY, behind closed doors, with NO DISTRACTIONS, and give Him your time. Prioritize a time when you can be set apart to hear Him; only one Word from Him can create your miracle healing.

In summary, READ the Word and HEAR the Word. When a portion of scripture resonates in your heart, read it over repeatedly and read it out loud. Sit with it. Chew on it. RECEIVE IT. BELIEVE IT. If there's something you need to do to activate it, do it!

Another common way God speaks to us is through prayer. Did you know that prayer is supposed to be a two-way conversation? Prayer was never meant to be a monologue, but a dialogue. Why is that important for healing? Well, a few pages back, I mentioned that disobedience can become a barrier or blockage to healing. I also mentioned that one could have a "heart issue" if they aren't willing to trust the Holy Spirit which can also block healing. This "heart issue" could be fear or it could be pride; either one will stop healing from manifesting. Here's the thing though. . . God wants you healed! And He is more than willing to tell you what is keeping your healing from manifesting! All we need to do is ask Him. Obviously, we then need to be open to hear His voice, discern what God is saying and be obedient. I've always loved King David's prayer in Psalm 139:23, "Search me, O God, and know my heart; test me and know my anxious thoughts. Point out anything in me that offends you, and lead me along the path of everlasting life" (NLT).

Jesus was excellent at hearing His Father's voice. We see this in operation as He healed various individuals using different actions and words. Throughout the Gospels, Jesus did not use any "cookie cutter" healing methods. Instead, He listened to His Father and His Father told Him what to do. Jesus' actions dealt with EVERYTHING that stood against a person's wellbeing—everything in his soul and body operating together to cause illness.

Some people Jesus touched. Some He didn't touch, and some touched Him. A few He had to deliver from evil spirits.[22] A few He anointed with His spit; one he mixed with dirt[23] and one He had to remove from the town and pray for twice.[24]

The man whose eyes were anointed with spit mixed with dirt, in John 9:1-7, was told to go wash in the pool of Siloam which means "sent," after which he was healed. Not every blind person who was healed had to do that—just him (that we know of). It follows then that there must have been purpose for the washing in that particular pool. Perhaps it had to do with washing away an old identity and ushering in a new one. With every splash of the water, he exercised his faith as he carried out this divinely appointed prophetic act, choosing to believe, accept, declare, and establish his new identity as a "sent" one.

The blind man from John 9 was born blind and Jesus specifically says in John 9:3, "It was not because of his sins or his parents' sins," Jesus answered. "This happened so the power of God could be seen in him" (NLT). However, this is not a blanket statement for all people who were blind or ill as Jesus also said to the man who was healed at the pool in John 5:14, "Now you are well; so stop sinning, or something even worse may happen to you" (NLT). There are different reasons for people to be ill and we must seek the Lord to know what those are.

Another healing I will emphasis is found in Mark 2:1-12. Here we see a man who was paralyzed being carried by four of his friends, trying to get close to Jesus as He preached in the home where He was staying. The home became so packed with visitors, no one else could even get in the door. As a result, the men got on the roof, opened it, and lowered the man down on

---

[22] Luke 13:10-17
[23] John 9:1-7
[24] Mark 8:22-26

his cot in front of Jesus. The man's friends wanted him healed physically, but Jesus' VERY FIRST words to the man are, "My child, your sins are forgiven" (Mark 2:5 NLT). Why? He didn't say this to the other people He healed. It's possible He said this to stir up the scribes that were there and to illustrate a point, but I believe, it was something else.

After reading Matthew's account of the same healing in Matthew 9, I believe the paralytic was vexed in his soul with grief and regret over his sin. Part of Matthew 9:2 says, "Son, BE OF GOOD CHEER; your sins are forgiven you" (NKJV, emphasis mine). That precious man needed to be cheered up and relieved of his regret before his body could be healed. Second Corinthians 7:10 says, "Godly sorrow brings repentance that leads to salvation and leaves no regret, but worldly sorrow brings death" (NIV). Friends of God, don't hang on to regret. Let it go. Don't be stuck in worldly sorrow which leads to hopelessness, illness, and death, but let Godly sorrow bring you to repentance and lead you all the way out. God says you are forgiven, so receive it and forgive yourself. Make the declaration over yourself, "I AM FORGIVEN." And I say to you, "Your sins are remitted, paid for and cancelled."

One time I went to a conference with a friend to a nearby city. We shared a hotel room and as I sat on the bed, criss-cross apple sauce, I felt the familiar sting in my left hip as my muscles and/or tendons refused to co-operate. I persevered singing a song that I had come to love, called "You Are My King (Amazing Love).[25] Perhaps you know it.

> "I'm forgiven because you were forsaken.
> I'm accepted. You were condemned.
> I'm alive and well. Your Spirit is within me.

---

[25] https://www.youtube.com/watch?v=C3E6ia8E74U

> Because you died and rose again.
>
> Chorus: Amazing love, how can it be?
> That you my King would die for me.
> Amazing love, I know it's true.
> It's my joy to honor you. (x2)
> In all I do, I honor you.
>
> YOU are my King.
> You are MY King.
> Jesus, You are my King.
> Jesus, You are MY King.[26]

As I sat on that bed, singing, and declaring that I was forgiven, suddenly the sting in my hip vanished. The pain was gone, and flexibility was restored. God's healing manifested in my body according to my confession of forgiveness.

God speaks. He's alive and He has a voice. He is speaking to us ALL the time. Sometimes He speaks through the pages of the Bible and in prayer. Other times He speaks through different things like dreams, books, and songs. Even other times He speaks through people—particularly when you're listening to a sermon online or when someone anointed prays for you or gives you a prophetic word. In addition, you may find God speaks to you through social media or even a billboard!

You may be asking, "How do I know if God is speaking to me when I read a billboard?" That's a good question. It's a little out of the box, isn't it? You will know it's God when it grabs your attention, convicts you, won't leave you alone, and perhaps confirms something you've already been thinking or praying about. Over time, you will begin to recognize His voice, how it makes you feel, and other signs that come with it.

---

[26] Written by Billy James Foote. 1999 worshiptogether.com Songs (ASCAP) (admin. by EMI CMG Publishing).

I'll never forget the first time I heard the voice of God in my head and spirit as I prayed. The Lord answered a question I had asked Him, responding with a clear Word of direction. It just about blew my mind.

I was standing at the sink washing dishes and I had just had a healing experience in the car on the way home from Toronto. As a passenger on a three-hour ride, there was a lot of time to think. Without even realizing it, God guided my thoughts as He opened my eyes to a hurtful event from my teen years and He led me to forgive someone who had stolen my innocence.

After the car ride as I stood at the sink, I had a new sense of peace; the anxiety, hate and emotional pain I had felt previously was gone and I was so thankful. I asked the Lord directly, "What do you want me to do with this now?" and IMMEDIATELY I heard God say in my thoughts, "Join the youth group." I was stunned. Becoming an adult sponsor for high schoolers was not even on my radar; it wasn't something I had thought about before. However, I did what God told me to do and I loved it. I became an adult sponsor for the youth group at our church; it stretched me, caused me to grow and it used my spiritual gifts to bless others. It was exactly where God wanted me to be at that time in my life.

One final way I will mention that God speaks is through dreams. This is a whole teaching by itself, but I will say this:

- Everyone has dreams whether we remember them or not.
- Not every dream is from God.
- Dreams from God are vivid and seem very real.
- God speaks in dreams through symbols and what they mean biblically and/or to you.
- Keep a journal by your bedside to journal your dream as soon as you wake up, before you forget.

- God dreams can be very helpful to you in life.
- The Holy Spirit will give you the interpretation of the dream if you ask Him.
- Talking your dream out sometimes gives you clues as to what it means.
- It is biblical.[27] Daniel and Joseph both interpreted God's messages in dreams.

Several years ago my daughter was at college and at the end of the school year, as she was getting off the campus bus, she slipped and hit her head on the step. We thought she was fine until she went back to school a few months later and began having severe headaches and difficulty with her memory. She finished the semester, took a break from college, and came home to rest and heal.

Shortly after she returned home, as I sought the Lord on her behalf, I had a dream:

> I was at a college campus in the campus bookstore, and I was in line, waiting to buy a scarf. The scarf was white and on the scarf were two handprints with the words, "They will lift you up." When I reached the cashier, she didn't know how to cash out that particular item, so I helped her out by cashing myself out on the bookstore's register.

I knew the Lord was speaking to me. I was at a college campus, so it was obviously referring to my daughter; she was the only one in the family at college. I was purchasing a scarf that was white which speaks of purity and the scarf speaks of a covering. MY purchasing the scarf was confirmation that I had successfully partnered with God to activate His covering over me

---

[27] "For God speaks again and again, though people do not recognize it. He speaks in dreams, in visions of the night, when deep sleep falls on people as they lie in their beds" (Job 33:14-15 NLT).

and my children; as her mother, the one in authority over her, my covering translated to her covering. Most powerfully though, the inscription on the scarf pointed me to the Word, Psalm 91:11-12:

> "For he will command his angels concerning you to guard you in all your ways; they will lift you up in their hands, so that you will not strike your foot against a stone (or your head against a step)" (NIV, brackets mine).

The next morning as I contemplated the dream and read the scripture, I realized by the Spirit in that moment, that God was actually changing history. As I caught revelation of His breath and voice on that Word from Psalm 91, I saw in my mind's eye, angels slipping their hands underneath my daughter's head as it hit the step, protecting her from the impact. From that moment on, she no longer had severe headaches due to a concussion or problems with her memory. (For more information about how God speaks in dreams, look for resources by Barbie Breathitt or James Goll.)

These are the foundations of connecting with God: an authentic salvation experience of heart transformation, baptism in the Holy Spirit, and hearing His voice followed by obedient action. All three set you up to begin and grow a vibrant, intimate relationship with God, through Jesus. They also set you up to be healed in every way. If you are convicted that you don't have all three of these elements, simply follow the Spirit and re-dedicate your life to Jesus as He leads you. This may look like:

- surrendering to Jesus afresh and accepting Him again (or for the first time) as your Savior AND Lord.
- asking God to fill you with Holy Spirit and new life.

- asking Jesus to baptize you IN the Holy Spirit to clothe you in His power so you can live for Him, be a witness wherever you go and serve Him well.
- getting to know God and His heart by reading His Word.
- memorizing verses that are special to you.
- praying and expecting to hear God's voice and asking the Lord to help you.
- giving the Holy Spirit an opportunity to speak to you by asking Him direct questions (Start simple).
- spending time with God and attuning your ear to the sound of His voice.
- allowing the Holy Spirit to pray through you however that looks and sounds.
- being open to praying in tongues—a heavenly language between you and God. Learn more from a book by John Bevere called, "The Holy Spirit: An introduction."
- praying in tongues often.

Chapter 5

AUTHORITY

When we are sick or burdened with an ongoing illness, as I've already said, one of the most beneficial things we can do for ourselves is to seek the Lord and ask Him WHY we are experiencing that illness. God wants us well, knows the solution to every problem and is more than happy to tell us what it is.

MOST illnesses and diseases do not manifest in our body without a root cause in our heart or our soul which is where our mind, emotions and will reside. Our body is an outward expression of our inner selves. All three parts of us are integrated together; our body does not operate by itself, independent of our spirit and soul. We are a FULLY integrated three-part being, made in the image of God; just as God the Father, God the Son and God the Spirit are all in unity and agreement with one another, so we are too. Our spirit, soul, and body work together; they are in agreement with one another. We are primarily spirit; we have a soul, and we live in a body.

Listen to Proverbs 4:23, "Guard your heart above all else, for it determines the course of your life" (NLT) or the New King

James Version, "Keep your heart with all diligence, For out of it spring the issues of life." "Heart" in these verses is referring to our inner man (our spirit and our soul).

Proverbs 23:6-7 tells us about a miser who tells a person with his mouth, "Eat and drink!" but in his heart he's resentful about what it's costing him to share his food. His words do not reflect the truth in his heart; he speaks falsehoods. Proverbs 23:7 tells us, "For as he thinks in his heart, SO IS HE" (NKJV, emphasis mine). In other words, it is what's in his heart that determines who he really is, not his empty, insincere words. The scripture goes on in verse 8 to tell us that if we do eat the miser's food, we will end up vomiting out the morsels we've consumed (I believe because we've eaten without his blessing but with a curse). These verses "bring home" for us the importance of the spiritual heart condition on our overall health.

Of course, some extreme negative environmental factors can affect the health of our bodies, but they are not the SOLE cause of disease. There are bad habits such as eating poorly or not exercising that can contribute to disease, but again are not the SOLE causing factor. I would also point out here that eating poorly and not taking care of oneself are behaviors that are rooted in deeper things—perhaps depression which very often is a spiritual attack on the mind or it can be a soul wound (sometimes more than one) that is perpetuating poor self-esteem, self-hate, loneliness, discouragement, and/or hopelessness. Over-eating or eating a lot of foods high in sugar are coping mechanisms—one way people try to cope with emotional pain and wounds in the soul.

Some medical doctors and therapists have *begun* to recognize the truth that disease is GREATLY caused by things like adversity in childhood, chronic fear and anxiety, lingering stress,

AUTHORITY

trauma, and repressed emotions.[28] But many doctors do not. Unfortunately, these factors are not frequently seen as causative nor addressed in the medical field. Many doctors even cringe at the suggestion. Nonetheless, it doesn't make it any less true. Generational iniquity (genetics as the world sees it) can also play a role in disease but that will be addressed in a later chapter.

If there is a soul-wound or repressed emotions that are contributing to your ill health, the Lord is more than happy to show you what those are. We are also more than able to exercise our free-will to repent and come out of agreement with any issue the Lord shows us. For instance, if God shows you that low self-esteem is a problem for you, it would be beneficial to ask the Lord where it came from. Where did you learn that you weren't good enough? When did you begin to accept that as truth? The Holy Spirit will show you and when He does, simply:

- agree with God (for example you might pray: "Yes Lord, that happened, and it hurt me deeply," or, "Yes Lord, I believed the lie that I was worthless because of that rejection").
- repent for accepting the lies regarding your worth.
- forgive anyone who hurt you or treated you unfairly.
- recognize the truth of who you are in God's eyes (read Psalm 139 to find out).
- forgive anyone who hasn't celebrated you as they should (a mom, dad, sibling, spouse, friend).
- thank God for how He made you and decide from this moment forward to celebrate God's creation—to celebrate you.

---

[28] See resources like *The Deepest Well* by Dr. Nadine Burke Harris, *Scared Sick* by Robin Karr-Morse with Meredith S. Wiley and *When the Body Says No* by Gabor Maté M.D.

You are God's unique and glorious creation—His work of art. Just as we don't appreciate criticism of our artwork, criticizing ourselves is not honoring to God. It is possible that there are DEEP wounds contributing to this, in which case, I would recommend seeing a pastor, prayer minister, or counselor to help you sort through it all. It is vital to NOT let these wounds and emotions fester in our heart. A "wound" that is not cleansed and treated becomes infected, causing us great harm, even manifesting into illness and disease.

What am I talking about when I say "wound?" I'm talking about any mark left on your soul that has hurt you. It could be the results of a long-term destructive habit that has undermined your wellness, a pattern of negative self-talk, the results of a bad choice, or it could be something someone has done to you, said to you, or said about you.

One time in prayer I was enjoying feeling the presence of God with me and "beholding" him as best I could. In the Spirit, I was looking intently at His being, His heart, His countenance, using my godly imagination in the Spirit trying to "see" Him and suddenly I realized, as I beheld Him, He was also beholding me. It startled me a bit and it caused me to quickly look away. I was uncomfortable with Him looking so intently at ME—seeing everything, seeing my imperfections and wrinkles and whatever else I felt insecure about. I had to do some repenting that day and come into an understanding that in His eyes I am beautiful just the way I am, and He loves me completely and perfectly. In fact, He doesn't even see my imperfections. I had to come INTO agreement with God about who I was as His masterpiece and OUT of agreement with every negative narrative I had learned since childhood.

I once started to read a book by Beth Moore entitled, "Get Out of that Pit." I don't believe I finished it, but I really liked the analogy she used about being in a pit emotionally. Wounds in our soul can cause us to be in a pit and we must get out to be free and to walk in divine health.

Sometimes we are in a pit because we jumped in (perhaps through sin of our own choosing). Sometimes we are in a pit because we accidentally fell in and sometimes, we are in a pit because we were pushed in. The good news is we CAN get out of every single one, no matter how we got there. We are never just stuck. If we will partner with God, acknowledge we are in the pit and truly desire to get out, Jesus will reach down and pull us out—EVERY time.[29]

We may have gone through some tough stuff in life. We may have been rejected and even betrayed by loved ones, but even though we have suffered injustice, we are NOT to remain victims. We are NOT to just sit in our pits and think that we better just get used to being there because we can't undo what someone has done. No, we can't erase the past, but we can change our perspective of it; we can choose to believe that it doesn't have to control us or hold us captive. We can choose to understand that it was a bad choice somebody else made that had more to do with their own pain than anything to do with us. We can choose to forgive our oppressor and not allow that wound to hold us captive.

This is the power we have as a human being. We have the capacity to choose our response to every action and every circumstance of life and with Christ, we have even greater power and even authority over our own mind, soul, and wounds.

In Paul's second letter to the Corinthians, he confronts the Corinthian church and boldly explains in chapter 10 that even though they (the Apostles) were in the world, their warfare was not waged in the earth realm. He says, "we do not wage battle according to the flesh, for the weapons of our warfare are not of

---

[29] Beth Moore, *Get Out of That Pit* (Nashville: Thomas Nelson, 2007). Print.

the flesh, but divinely powerful" (2 Cor. 10:3-4 NASB). Those weapons Paul referred to are the spiritual weapons of God including divine authority, the fellowship and power of the Spirit, the Word of God (spoken/ prophetic and written/Bible), our confession/testimony, the name of Jesus, the blood of Jesus, praying in tongues, praise, and worship, among others. Paul then continues to tell the Corinthians that in their prayers, the Apostles were taking authority over and destroying every high and lofty argument and thought pattern raised up against the knowledge of God. He even tells them that they (the Apostles) were taking every thought plaguing the minds of the Corinthians captive and making them obedient to Christ (2 Cor. 10:5).

This is the same warfare that we must wage, against any prideful arguments in our own mind against the truth, any lies the devil has sown into our heart which we have believed and any thought that enters our mind which is contrary to God, including any thought that is for instance, lustful, slanderous, fearful, anxious, critical, bitter, prideful, vengeful, full of grumbling and complaining, ungrateful, argumentative, contentious, not loving, not peaceful and not joyful. We must capture every thought in our mind and make sure it lines up with God.

Did you know that we can control our own thinking? Well, if you didn't, you do now! Stop just allowing your mind to wander away into ungodliness. Take authority over your mind and demand holiness there. Repent for thinking in an ungodly way. Controlling your thoughts will bear tremendous fruit; you will find that controlling your thoughts will produce controlled emotions and stable moods. It may even begin to lead you out of mental health issues like depression and others.

One day I was driving to the local pregnancy center where I was volunteering. I was very upset about a ministry venture I had attempted that afternoon, which in the natural appeared as having failed. Random accusing thoughts about being a failure plagued my mind as hot tears streamed down my face in droves. *I need to get it together*, I thought, *I can't show up and work like this*, but no matter how hard I tried, I could not seem to make myself stop crying. Immediately, Holy Spirit helped me realize that my thoughts were the root of my emotional breakdown, and He led me to take authority over them. I put my hand on my head and said, "In Jesus' name, every voice that is not God, I command you to shut up right now!" Instantly, I mean INSTANTLY, like a switch had been flipped, the tears that had been coming fast and furious before, in the blink of an eye, just simply stopped. One second, I had no control over my emotions and the next, I was as cool as a cucumber. I was stunned that my state had changed so drastically, so quickly. Only the power of God has that effect.

Ephesians 6:10-12 says:

"A final word: Be strong in the Lord and in his mighty power. Put on all of God's armor so that you will be able to stand firm against all strategies of the devil. For we are not fighting against flesh-and-blood enemies, but against evil rulers and authorities of the unseen world, against mighty powers in this dark world, and against evil spirits in the heavenly places" (NLT).

From this scripture we learn there are dark spirits, "evil rulers and authorities," "mighty powers," and "evil spirits" that war against us. They want us to stay in our pits. They want us to be in fear, frustration, discouragement and to give up; they want us to be contentious with one another, to be in strife, and to argue against the truth.

While reading this book, perhaps you have had thoughts in your mind, telling you, *there's no use, I've tried everything, it's hopeless, I'll never get well*, even perhaps, *this author is nuts; she's speaking heresy.* These thoughts are not your thoughts!

And they certainly are not from God! Those thoughts are evil spirits trying to control the narrative in your mind and your circumstances. We must recognize their source and deal with them. Put your hand on your head and take authority over those thoughts right now! Pray and declare, "In the name of Jesus, I reject and renounce every lie and every evil thought, and I repent for entertaining them. I now bind and take authority over every prideful, evil, and lying thought in my mind, and I command them to be silent NOW! I MUZZLE EVERY EVIL SPIRIT and break its power over me, in Jesus' name." This is praying in the authority Jesus gave us.

Jesus said in Luke 10:19, "I have given you authority to trample on snakes and scorpions and to overcome ALL the power of the enemy; NOTHING WILL HARM YOU" (NIV, emphasis mine). Now, exercise your authority in Christ for yourself. You have been given the ability to be an OVERCOMER in EVERY situation! Jesus paid dearly to give you authority and power over the enemy, so use it—don't let it go to waste.

Now, as we continue to build on this knowledge, don't be overwhelmed. This may be new to some but remember how BIG our God is. He created the universe, and He tells the sun when to shine and the moon when to appear. He draws the line in the sand for the waters and says, "this far and no farther." He names the stars, and He knows the number of hairs on your head. He is with you, and He is for you. His eye is on you, and He never forgets about you. "For the eyes of the LORD run to and fro throughout the whole earth, to show Himself strong on behalf of those whose heart is loyal to Him" (2 Chronicles 16:9 NKJV). He sees you and He loves you with an everlasting love. With those reminders at the forefront of your mind, let's continue.

In addition to evil spirits putting thoughts into our mind, evil spirits can also attach themselves to our soul when given the opportunity (through repetitive sin, wrong heart attitudes or iniquity) and cause illness. This is illustrated well in Luke 13:10-13:

> "Now Jesus was teaching in one of the synagogues on the Sabbath. And there was a woman who for eighteen years had had an illness caused by a spirit (demon). She was bent double and could not straighten up at all. When Jesus saw her, He called her over and said to her, "Woman, you are released from your illness." Then He laid His hands on her; and immediately she stood erect again and she began glorifying and praising God" (AMP).

Now, let's be wise and understanding. Just because in this passage of scripture, the evil spirit caused a problem with the woman's spine, DOES NOT mean every person with a spinal issue is demonized nor does it mean this is the only illness a demon can cause. Let's not get religious! Let's not create any rules or patterns out of this but realize we need to be discerning about the root cause of illness.

This discussion, unfortunately, may cause disagreements, as many Christians assume that evil spirits cannot be in them nor cause illness. This is not true. While it is true, a Christian cannot be POSSESSED by evil spirits, as possession is about ownership and every Christian is owned and possessed by Christ. However, a Christian can be demonized, which can be understood as being OPPRESSED of soul. Oppression means, subject to harsh or authoritarian treatment, burdened with cruel or unjust impositions or restraints, and subjected to a burdensome or harsh exercise of authority or power.[30] I think you're beginning to get the picture. When we are oppressed by demons, the enemy is successfully exercising his power over us, influencing

---

[30] Various online dictionaries

us in our thoughts, moods, emotions, words, choices, and behaviors and ATTEMPTING to control us.

Remember our discussion from before. When we are saved, our spirits are immediately re-created and made brand new, but our souls are not. Our soul is healed over time in a process, so parts of our soul can be unhealed. This is the part where demons can be attached to.

Sometimes a word picture or illustration can help us understand difficult concepts. Let's consider this illustration to help us understand how we become OPPRESSED by demons:

Imagine you lease a car.[31] You don't own the car; it belongs to someone else, but it's on loan to you. You can drive the car anywhere you want and use it for whatever purpose you want. You can also open the passenger door to anyone. You can invite whomever you wish into your car and allow them to ride with you for however long you want. Imagine also, that certain "less-desirable" passengers get to ride with you BY DEFAULT, even if you don't want them to, based on things like repeated sinful actions not repented for, un-healed emotional wounds, long-held wrong beliefs, deep hatred and/or bitterness, etc. These "less-desirable" passengers don't have to get out of the car until you stop giving them access and you tell them to get out. You oversee that car on loan to you; you're responsible to take care of it properly. The OWNER of the car is NOT responsible to control who rides with you—that is your job. I will say that again! The OWNER of the car is NOT responsible to control who rides with you!!! That is your job.

Do you see the parallel? The Lord has given us free-will and the choice to live however we wish. We have personal autonomy, and the Spirit of God does not over-ride our choices. God will try to lead us His way, but the final choice is ours. Having

---

[31] Thanks to Dr. Bernardine Daniels for introducing this illustration.

AUTHORITY

choices is good, but we also need to realize that we will experience the consequences of those choices. Demons may ride along with us accordingly, whether we want them to or not. It IS possible to allow the Holy Spirit to drive our car but getting to that point of COMPLETE surrender and perfect discernment is a process and we spend many years driving our car with the Holy Spirit in the back seat, allowing less-desirable passengers to ride along with us.

Demons can attach to our soul through many things—trauma, wounds, repetitive sin, and generational iniquity are just a few common examples. But don't fret! NEVER should we be afraid of them, be embarrassed about it, or feel condemned. Evil spirits are EASILY DEALT WITH! They just need to be discerned and cast out.

Remember, we are NOT dealing with a situation, like that from the 1973 movie, "The Exorcist." No one's head is spinning around! Hollywood has done a great job of freaking people out and sowing fear into hearts around this issue but casting demons out of a Christian can be very simple and does not have to be dramatic. We can even do this for ourselves when we close the points of entry demons have used (through repentance and renunciation), as well as understand who we are in Christ and the authority Jesus has given us over the devil.

The full truth of what Jesus accomplished on the cross for us is so much more than a ticket to heaven when we pass from this earth. We MUST understand how Jesus has transformed our identity completely and purchased us as His very own possession. When we believe and surrender to Christ, we belong to Him, and we become a brand-new spiritual creation. Second Corinthians 5:17 says, "Therefore, if anyone is in Christ, he is a new creation; old things have passed away; behold, all things have become new" (NKJV).

Understand that we have not been *renovated* or *upgraded*. No! We have been COMPLETELY renewed and REBORN as a child of God—born of God with a completely new *spiritual* identity as a son or daughter of God. ALL things have passed away, and ALL things have become new. Ephesians 2:4-7 says:

> "But because of his great love for us, God, who is rich in mercy, made us alive with Christ even when we were dead in transgressions—it is by grace you have been saved. And God raised us up with Christ AND SEATED US WITH HIM IN THE HEAVENLY REALMS in Christ Jesus, in order that in the coming ages he might show the incomparable riches of his grace, expressed in his kindness to us in Christ Jesus" (NIV, emphasis mine).

Our spiritual identity is now found "IN" Christ Jesus. Think about what it means to be "IN" something. It means you are "inside of" which means you are contained by it—you are surrounded by it on all sides and if we are "IN" Christ, we MUST be where He is!! We are seated in Heavenly places with Him, far above all principalities and evil spirits. Physically we live in this natural world, but spiritually we have been given citizenship in heaven, a victorious position far above the devil AND a heavenly perspective to see things with the wisdom of God.

According to the Word of God, in Christ, spiritually we are:

- the salt of the earth (Matt. 5:13).
- the light of the world (Matt. 5:14).
- children of God (John 1:12).
- part of the true vine, a channel of Christ's life (John 15:1&5).
- chosen and appointed by Christ (John 15:16).
- slaves to righteousness (Romans 6:18).

- joint heirs with Christ, sharing His inheritance (Romans 8:17).
- the dwelling place of God (1 Cor.3:16, 6:19).
- united with the Lord and one spirit with Him (1 Cor. 6:17).
- members of Christ's body (1 Cor.12:27, Eph. 5:30).
- saints (1 Cor. 1:2, Eph. 1:1, Phil. 1:1, Col. 1:2).
- God's workmanship (Eph. 2:10).
- righteous and holy (Eph. 4:24).
- hidden with Christ in God (Col. 3:3).
- chosen of God, holy and dearly loved (Col. 3:12, 1 Thess. 1:4).
- a son of light (1 Thess. 5:5).
- a holy partaker of a heavenly calling (Heb. 3:1).
- God's living stones, being built up in Christ as a spiritual house (1 Peter 2:5).
- members of a chosen race, a royal priesthood, and a people for God's own possession (1 Peter 2:9-10).
- enemies of the devil (1 Peter 5:8).
- born of God and protected from the devil (1 John 5:18).

All these statements are true of us WHEN we surrender to Christ. In and of ourselves, we are nothing, but with Christ and in Christ, we are everything, ONLY because of Him and His Spirit living in us. God plus nothing equals everything. We do not add anything to God, but God adds EVERTHING to us. We may not walk in our new identity perfectly, but that's where grace comes in. God has given us everything up front but then teaches us how to walk it out in this world. Spiritually, we are already perfected; naturally, we are not. We are in process.

Finally, let's remember that the devil is a fallen angel who was created by God; NO creation is EVER greater or even on parr with its CREATOR. God is the supreme Creator and is far above any other spiritual power, including the devil. Jesus has triumphed over the devil, disarmed the false powers and authorities, and made a public spectacle of them all.[32]

In the Bible, when kings went to war and won, the triumphant king would parade his defeated foe through the streets in humiliation, dragging the enemy's body behind him. Spiritually speaking, Jesus, our TRIUMPHANT KING did this same thing to the devil and all his cohorts. This SAME Jesus lives IN us giving US that same victory!

If you're still having difficulty understanding or believing for your authority over the devil, please pick up and read, *Victory Over the Darkness,* by Neil T. Anderson; it will lead you to all the truth from God's Word that you need to stand in Christ. There is never any need for Spirit-filled, Spirit-baptized, born-again believers to be afraid of the devil. In fact, in Christ, YOU are a threat to him. A demon may try to intimidate us but all we need to do is:

1. repent for whatever Holy Spirit convicts us of.
2. renounce wrong motives, thoughts, attitudes, behaviors, and associations.
3. bind the demons with our words as led by Holy Spirit.
4. declare the demons ineffective and powerless over us because of the blood of Jesus and Who our Father is.
5. in faith and confidence, tell them to get out and leave us RIGHT NOW!
6. ask Father to send Holy Spirit to fill us afresh.

---

[32] "In this way, he disarmed the spiritual rulers and authorities. He shamed them publicly by his victory over them on the cross" (Colossians 2:15 NLT).

There will be prayers throughout the book that will give you specific words to pray. Also Dr. Douglas E. Carr has some great resources that will give you specific direction on how to identify and deal with demons. His first book, *Free Indeed,* is a great overview and his new book, *Breaking Patterns of Perversity: Freedom from Iniquity,* will help you be free from iniquity (and associated spirits) passed on through the generations of your family (more on that later). All his books can be purchased from Amazon. If you are unsure of your status as a born-again believer, or feel nervous about casting out demons, ask the Lord to lead you to someone who can help.

It goes without saying that in order to cast out demons, one must pray in faith and authority. It is also true that when we pray for healing in our body, our prayers are more effective when we again, pray in faith and authority. Praying for what we already have or begging God to heal us, is NOT praying in faith.

Have you ever prayed and asked God to be with you? I've done it many times, but God's Word has already told us that He will never leave us or forsake us.[33] We would do well to believe what God has already said and pray from a place of belief and faith. Even if we don't FEEL God with us, He IS there. So, it would be better to pray, "Lord, thank you that you are always with me; you have promised it in your Word and I believe it. Help me to sense your presence. Help me to sense your love and your comfort. Open my spiritual senses God to Who you are, in Jesus' name."

Similarly, God has already done everything necessary to make healing available to us—we just need to access it. So, don't pray, "Lord, please heal me." Pray, "Thank you God for healing

---

[33] "I will never leave you nor forsake you" (Joshua 1:5 NIV). "God has said, "Never will I leave you; never will I forsake you." So we say with confidence, "The Lord is my helper; I will not be afraid. What can mere mortals to do me" (Hebrews 13:5-6 NIV)?

me, spirit, soul, and body. Your Word says that by His wounds, I AM healed,[34] and I choose to believe your Word with every fibre of my being. I renounce unbelief and I ask you Lord to root it out and rid me of it. I pray God that your Spirit, by whose power Christ was raised, would cause every cell in my body to line up with the truth and be made whole, and brought back to life. I open myself up to you completely right now; I command my soul to open to Holy Spirit now and I give you Holy Spirit, access to every part of me. I ask Lord that every truth in heaven would be made manifest in my body, right now, in Jesus' name." We can even take our faith and authority further and begin to GOVERN our natural circumstances and our physical health through binding, loosing, commanding, and making declarations into the spirit realm.

About ten years ago I started a journey with Holy Spirit as He began to teach me about praying with authority. As I mentioned earlier, Jesus gave us authority to trample on snakes and scorpions and ALL the power of the enemy (Luke 10:19). In addition, we have been given the keys of the Kingdom according to Matthew 16:19:

> "I will give you the keys (authority) of the kingdom of heaven; and whatever you bind [forbid, declare to be improper and unlawful] on earth will have [already] been bound in heaven, and whatever you loose [permit declare lawful] on earth will have [already] been loosed in heaven" (AMP).

---

[34] "He himself bore our sins" in his body on the cross, so that we might die to sins and live for righteousness; "by his wounds you have been healed" (1 Peter 2:24 NIV). Also Isaiah 53:5

As I sought the Lord, He began to show me that He has already blessed us in the heavenly realms with EVERY spiritual blessing[35] and to see them manifest in the natural realm, I had to begin to "command" my blessing and pull them into the earth realm.

He also reminded me of how in Daniel 10:10-14, Daniel had to fast 21 days to receive understanding of a message the Lord gave him. When Daniel finally received his answer, the messenger (angel) of the Lord revealed that he (the messenger) had been resisted in the heavenly realm by the prince of Persia (a demonic entity) and needed help to break through.[36] The moment Daniel prayed, his answer was released from heaven, but the angel was engaged in warfare through the heavenlies for twenty-one days. So, it is clear, the enemy resists our blessings, and we need to take authority over that resistance in order to see them manifest. As a result, I began to command my blessings through the heavenlies into the earth realm.

After that, I began reading a book by Dutch Sheets called, *Authority in Prayer*, and I learned even more. You'll have to read the book for yourself to get the humor about the dog, but he begins by asking a thought-provoking question and making an incredible statement: "Who is ruling your world? I'm not referring to the big one, as in planet earth. At least not yet. I'm talking about the world you live in every day, your personal world. I'm speaking of your home, family, job, health, dog—well, okay maybe not your dog. God doesn't intend that any outside

---

[35] "All praise to God, the Father of our Lord Jesus Christ, who has blessed us with every spiritual blessing in the heavenly realms because we are united with Christ" (Ephesians 1:3 NLT).

[36] "But for twenty-one days the spirit prince of the kingdom of Persia blocked my way. Then Michael, one of the archangels, came to help me, and I left him there with the spirit prince of the kingdom of Persia" (Daniel 10:13 NLT).

force dominate you. He has given you jurisdiction over your life."[37] By page eight, he had my attention.

Dutch continues to tell a story very humorously about how God began to teach him how to govern his life and circumstances. It all began when he was at the airport, on his way to an important speaking engagement, in a very long line of unruly passengers waiting to check in. After some time, Dutch became concerned he might miss his flight, so he began to ask the Lord to intervene. The Lord then informed Dutch that all the chaos happening in the line was all because of him and the demonic resistance to his assignment.

Interestingly enough, after Dutch asked the Lord again to please do something about the situation, the Lord responded, "No, you do something about it. Move in the authority I have given you and command the demonic hindrances of your assignment to be ineffective. Declare that you have favor and will get to your meeting on time."[38] Dutch then wraps up the story by doing as he was told and following every detail of additional instruction God gave him. Dutch ended up experiencing supernatural favor by skipping the line, getting an up-grade to first-class AND reaching his meeting on time!

After reading Dutch's story, I immediately had an opportunity to test what I had been learning—to govern my own circumstances to see change. My daughter was pitching for her school's softball team, and they were in the playoffs that weekend. Her team had made it all the way to the finals two years in a row but the year prior they lost to a tough rival school who took great pleasure in speaking all kinds of nasty things against them. They suffered great humiliation after working hard all season.

---

[37] Dutch Sheets, *Authority in Prayer: Praying with Power and Purpose* (Minneapolis: Bethany House, 2006) 8-9. Print.

[38] Sheets, *Authority in Prayer*, 11. Print.

That Saturday they first played the finals for their division and won. Then they had to face the same team that had previously humiliated them; in the same fashion, they spoke hateful, crude remarks against the girls as they played. I began to recognize that something spiritual was at work.

Our team was not playing well; the oppression around them was affecting them greatly. They missed fly-balls and infield hits that they normally would have easily picked up and thrown out. They continually over-threw the ball; it was a comedy of errors, except no one was laughing. The opposing team seemed to hit the ball unusually well and were making every catch and every throw on target. If you've ever seen the movie, "Angels in the Outfield," it was kind of like that only it was demons who were controlling the game.

Two thirds of the way through the game, our girls were losing miserably, and I wondered what would happen if I began to govern the circumstances by binding the evil spirits at work, loosing the Holy Spirit over the game and declaring favor over my daughter and her team—so I did. It took about two minutes for the game to begin to turn and only about one inning for the girls to be totally back on their game! They had a huge come-back and ended up winning the game, PLUS the season, over the ENTIRE region where we live—BOTH city and rural divisions. The girls were over-the-moon. It was such a blessing.

The press was there and when they interviewed one of the girls on the opposing team, she said, "It was like out bats just stopped working." Grin. It is noteworthy to say here that I did not pray against the girls on the opposing team; I prayed against the demons in the atmosphere. I simply shifted the atmosphere to dis-empower evil and empower Holy Spirit through binding and loosing. I used my Kingdom keys just as we are supposed to.

We have the ability to lock and un-lock spiritual activity in the heavenly realm with the authority Christ has given us. We do that by opening our mouths in prayer, making decrees and declarations based on the Word of God into the atmosphere which let demons know what is allowed and what is not. We don't let the devil push us around! We govern the spirits which then leads to governing our circumstances. Remember, the Apostles said in 2 Corinthians 10:3, they did not wage war as the world does and neither do we. We have been given access to spiritual weapons that are mighty and powerful in Christ, and we have been given the FULLNESS of Christ dwelling within us.[39]

Is it possible to undermine the authority Christ has given us? Have you ever known someone in authority who didn't act the way they should? Have you ever heard of or known a corrupt police officer, an adulterous pastor, or an abusive parent? Did you lose respect for them and as a result see them as less of an authority figure in your life? I am going to venture a guess that you answered "yes" to that last question.

When those in authority don't steward that authority well, they undermine themselves and as a result will fail to continue to operate in that authority. We stop listening to the sermons of that adulterous pastor and stop seeking counsel from them, don't we? A corrupt police officer is stripped of his badge and held accountable for his actions. An abusive parent is held accountable by God, and the law if caught, and will likely lose relationship with their adult children.

What about us? Do we lose our spiritual authority when we don't bridle the flesh, put to death its sinful desires and exercise self-control? Do we undermine our authority in the spirit realm when we continue to live in sin even after we've repented? Yes, we do. We can't pick and choose what areas we want to submit to God in. It's all or nothing. God wants it all and He deserves it

---

[39] "For in Christ lives all the fullness of God in a human body. So you also are complete through your union with Christ, who is the head over every ruler and authority" (Colossians 2:9-10 NLT).

all! Doesn't He? He gave us His all and we need to reciprocate with the same devotion.

As we grow spiritually in our faith-walk and gain personal victories, overcoming temptation and destructive heart attitudes, our spiritual power and authority begin to "work" for us in greater and greater measure. Do you remember back in chapter 2 when we talked about Jesus being baptized? We looked at how Jesus was filled by the Holy Spirit at His baptism but was EMPOWERED[40] (miracle working power/strength/virtue) by the Holy Spirit AFTER He emerged out of the desert having OVERCOME the temptations the devil threw at Him.[41] Based on that revelation, here's what I believe Holy Spirit is saying to us right now:

OVERCOMING activates MY power and authority in YOU.

God calls us ALL to be OVERCOMERS with His help! What do you think being an overcomer looks like? To overcome something means to defeat something—to succeed, prevail over, to have the victory, to gain mastery over, to conquer. To be an overcomer means to be someone who stands in victory, who isn't mastered by a thing but has mastery over it. Nothing controls an overcomer except Christ. No habit, no need, no other person controls them.

Is there anything or anyone in your life that you feel controlled by? If so, this is one area the Lord is putting His finger on right now and calling you to deal with. Pray beloved! This could be something that is connected to ill health in your body. Remember, God, Jesus and Holy Spirit are gentle, and they are

---

[40] The word "power" is translated in Luke 4:14 from the Greek word dunamis which means miracle working power, might, ability, virtue (blueletterbible.org).

[41] "Then Jesus returned in the power of the Spirit to Galilee, and news of Him went out through all the surrounding region" (Luke 4:14 NKJV).

NOT into controlling us or overriding our free-will. Only the devil controls. So, if we are feeling controlled in an area, that is the devil at work. We must come out from under that and gain the victory. When we pass the test, just as Jesus passed His tests, we gain ground, and we are activated in more supernatural ability and authority.

There are 2 different words in the Greek that are translated "power," in various passages, even though one of them doesn't really mean power. Those words are, "dunamis" which means miraculous power, ability, and strength, and "exousia," which more accurately means AUTHORITY. Some passages use dunamis and some use exousia, but how many of you know, authority is useless unless you've also got the power? You can have power without authority but if you've got supernatural authority, you MUST also have supernatural power to back it up. As well, those with power AND authority are greater than those with only power. What good is power when you don't have the authority or right to use it?

With that understanding, listen again to Luke 10:19, "Behold, I give you the AUTHORITY to trample on serpents and scorpions, and over all the POWER of the enemy, and nothing shall by any means hurt you" (NKJV). What has Jesus given us? Authority. What does the devil have? Power, but no authority to use it.

Also, check out Luke 9:1-2, "Then He called His twelve disciples together and gave them POWER and AUTHORITY over all demons, and to cure diseases" (NKJV, emphasis mine). Then in Luke 10, He sends out seventy others, anointing them with the same power and authority saying to them, "Whatever city you enter, and they receive you, eat such things as are set before you. And heal the sick there, and say to them, 'The kingdom of God has come near to you" (Luke 10:8-9 NKJV). Just as Jesus sent the seventy and anointed them with power and authority, so He has sent us and anointed us, as we are faithful to overcome.

Lastly, when Jesus told the disciples to wait in Jerusalem for the gift of the Holy Spirit, He said to them, "But you shall receive POWER (dunamis: miraculous power) when the Holy Spirit has come upon you; and you shall be witnesses to Me in Jerusalem, and in all Judea and Samaria, and to the end of the earth" (NKJV, emphasis and brackets mine). It is the baptism of the Holy Spirit that gives us dunamis. And dunamis is the root word of our English word dynamite! The power of God in you works like dynamite to blow up and obliterate anything not of Him!

Have you been baptized in the Holy Spirit? If so, you have the dynamite, miracle working power of the Kingdom of God available to you. Make sure it is activated by being an overcomer and passing the tests God puts on your path. When we are faithful to persevere, letting go of every bad attitude, overcoming temptation, offense, bitterness, and everything that binds, God knows we can be trusted with His power and authority.

If you're not yet baptized in the Holy Spirit, ask Jesus NOW! Don't wait any longer. Cry out to Him for everything He has for you. "Jesus! Baptize me in the Holy Spirit! Would you cause the very Spirit of God to descend upon me and consume me now! I repent for not submitting nor accepting His baptism but NOW I'm ready! I humble myself under His mighty hand and open myself to His authority and control—in Jesus' name. Holy Spirit come! Consume me! Possess me now. Amen." And watch what happens. Hear the voice of the Lord. Is there something you must do to align yourself first? If so, do it! If something is causing you to sin, get rid of it! Is your Netflix subscription tripping you up? Get rid of it! Cut it out. Be obedient and open yourself up to God to take control of your desires, your heart, and your behaviors.

Beloved, God's got you. Do you know what "beloved" means? It means, "the one who is loved." Why do I keep calling you "beloved?" Is it because I'm just sappy? Is it just me and my personality? No! It's the Holy Spirit. The Holy Spirit is putting that word in my heart to describe you. To Him, you are His beloved, no matter what. He loves you! YOU are "the loved one" of the Lord. Even though He sees EVERYTHING you don't want anyone to see, He still loves you all the same. Receive Him. Receive all of Him. Don't refuse any gift God has for you. He knows what you need, and He knows how to bless you perfectly.

Chapter 6

PRAISE AND WORSHIP

What breaks the enemy's oppression over us faster than anything else? Praise and worship! Opening our mouths and choosing to celebrate God for Who He is, singing His praises, declaring His goodness and mercy, THROUGH EVERY CIRCUMSTANCE sends the devil running every time. The devil hates it. The devil wants us to wallow in disappointment and fear, feeling sorry for ourselves sitting under defeat. He wants us to focus on what's not working out for us so that it consumes us and controls us. God on the other hand wants us to focus on Him and His victory, shouting out His praises with a voice of triumph, ALL THE TIME, even when we don't feel like it. We may have to push our flesh, but when we do, we will win and maintain the victory we already have in Christ.

In 2001, my husband and I went through a very difficult time. We were expecting our third child but days after my eighteen-week ultrasound, we were informed that our baby had no heartbeat. It was heart-wrenching to say the least.

During and right after the ultrasound, I sensed something wasn't quite right and agonized about it until we finally got the call from the doctor's office. We got the bad news on a Friday and were told that my body would likely miscarry over the weekend, so that is where it was left. Two days later, on Sunday morning, I was feeling fine physically but emotionally wasn't and didn't *feel* like going to church. However, because I am *always* connected to the Spirit, I heard His gentle, still small voice inside, "Why do you go to church?" I answered *to worship God*. Then I heard, "Am I not worthy to be worshipped this morning? Have I changed? Have I somehow lost my holiness?" I think my heart may have stopped for a millisecond right there as the answer was obvious.

Well, you can probably guess the rest of the story. What would you do? Of course, God is worthy to be worshipped, at all times, so we went to church and sat near the front as we always did. I couldn't sing much because of the massive lump in my throat, as I tried desperately not to ugly cry in front of everyone, but I worshipped God in my heart with all sincerity. It was the strangest mixture of grief and praise and worship all at once. That morning, I learned, we are to worship, love and honor God for *Who* He is, not only for what He does, regardless of our circumstances.

Unfortunately, ten days later I still had not miscarried and I was admitted to the hospital for an induction. Our little one was stillborn, almost fully formed having survived about twelve weeks gestation. I don't know why this happened to us, but I chose to continue to trust in the goodness of God and I greatly valued my Sunday morning lesson in honoring God well.

God did not allow me to get away with not worshipping Him and I am so very grateful! Human reasoning told me it was okay to stay home and have a pity party, but God knew what I needed to do to stay aligned with Him and remain in victory. Praise and worship amidst sorrow and pain opened the way for God to manifest great favor in our lives. Just two months after my "missed miscarriage" I was pregnant again, but this time with twins. Gabriel and Jonathan, identical twins, were both born healthy in August of 2002. Praise God!

Psalm 100 says:

"Shout with joy to the LORD, all the earth! Worship the LORD with gladness. Come before him, singing with joy. Acknowledge that the LORD is God! He made us, and we are his. We are his people, the sheep of his pasture. Enter his gates with thanksgiving; go into his courts with praise. Give thanks to him and praise his name. For the LORD is good. His unfailing love continues forever, and his faithfulness continues to each generation" (NLT).

Exuberant praise should come first. Don't even think about holding back! Praise ushers us into His courts and His presence and He is worthy of it all. He is worthy to be praised with every fibre of our being, with prayer, words, and shouts—with instruments, flags, songs, and even dance. Yes! I said dance! Don't hold back.

I will never forget the first time I broke out in exuberant dance while praising the Lord. As I simply just let go of my self-imposed, self-conscious boundaries and limitations, the freedom and joy I felt was extraordinary. It was a Tuesday night meeting at a friend's home. As the live musicians strummed and beat their instruments and the vocalist sang in the Spirit, we moved seamlessly from praise to worship and back to praise as the Spirit led. It was beautiful. There was freedom as everyone did what the Spirit put on their heart to do. Some stood with hands raised, some knelt, some sat quiet with eyes closed and some lay prostrate on the floor. A holy hush had come over us as the music stopped and the presence of God filled the room. Moments of complete silence passed as we simply adored Him.

Suddenly, as the musicians followed the Spirit, an exuberant sound erupted and beckoned me to dance. Before I even knew what I was doing, I began to dance—to war dance. The Spirit propelled me, and I was completely submitted. My brain wanted to stop. My brain was concerned about who was watching me, but I persisted anyway. It was amazing. I know that personally, I overcame the need to impress others and the concern of what others thought of me but I'm sure it accomplished so much more than that in the Spirit as it was an intercessors' dance and a prophetic demonstration all its own.

I am reminded of another person who broke out in dance before the Lord; his name was King David. Second Samuel 6:12-15 tells the story:

> "...So David went and brought up the ark of God from the house of Obed-edom to the City of David with gladness. And so it was, when those bearing the ark of the Lord had gone six paces, that he sacrificed oxen and fatted sheep. Then David danced before the Lord WITH ALL HIS MIGHT; and David was wearing a linen ephod. So David and all the house of Israel brought up the ark of the Lord with shouting and with the sound of the trumpet" (NKJV, emphasis added).

King David danced WITH ALL HIS MIGHT; he held nothing back and he didn't care what others thought. Was he criticized for it? Yes, he was. His wife, Michal, daughter of Saul, saw him and verse 16 says that she "despised him in her heart." King David responds to her criticism and says in verse 21 and 22:

> "It was before the LORD, who chose me rather than your father or anyone from his house when he appointed me ruler over the LORD's people Israel—I will celebrate

before the LORD. I will become even more undignified than this, and I will be humiliated in my own eyes. But by these slave girls you spoke of, I will be held in honor" (2 Samuel 6:21-22 NIV).

King David had no problem humiliating himself for the sake of worshipping God and pleasing Him. Impressing others was of no importance but impressing God was. He danced for an audience of One!

Praise recognizes God for WHO He is. Praise celebrates Him and all His amazing characteristics: His goodness and holiness, His amazing power, authority, greatness, and beauty. Praise is exuberant, loud, and expressive. It stirs up joy from our inner most being, leads us into His presence and elevates us into a spirit of worship.

Praise shifts to worship as we are overtaken by His love. Praise gets us in the door, but the presence of God brings us to our knees. When the beautiful spirit of worship overtakes us, suddenly everyone else in the room disappears and it becomes just us and God together as one. We go from a party in praise with many others to complete seclusion, privacy, and intimacy with the One we love, where we simply behold and adore Him.[42] As we worship, we are overtaken by His love and end up receiving much more than what we've given.

Worship itself *begins* with a reverent heart toward God but many Christians choose to stay there; sadly, they choose not to press through into adoration. We can go higher! We can go higher if we will allow ourselves to fall deeply in love with Him, adore Him and become ravished by His love.

Worship is about turning our hearts completely toward God, putting everything else out of our mind and focusing

---

[42] Ruth Ward Heflin, *Glory: Experiencing the Atmosphere of Heaven* (Maryland: McDougal Publishing, 1990, 2000) 88-89. Print.

SOLELY on Him. As we do, we offer Him ALL our heart and ALL our adoration; we let go of every "lesser lover" we have entertained in the past. The more we are willing to focus our attention on God and *demonstrate* our love to Him, the higher we can rise. If you've not forgotten where you are while in worship, you've not yet come high enough.

Luke 7:36-50 tells us of a sinful woman who knew how to *demonstrate* her worship. A Pharisee by the name of Simon invited Jesus to his home for a meal and an uninvited woman with a colorful, sinful lifestyle boldly inserted herself there. We see two very different levels of love and worship being expressed to Jesus between the Pharisee and the woman. Let's have a look at the woman's actions:

> "Now one of the Pharisees was requesting Him to dine with him, and He entered the Pharisee's house and reclined at the table. And there was a woman in the city who was a sinner; and when she learned that He was reclining at the table in the Pharisee's house, she brought an alabaster vial of perfume, and standing behind Him at His feet, weeping, she began to wet His feet with her tears, and kept wiping them with the hair of her head, and kissing His feet and anointing them with the perfume. Now when the Pharisee who had invited Him saw this, he said to himself, "If this man were a prophet He would know who and what sort of person this woman is who is touching Him, that she is a sinner" (Luke 7:36-39 NASB).

This precious woman washed Jesus' feet with her tears, dried them with her hair, kissed his feet and anointed them with costly perfume. The Pharisee, on the other hand, didn't offer Jesus any such admiration—not even the basic foot washing when He arrived. The woman's demonstration of worship indicates the depth of her love for Jesus and the tenacity of her faith. Jesus says in verse 47, "... whoever has been forgiven little loves little" (Luke 7:47 NIV).

We all have a decision to make. How will we worship? Will we worship like the sinful woman, humbling ourselves offering the Lord all our heart and affection, or will we hold back and worship like the Pharisee? Will we allow Holy Spirit to give us revelation on how much we have truly been forgiven as well as the holiness of Christ and worship Him accordingly or will we stay in our limited carnal understanding, pride, and deception thinking we're not all that bad, staying in complacency? I pray you are willing to challenge yourself and push your flesh outside of your comfort zone, into a whole new level of praise and worship.

When the unction comes upon you from Holy Spirit to raise your hands, to kneel, to dance, to lay prostrate on the floor, DON'T HOLD BACK my friend! This grieves the Holy Spirit. Break through your fear. Break through whatever is holding you back and GO FOR IT! I promise you—you will be so blessed by it.

Chuck D. Pierce wrote a book called, *God's Now Time for Your Life*. In it, he gives his and his wife's testimony over barrenness. The final step to their healing was for Pam to worship the Lord in a brand-new way. Apostle Pierce lists twelve steps they had to take as a couple to see the fulfillment of their promise including attending a conference that they would not have normally attended and then he writes:

> "As a result of following these steps of obedience, culminating at the conference when Pam, against her nature, raised her hands in worship to God, Pam was healed instantly by the power of God invading her body and actually knocking out the clots that were in her uterus."[43]

---

[43] Chuck D. Pierce and Rebecca Wagner Systema, God's Now Time for Your Life: Enter Your Prophetic Destiny (Ventura: Regal Books from Gospel Light, 2005), 13. Print.

Wow! Healing manifested in her body the minute she was obedient to the Spirit's lead to raise her hands in worship. What have we missed out on by not raising our hands in worship!? What have we missed out on by not being obedient? God only knows. I pray Holy Spirit is opening your eyes to how important this is for your healing. And I pray, the next time Holy Spirit prompts you to express worship in a tangible way, you will do it, without hesitation.

The Lord is worthy of everything we can give. He is worthy of our words, shouts, adoration, and every expression of the physical body. If we want healing in our physical body, we better be willing to worship with our physical body on the outside and not just in our heart.

Here's the thing: if we are completely honest, we would admit that we don't raise our hands or dance or whatever because we don't want to look stupid to others. Come on! Let's just get real. It is an invisible social boundary that we have been trained to adhere to. Don't be weird. Fit in. Do what everyone else is doing and nothing more. Right? The spirit of the world causes us to be ashamed of our passion for the Lord. The spirit of the world convinces us that we shouldn't be "religious fanatics." Well, that belief is killing us, my friend.

The belief that we are crazy or fanatical or whatever when we raise our hands in worship is of the devil and it keeps people in bondage to the world, including sickness and disease. Don't be of the world! We are called to be "in the world" but NOT of it. God has called us out and right now, I speak courage to you in Jesus' name to be a "called out one," to be separated, and to be a possession of the Lord who is different, holy, righteous, and "on fire" for God. May our hearts burn for Him! May we be more concerned about God's approval than man's.

Are you with me?

Chapter 7

LIVING BY THE SPIRIT

Romans 8 is so rich with truth regarding how to lay hold of healing in our body and see it manifest now. Let's have a look at it:

"Therefore, there is now no condemnation for those who are in Christ Jesus, because through Christ Jesus the law of the Spirit who gives life has set you free from the law of sin and death. For what the law was powerless to do because it was weakened by the flesh, God did by sending his own Son in the likeness of sinful flesh to be a sin offering. And so he condemned sin in the flesh, in order that the righteous requirement of the law might be fully met in us, who do not live according to the flesh but according to the Spirit. Those who live according to the flesh have their minds set on what the flesh desires; but those who live in accordance with the Spirit have their minds set on what the Spirit desires. The mind governed by the flesh is death, but the mind governed by the Spirit is life and peace. The mind governed by the flesh is hostile to

God; it does not submit to God's law, nor can it do so. Those who are in the realm of the flesh cannot please God. You however, are not in the realm of the flesh but are in the realm of the Spirit, if indeed the Spirit of God lives in you. And if anyone does not have the Spirit of Christ, they do not belong to Christ. But if Christ is in you, then even though your body is subject to death because of sin, the Spirit gives life because of righteousness. And if the Spirit of him who raised Jesus from the dead is living in you, he who raised Christ from the dead will also give life to your mortal bodies because of his Spirit who lives in you. Therefore, brothers and sisters, we have an obligation—but it is not to the flesh, to live according to it. For if you live according to the flesh, you will die; but if by the Spirit you put to death the misdeeds of the body, you will live" (Romans 8:1-13 NIV).

That's a mouthful! But let's pull out some key points.

1. There is a "law" of the Spirit—that is the Holy Spirit, and that LAW states that the Spirit gives Life. Wherever the Spirit is, there is life. They are inseparable. Just like the law of gravity operates in the natural realm without partiality, so does the LAW of the Spirit operate on behalf of those living by the Spirit, in Christ Jesus.

2. There is also a law of sin and death which is the law of the flesh that states, wherever sin is, death is. Sin and death (or the process of death) are inseparable. Anyone living by the flesh, will experience the LAW of sin and death. It will operate without partiality; it is a law.

3. The Spirit sets us free from the law of sin and death, through Christ Jesus.

4. We will TRULY LIVE when we live by the Holy Spirit within us—by His power, His enabling, and His leading.
5. Living by the Spirit brings TRUE LIFE (vitality and health—life according to God's timetable).
6. Living by the flesh brings death (sickness, disease, and early death).

Unfortunately, while living on the earth, there is no delete button for the sinful nature; we still carry it around in our body, but by the Spirit it has been disempowered and crucified with Christ. To reinforce that truth, we also need to, in the power of the Holy Spirit, willfully put to death the misdeeds of the body (stop using our body as an instrument of unrighteousness) and CHOOSE to live by the Spirit. We need to let our dead "sin nature" STAY dead—without resurrecting it by our own will and wrong desires.

"Living by the Spirit"—I wonder if we really understand what that looks like. We tend to live by what we see and feel in the natural realm as it is obvious, easy, and right here in front of us. Living by the Spirit, takes great intentionality and focus—a choice to sometimes ignore what I see with my natural eyes, and allow what I see with my spiritual eyes to become superior. Living by the Spirit is something else—something other.

As a human being, we are primarily spiritual beings. We are spirit. We have a soul where our mind, will and emotions reside, and we live in a body. Our body is like a tent or a house our inner man lives in. Before we are saved, we are led by our souls and our feelings. After we are saved, the Holy Spirit becomes one with our spirit, giving us renewed inner life. We then need to command our soul to submit to the Spirit and allow the Holy Spirit to lead our lives. Living by the Spirit looks like seeking God's ways, God's heart, and God's perspective on everything, hearing His voice, obeying His direction, submitting our mind and will to His, thinking His thoughts, relying on Him in all of life and allowing His gifts to flow out of us.

Because I am a practical person and I like to use word pictures, imagine you accidently cut in line at the grocery store and someone gets mad and starts yelling at you, even calling you names. What do you do? If you were living by the flesh, you might have a few different responses depending on your personality and past woundedness. You might say, "I'm so sorry" repeatedly, be horribly embarrassed and leave the store in tears, struggling with your self-esteem. You may even have thoughts like, "I'm such an idiot!"

Someone else, living by the flesh, might respond with the same aggression, get angry and yell back, shooting a few choice names and/or saying something like, "Calm down!" or "Take it easy! It was an honest mistake," in defense of yourself. Either way, both responses are from your own feelings, soul, and flesh.

Contrarily, if you were living by the Spirit, how would you respond? Well, you would respond as if you were Jesus. First, their words would not penetrate your heart. It wouldn't hurt you or offend you in any way. Why? Because you know it was an honest mistake and you know who you are in God. You know you are right before God and it's only God's opinion of you that matters. You would say, "I'm sorry, I didn't realize the line was there. Please forgive me," because you did make a mistake and it would only be right to apologize but, you would also be able to ignore all other rants being spewed at you without reaction or inclination to defend yourself. Additionally, you would have compassion and empathy for the other person and "see" them from God's perspective. Perhaps the Spirit would even show you his/her heart and give you understanding of why he/she is responding the way he/she is. Perhaps the Spirit would show you that they are just tired and weary from a long day. The Spirit may even move you to do something for the person to make up for your mistake, but the key is to hear the inner leading of the Spirit of God and be obedient.

Another good example (given that this book is about the healing of illness) is what we do when we get sick. If I'm living according to the flesh, I do whatever feels right to my flesh, whatever the world has educated me to do or whatever is easiest. Perhaps I pop a few pills, or I run to the doctor immediately, for a diagnosis. But, if I'm living by the Spirit, the first thing I do is pray. I ask God. "Jesus, I have this pain in my side, let your Spirit flow in my body to bring your healing power. In the name of Jesus, I rebuke this pain now and command it to go. I do not receive it. It is not part of who I am in Jesus. I have been set free from the law of sin and death by the law of the Spirit of life. I am a brand-new creation in Jesus. By His stripes I am healed Now!" Pray over yourself. If the pain goes, great!! If the pain doesn't go, continue to pray, and ask the Lord to give you wisdom and knowledge on how to proceed. Ask Him what is causing the pain. Wait on Him to answer you. Spend time in worship and pray in tongues to stir up your spirit to hear Holy Spirit. Ask Him if there is something in your heart at the root of the pain. What happened right before the pain started; did you get angry at someone? Did you talk badly of someone? Ask God if you need to forgive someone. Ask Him if you have sinned somehow. Finally, ask Him if you should go to the doctor. (If you're struggling to hear the Lord, there is no shame in going to the doctor but at least pray first and give God an opportunity to speak to you. Ask the Lord to lead the doctor, give the doctor wisdom and to protect you as you go.) The key here is to seek the Lord FIRST for an answer and the doctor second. There is no sin in taking medication or a pain reliever but taking too much can affect your health as well. "Living by the Spirit" is living by the wisdom of God (not worldly wisdom) and allowing the Spirit of God to take control.

In this world, we think more knowledge is what we need so we get this degree and that degree, even going to seminary and letting other people (without the Spirit's lead) tell us how to interpret the Bible, but human or worldly knowledge does not give us true life. It may help us get a job or career but it's not going to give us eternal life or divine health—only Holy Spirit can do that.

Unfortunately, when we RELY on worldly knowledge it can become even more difficult than usual, to live by the Spirit, because we think we know everything! Thinking that worldly knowledge is the answer and seeking it out like one should seek God is dangerous and can get us entangled with demons of humanism and intellectualism (Matthew 6:33 tells us to seek first the Kingdom of God, not the world). Many Christians live this way. They've given mental assent to the Gospel, even received salvation, but they ignore the Holy Spirit and live by their own logic, knowledge, and wisdom rather than God's. Apart from the mercy of God, someone living this way would need to repent and possibly get delivered from a spirit of humanism, intellectualism and even idolatry, to be healed.

Holy Spirit should ALWAYS be our MAIN source of knowledge, wisdom and understanding, especially if it is our desire to live by the Spirit. Don't confuse human wisdom for God's wisdom. Ask the Lord for discernment to tell the difference and get to know the sound of the Lord's voice to distinguish it from your soul.

God's wisdom is going to sound foolish to your flesh/intellect but it's actually the opposite that is true; first Corinthians 3:19 tells us that to God, it's the wisdom of this world that is foolish. James 3:17 gives us clues to help recognize the wisdom of God, "But the wisdom from above is first of all pure. It is also peace loving, gentle at all times, and willing to yield to others. It is full of mercy and the fruit of good deeds. It shows no favoritism and is always sincere" (NLT).

First Corinthians 12:4-11 advises us of the manifestation gifts given to men by the Holy Spirit. Recognizing and moving in these gifts is part of living by the Spirit:

> "There are diversities of gifts, but the same Spirit. There are differences of ministries, but the same Lord. And there are diversities of activities, but it is the same God who works all in all. But the manifestation of the Spirit is given to each one for the profit of all: for to one is given the word of wisdom through the Spirit, to another the word of knowledge through the same Spirit, to another faith by the same Spirit, to another gifts of healing by the same Spirit, to another the working of miracles, to another prophecy, to another discerning of spirits, to another different kinds of tongues, to another the interpretation of tongues. But one and the same Spirit works all these things, distributing to each one individually as He wills" (1 Corinthians 12:4-11 NKJV).

These gifts are as follows:
1. Word of wisdom
2. Word of knowledge
3. Gift of faith
4. Gift of healing
5. Working of miracles
6. Prophecy
7. Discerning of spirits
8. Different kinds of tongues
9. Interpretation of tongues

Word of Wisdom

A word of wisdom is a supernatural enabling of the Spirit, to hear for yourself and/or deliver to someone else, a word from God that gives you/them Godly wisdom which perhaps addresses a current issue or question in their life. Wisdom is the correct or needed application of knowledge, experience and/or good judgment required for a situation. This wisdom is not from our own knowledge or experience but from God which goes beyond what we would naturally know or be able to communicate.

There are many examples in the Bible of when the Spirit gave a Word of wisdom to Jesus and others. For example, when Jesus healed the blind man from Bethsaida, in Mark 8:22-26, Jesus first took him out of the town and then healed him. Jesus put spit in his eyes and put His hands on him, twice. Jesus also made him "look up." Why? Because Jesus looked to His Father on what needed to be done and He told Him by the Spirit. Jesus received Words of wisdom on how to heal this man. Each action was significant to his healing, addressing root issues, directed by the Holy Spirit's wisdom.

Remember, Jesus, even though He was with the Father from the beginning of time, divine in every respect, He came to earth as a man only and He ministered on the earth through the empowering of the Holy Spirit. He had to submit completely to Holy Spirit and operate in the gifts of the Holy Spirit to be effective.

In John 2:1-10, Jesus does His first miracle when He turns water into wine. Mary, mother of Jesus, says to Him, "They have no wine" (vs. 3). Jesus says what does that have to do with me? "My hour has not yet come" (vs. 4). Despite that, Mary says to the servants, "Whatever He says to you, do it" (vs. 5). Mary somehow knew God was going to move on their behalf. She knew it before Jesus did! Moments later, Jesus begins to give the servants direction. "Fill the waterpots with water" (vs.7). Why?

Did Jesus simply change His mind? Did His mother's influence somehow affect His decision? No. Jesus only did what He saw His Father doing. One minute, the Father wasn't doing anything; the next, He was giving direction to Jesus on how to turn water into wine. Jesus received a word of wisdom and instruction through the Holy Spirit that He didn't anticipate.

What is interesting to me about this account also is why the waterpots were filled and not the containers the previous wine was in. They had wine up to that point at the wedding. The wine had to be contained in something. Why not fill those containers with water?

The scripture says, "Now there were set there six waterpots of stone, according to the manner of purification of the Jews, containing twenty or thirty gallons apiece" (John 2:6 NKJV). These jars were used by the Jews for ceremonial washing. Interesting. Jesus received a Word of wisdom from Holy Spirit to do what He did. In fact, through that miracle, Jesus foreshadowed that the Jews would cease to be cleansed with water but would be cleansed with the wine of the New Covenant, His blood, and it would happen at a covenant sealing moment, such as a wedding, when they and all of us would willingly and spiritually betroth ourselves to our Bridegroom King, Jesus. Very cool imagery here!

One last example, from the Bible, of a word of wisdom is found in the healing of the woman who suffered from continuous bleeding, found in Mark 5:25-34. We've already talked about that healing, but I just want to point out here, that it wasn't her good idea that led her to seek Jesus out. She was tired and weak; her flesh wanted to stay in bed! I'm sure of it! It would have made no good sense to any logical mind for her to get up and go anywhere. No, it was the Spirit that gave her a Word of wisdom, to get up, seek Jesus out, and touch the hem of His garment. It was also the Spirit that gave her the faith for her healing.

I remember a time when I was facilitating a small group discussion at church after a conference and there was a woman who was very discouraged about her small business. She owned and ran a salon/spa and was feeling that maybe what she was doing was not spiritual enough and a waste of time. We had just finished listening to some great speakers on how God was doing amazing things through them—rescuing children from child labour in India etc. and her little business suddenly felt too insignificant to matter. The business wasn't overly successful, and she was thinking that maybe she should close shop.

Two minutes after first speaking with her, the power and anointing of Holy Spirit rose up in me strongly and I began prophesying to her, encouraging her on how God wanted to touch people through her, and relaying a number of words of wisdom on how to level up her business. Included was instruction on creating more of an atmosphere of peace by reducing clutter and organizing things better, creating order out of chaos, praying in her space, and asking Holy Spirit to fill it. (There were other words too, but this is what I remember.) Now, many years later, she is still in business, and her shop is lovely. She is one of the higher end salons in town.

Word of Knowledge

A word of knowledge is information given to you by the Holy Spirit that gives you information that you do not naturally know about someone or knowledge about what God wants to do or heal. Knowing that Holy Spirit would tell someone information about you is a bit unnerving, however, it is ALWAYS for a good purpose, and He only tells those whom He can trust.

Jesus moved in words of knowledge when He spoke to the woman at the well and said to her, "for you have had five husbands, and the one whom you now have is not your husband" (John 4:18 NKJV). Jesus did not know this on His own; He knew it by the Holy Spirit.

Jesus also moved in words of knowledge in John 1:47-48 when He recognized Nathanael even before meeting him physically and said, "Behold, an Israelite indeed, in whom is no deceit" (vs.47 NKJV)! Nathanael was confused and wondered how Jesus knew him. Jesus said, "Before Phillip called you, when you were under the fig tree, I saw you" (vs.48 NKJV). This was all it took for Nathanael to recognize Jesus as the Son of God. Love Nathanael!

Words of knowledge are especially useful in evangelism and Holy Spirit uses it often with those who are open to it. For instance, if there was a person on the street that Jesus wanted to reach, a Spirit-filled, Spirit-baptized Christian who is open to being used this way could speak to that individual and deliver a message right from Holy Spirit that pierces their heart. For example, you might be on the street, and you notice something about someone (something stands out to you), and compassion begins to stir in your heart for them. This is how you know Holy Spirit is at work.

A good question to the Lord would be, "What do you want to do in this moment for that person?" Holy Spirit may answer you directly or show you an area in their life where they need care, love, or encouragement. Holy Spirit may say, "They struggle with fear," or "They're having nightmares," or "They're suicidal," or give you some sort of tidbit of knowledge about them that will give you a launching pad for witnessing and ministry to them. The beauty of this gift is it communicates clearly that God is real, God cares, and God sees what they're struggling with.

Another type of word of knowledge is when Holy Spirit reveals to you what He wants to do, or what He wants to heal in that moment, for a particular person, people group, or in a meeting—wherever you are. I was involved with a church group who purposefully went out into the street, stores, and public places to move in this type of gifting. We would pray ahead of time and ask God to show us the people He wanted us to connect with and we would make notes on the features of the people God showed us. We would also ask if there was something, in particular, God wanted us to share with them or God wanted to heal (based on an evangelism method called Treasure Hunting).[44] Sometimes God would give us details ahead of time but sometimes He would wait until we were speaking to the person we found.

One time we had been ministering in Meijer and at some point surrounding that event, God dropped an image in my mind of a tall young man (early twenties perhaps) with friends, standing in front of the dairy section. The Lord then dropped the words, "shin splint" in my mind. Then, in my mind's eye, I saw myself ministering to this young man, and I heard the words, "You have pain in the front of your shin (pointing to the left one), and God wants to heal it. You have been playing soccer, though most people assume you play basketball, and you injured yourself playing the game, with such intensity. You're very good at it! The Lord wants to heal you, but He also wants you to come back to Him. When you were a child, you used to kneel at the edge of your bed and pray but as you grew, you stopped doing that. The Lord misses you. The Lord misses hearing your voice. Return to Jesus. He loves you with an everlasting love. If you will once again kneel and pray to your Savior acknowledging Him, He will heal you."

---

[44] Kevin Dedmon, *The Ultimate Treasure Hunt* (Shippensburg: Destiny Image Publishers, 2007).

I didn't have the opportunity to deliver that word to anyone that night as I didn't see anyone that fit that description. I'm not sure why. Perhaps I missed him or perhaps I have not yet met him. Regardless, the word I received was FULL of supernatural words of knowledge from Holy Spirit.

We did speak with a few people in Meijer at the outreach event previously mentioned. I don't usually remember exactly what I say to people as I am in the Spirit when I speak, but I do remember speaking to one young woman and delivering a word of encouragement to her about something she was worried and concerned about—that God was intervening on her behalf etc. I remember she was overcome by emotion as Holy Spirit ministered to her heart, and she revealed to us that her cat was sick, and no one could figure out what was wrong. She received encouragement and a sense of peace about the situation, and we parted ways. She already knew Jesus and just needed a touch from Him.

Gift of Faith
The gift of faith from Holy Spirit is a supernatural deposit of massive, fully persuaded faith that suddenly drops in our spirit which supercharges the faith we already carry. It is over and above the faith that is in our spirit every day and shifts us into sudden, aggressive faith for something we may not have been FULLY persuaded of before. It very often will propel us into action.

Gift of Healing
The gift of healing is the supernatural ability to heal others by the Holy Spirit which is above and beyond the normal supernatural working of Holy Spirit resident in every Spirit-baptized believer. "Healing" implies that what is already in existence is put into order according to God's will. For example: to heal someone who is now blind but was born seeing.

Working of Miracles

The working of miracles is a gift which provides believers the supernatural ability, by Holy Spirit, to heal an issue that would require the creation of something that is not already in existence. For example: to heal a person who was born blind without the necessary physical organs in their eyes to see or born with no eyes at all.

Prophecy

Prophecy is a gift of Holy Spirit giving believers the ability to see and/or hear and discern in various ways the heart, will, and voice of God regarding people (personal prophecy) and/or geographical regions and could include (but not always) the foretelling of events to come.

Paul tells us in 1 Corinthians 14:1-3 to earnestly desire the gifts, especially the gift of prophecy:

> "Pursue [this] love [with eagerness, make it your goal], yet earnestly desire and cultivate the spiritual gifts [to be used by believers for the benefit of the church], but especially that you may prophesy [to foretell the future, to speak a new message from God to the people]. For one who speaks in an unknown tongue does not speak to people but to God; for no one understands him or catches his meaning, but by the Spirit he speaks mysteries [secret truths, hidden things]. But [on the other hand] the one who prophesies speaks to people for edification [to promote their spiritual growth] and [speaks words of] encouragement [to uphold and advise them concerning the matters of God] and [speaks words of] consolation [to compassionately comfort them]" (1 Corinthians 14:1-3 AMP).

Discerning of Spirits

The gift of discerning of spirits is a gift of Holy Spirit giving believers the ability to know when Holy Spirit is at work and when a demon is at work. It also gives the believer the ability to know WHAT demon, in particular, is at work around them, in the atmosphere, in people and in geographical regions with the purpose of dealing with it in prayer and/or casting it out.

Different Kinds of Tongues

The gift of tongues is a supernatural ability to speak another earthly language unknown to the speaker or a heavenly language for the purpose of delivering a message from God in a corporate setting (when in order) or to use in personal prayer to draw closer to God, hit the mark in prayer, stir oneself up in the spiritual realm to activate discernment and/or to war in the spirit realm. There are whole books written on why we should pray in tongues so the benefits I've listed are in NO way the only benefits, just the ones off the top of my head.

Interpretation of Tongues

The gift of interpretation of tongues is a message from the Holy Spirit, given in the language of the corporate setting, which interprets an utterance already given in a heavenly language.

These are the manifestation gifts of Holy Spirit, and He wants us to move in them as He releases them and empowers us. They are for our benefit and the benefit of everyone around us and can cause a pre-believer to take the leap into relationship with Christ. Embracing or rejecting the gifts is your choice but rejecting them could have consequences.

Have you ever given a gift only to have it rejected by the person it was given to? No? Me neither. That would be rude, wouldn't it? Well, in this conversation we are talking about God, not people. The last thing I would want to be to God, is rude. It wouldn't help in our relationship and our fellowship together. It would only hinder. It's okay to be a bit nervous and it's okay to be unsure. Moving in the gifts of the Spirit takes practice so get with some spiritual Christians who are like-minded, who are forgiving and will allow you to make mistakes.

Above all, honour the Holy Spirit. Welcome Him in your presence and give Him the space and opportunity to move in your life. If you haven't honored Him, repent, change your mind, and turn back toward goodness, thankfulness, honor, and righteousness. Throwing the baby out with the bath water because of fear only produces religion without power and that's no good to anyone. So, embrace the supernatural instead of running from it or rejecting it. It is ONLY by the breaking in of supernatural power from Holy Spirit that we will be healed in this earthly realm.

Chapter 8

THE LORD'S SUPPER

In John 6, Jesus speaks a Word in the synagogue at Capernaum which challenges the crowd beginning with: "I am the bread of life. Whoever comes to me will never be hungry again. Whoever believes in me will never be thirsty" (John 6:35 NLT). Jesus continues in verse 47:

> "I tell you the truth, anyone who believes has eternal life. Yes, I am the bread of life! Your ancestors ate manna in the wilderness, but they all died. Anyone who eats the bread from heaven, however, will never die. I am the living bread that came down from heaven. Anyone who eats this bread will live forever; and this bread, which I will offer so the world may live, is my flesh (John 6:47-51 NLT).

This Word causes arguments among the people and offends the minds of many, "How can this man give us his flesh to eat" (John 6:52 NLT)? They had no clue what He was talking about as they didn't know Jesus was about to willingly give up His life for them and allow the brutal beating and crucifixion of His own body for them and us.

Jesus continues to speak even more blatantly:

> "I tell you the truth, unless you eat the flesh of the Son of Man and drink his blood, you cannot have eternal life within you. But anyone who eats my flesh and drinks my blood has eternal life, and I will raise that person at the last day. For my flesh is true food, and my blood is true drink. Anyone who eats my flesh and drinks my blood remains in me, and I in him. I live because of the living Father who sent me; in the same way, anyone who feeds on me will live because of me. I am the true bread that came down from heaven. Anyone who eats this bread will not die as your ancestors did (even though they ate the manna) but will live forever" (John 6:53-58 NLT).

Many of Jesus' disciples left Him because of this Word. They could not understand it. However, *we* can understand it being on this side of the cross. Jesus demonstrates what He means at the Passover meal which He shares with His disciples right before His arrest:

> "I have been very eager to eat this Passover meal with you before my suffering begins. For I tell you now that I won't eat this meal again until its meaning is fulfilled in the Kingdom of God." [19]He took some bread and gave thanks to God for it. Then he broke it in pieces and gave it to the disciples, saying, "This is my body, which is given for you. Do this in remembrance of me." After supper he took another cup of wine and said, "This cup is the new covenant between God and his people—an agreement confirmed with my blood, which is poured out as a sacrifice for you" (Luke 22:15-16, 19-20 NLT).

Jesus demonstrates for us how to partake of His blood and broken body *by faith*, by using symbols of bread and wine. The church has implemented this as a corporate act once a month or once a quarter, depending on the church, but there is no reason why we can't do this at home by ourselves, every single day—especially if we're ill. It does not have to be given by a pastor, priest, or minister; we can simply take a little cup of wine or grape juice and a piece of unleavened bread or cracker, pray over them, and exercise our faith to partake and receive the renewing power of Jesus' life.

How we take the Lord's supper is also important. First Corinthians 11:27-30 tells us to examine ourselves *before* we partake so we don't partake in an unworthy manner.

> "So anyone who eats this bread or drinks this cup of the Lord unworthily is guilty of sinning against the body and blood of the Lord. That is why you should examine yourself before eating the bread and drinking the cup. For if you eat the bread or drink the cup without honoring the body of Christ, you are eating and drinking God's judgment upon yourself. That is why many of you are weak and sick and some have even died" (1 Corinthians 11:27-30 NLT).

I remember being at a women's renewal weekend and we were about to take communion on Sunday morning; it had been a great weekend with the Spirit moving powerfully in my heart. As I held the bread between my fingers, the Spirit reminded me of a painful event in my teen years; I had forgiven the other person involved but I knew it wasn't all his fault. I knew I had a part to play in it too. As I contemplated everything, still seeing the regret in my heart, I heard the Lord say CLEAR AS DAY, "Don't you dare put that bread in your mouth until you forgive yourself."

A little stunned, I sat there, motionless for a minute. Frozen in the fear of the Lord, physically unable to put the bread in my mouth. And here was yet another moment when I knew that I knew God was VERY real, alive, and active in my life. I was not going to get away with anything.

Tears quietly leaked from my eyes as I said, "Yes, Lord." With eyes closed, I brought my heart into alignment with His will and once again, just like He had done many times before, He gave me a wonderful picture confirming my surrender and His acceptance. As a young girl dressed in white, I saw myself in the throne room, before my Father, twirling and dancing before Him. He had such a look of delight on His face! And there was so much freedom in my childlike display. As this wonderful scene played out in my mind, I quietly slipped the bread into my mouth and peace overcame my heart and mind.

Before taking communion, be sure to ask the Lord to search your heart and show you anything there that would cause you to partake in an unworthy manner. Perhaps repent for taking the Lord's supper in an unworthy manner before if this discussion has convicted your heart.

My suggestion for you would be to work through the remainder of this book, then begin to take communion everyday as follows:

Take your bread or cracker and pray:
"Lord, before I partake of these elements, search my heart O God, and renew a right spirit within me. Is there anything I need to repent for or anyone I need to forgive? [Allow Holy Spirit to search your heart and then repent for anything the Lord shows you and forgive those who you haven't forgiven. Then continue...] On the night He was betrayed, Jesus took bread, gave thanks to God, and gave it to His disciples saying, 'This is my body which is given for you. Do this

in remembrance of me.' Thank you, God, for this bread/cracker which represents the broken body of your Son, Jesus. Thank you that His body was broken for my healing and as I eat His body, eternal life is made manifest in mine. As I partake, I remember and honor His sacrifice. I live because He lives [break the cracker and partake]."

Take your juice and pray:
"Also on the night He was betrayed, Jesus took a cup and said, 'This cup is the new covenant between God and his people—an agreement confirmed with my blood, which is poured out as a sacrifice for you.' Thank you, God, for this wine/juice which represents your blood poured out for me for the forgiveness of my sins, sealing our covenantal promise together. As I partake, putting my faith behind my action, may your blood wash me clean. [Partake of the juice/wine.] Thank you, Lord. I bless you and worship you with all that I am. Amen."

This concludes the first part of *Position Yourself for Healing*. We have laid a foundation for divine healing as well as an expectation for it. We have also talked in generalities about attitudes of the heart and various other things that could block us from receiving our healing so now we're going to get more specific. And we're going to dive into some prayer examples to get you praying in faith, authority and boldness as the Spirit leads and wants you to.

PART II

ELIMINATING
BLOCKAGES
TO HEALING

BLOCKAGES

Ever had a blocked drain in your kitchen? Ever had a blockage so bad a professional had to come in with a drain snake? We have. For some reason, our last house seemed to be particularly bad for this. The plumber had to snake the pipes all the way down under ground and we had to become extra vigilant at not allowing food particles to go down the drain. It became quite a nuisance.

Ever had a plugged toilet? If you've had young children growing up in your home, you've probably become an expert with the plunger. Perhaps you've had unexpected things block your toilet, like us. I think the worst blockage we had was after our 4-year-old tried to flush a bottle of Calamine lotion. My husband had to completely remove the toilet to get it out. Toddlers love to put all kinds of random things in the toilet, don't they? Hopefully, you've not had to part with anything valuable due to a toddler's obsession with the flush.

Why do I bring up pipes, toilets, and blockages of all kinds? Because it's possible for our healing and our blessings from the Lord, financial and otherwise, to be held back or blocked from reaching us, because of issues in our soul which have not been dealt with.

In the Old Testament, we see an example of a gate or portal to heaven in Genesis 28:10-17. Jacob had a dream and saw a ladder stretching into heaven, upon which angels ascended and descended. In verse 17, Jacob says, "How awesome is this place! This is none other than the house of God, and this is the gate of heaven" (Genesis 28:17 NKJV)! How awesome for Jacob to have discovered that place and connected with God's presence there; it was rare for those in the Old Testament to experience such a thing. Conversely, under the New Covenant, we are honored and privileged to be blessed with all the benefits of being reconciled to God. One of those benefits is to have the very presence of God living within us and another is being welcomed right into the throne room, should we wish to go.[45]

John of Patmos is given one such invitation as seen in Revelation 4. "Come up here," said the Lord. A divine portal or door suddenly became manifest to John's spiritual eyes in a vision. "Then as I looked, I saw a door standing open in heaven…" (Revelation 4:1 NLT).

As Christ's own beloved, the Spirit of God lives within us, and WE have now become God's dwelling place. We don't need to travel to any geographical location to find the presence of God. He is as close to us as we are to ourselves. We as believers are temples of the Holy Spirit.[46] The Spirit of Jesus dwells within us and we have become the point of connection where the natural realm meets the spiritual, where angels ascend and descend.

Inside all of us is a gateway, passageway, or portal to heaven. Jesus said, "I am the way…" Jesus also said, "I am the door…" (John 10:9 NKJV). The Spirit of Jesus in us, provides a point of access, for us to reach God and the heavenly realm, and for God to reach us. This door, where the natural and supernatural meet—where divine power passes from one reality to another, is the meeting place—the touching point, where Holy Spirit meets our spirit and soul. It's a place of supernatural exchange and each time divine power crosses over, healing and transformation happens.

---

[45] "So let us come boldly to the throne of our gracious God. There we will receive his mercy, and we will find grace to help us when we need it most" (Hebrews 4:16 NLT).

[46] "Don't you realize that your body is the temple of the Holy Spirit, who lives in you and was given to you by God? You do not belong to yourself, for God bought you with a high price. So you must honor God with your body" (1 Corinthians 6:19-20 NLT).

But what if we don't properly honor the Spirit of Jesus in us, or submit to Holy Spirit? What if we don't honor our body which is the temple or abiding place of God? What if we try to take advantage of grace and continue to partner with sin after being saved? What if we don't exercise our freedom over sin by saying "no" to it? What if we live in falsehood by not recognizing the negative attitudes in our heart and repenting? In each of these cases, the doorway between Holy Spirit and our inner man gets blocked and if our access is blocked, we have trouble connecting to God and hearing His voice. As a result, the healing we desire which is supernaturally present in His love and power, can't reach us.

The scriptures confirm that we are BOTH sanctified[47] AND in the PROCESS of being sanctified[48] as the natural has not yet been perfected. And just like food particles and grease can stick to the inside of a pipe and prevent water from flowing through it, the junk in our soul prevents supernatural healing power from flowing to us. If there are things in our soul that prevent us from being able to receive from the Lord, we would want to clear those blockages, wouldn't we? I know I would. I want to experience every benefit of the cross I can, here, now, on this side of eternity.[49] Why live any less triumphantly than what we were intended to?

Many things can block us from receiving, but they all have one thing in common: they all interfere with our ability to love God, love others, and love ourselves, as we are called to. How are we called to love? Jesus tells us in Matthew 22:37-39, "Love

---

[47] 2 Corinthians 5:17, Romans 8:30

[48] Philippians 2:12, 2 Corinthians 3:18

[49] "Bless the LORD, O my soul; And all that is within me, *bless* His holy name! Bless the LORD, O my soul, And forget not all His benefits: Who forgives all your iniquities, Who heals all your diseases, Who redeems your life from destruction, Who crowns you with lovingkindness and tender mercies, Who satisfies your mouth with good things, So that your youth is renewed like the eagle's" (Psalm 103:1-5 NKJV).

the Lord your God with ALL your heart and with ALL your soul and with ALL your mind.' This is the first and greatest commandment. And the second is like it: 'Love your neighbor as yourself'" (NIV, emphasis added).

Loving God with ALL our heart looks like guarding our heart and not allowing anything contrary to love, according to 1 Corinthians 13:4-7, to live there, hide there, or even visit there. Loving God with all our soul, is the same principle. We love God with ALL our soul when we do not tolerate, hold, or allow to remain, ANYTHING in our soul that is contrary to love—not an ounce of hurt, offense or ill-will toward ANYONE, including those who have hurt, offended, cheated, and/or not liked us. And it goes even further than that! LOVE not only doesn't curse but has a desire to bless. Love goes out of its way to do good to its enemies.[50]

Lastly, loving God with ALL our mind looks like not entertaining any thought or thinking pattern contrary to love and righteousness and not *feeding* our mind anything of the same. It means keeping our mind fixed on the things of God, including whatever things are true, good, pure, just, noble, lovely, and praiseworthy.[51] Loving others and loving ourselves is a natural outflow of loving God with ALL we are.

Are you beginning to see the blockages? If we were honest, we would admit, we have A LOT of work to do—we have a lot of healing that needs to happen on the inside before it can manifest on the outside.

---

[50] "'You have heard that it was said, 'You shall love your neighbor and hate your enemy.' But I say to you, love your enemies, bless those who curse you, do good to those who hate you, and pray for those who spitefully use you and persecute you, that you may be sons of your Father in heaven" (Matthew 5:43-45a NKJV).

[51] "Finally, brethren, whatever things are true, whatever things are noble, whatever things are just, whatever things are pure, whatever things are lovely, whatever things are of good report, if there is any virtue and if there is anything praiseworthy—meditate on these things" (Philippians 4:8 NKJV).

There can be MANY things blocking our healing, but there is still hope; it is possible for the greatness of God's mercy to bust right through and manifest at any time, AS GOD CHOOSES and enables according to our heart. Nevertheless, the issues Holy Spirit *makes us aware of*, are our responsibility to deal with through repentance and renunciation. Never should we just ignore the conviction of Holy Spirit expecting God to just overlook what He puts His finger on. Holy Spirit convicts us to help us come into the fullness of resurrection life. We CAN expect God's mercy to bust through those things we *aren't aware of*, as long as our heart is soft and open to His leading.

There are too many issues to address in one book, but you will get a feel for how to pray through as we cover the following:

- the religious spirit or mindset
- anger and forgiveness
- idolatry
- iniquity
- words and power
- negative body perspectives
- repressed emotions
- injustice
- shame and self-hate/rejection
- the orphan spirit or mindset
- false religions and secret societies

Every prayer to gain freedom will follow a pattern with multiple steps. One does not always need deliverance from a demon but when you do, the steps are as follows:

1. Confess and Repent
2. Renounce
3. Ask for mercy for what you've missed

4. Bind demons
5. Cast demons out
6. Declare every curse broken
7. Ask Father to send Holy Spirit to completely fill you

Confess and Repent
Effective prayer to be free from sin, heart attitudes that don't glorify God, and the influence of demons always begins with confession. How have you partnered, knowingly or unknowingly, with the demon you are attempting to break agreement with and cast out? What bad fruit has come up in your life that is connected to that demon? These are the things you will need to confess. For example, if you have been bound by a spirit of fear, you have likely participated in worry. You may have also participated with a spirit of procrastination and indecisiveness which may in turn have caused grief for your family members. When we are living in fear, we cannot and do not love well. Fear can also nullify faith and trust in God. In summary, confession will need to include worry, lack of faith, lack of trust in God, procrastination, indecision, lack of love, causing others grief and perhaps not fulfilling your God-given role in your family. You will need to seek the leading of Holy Spirit, to know exactly what you need to confess and repent for. Let the Spirit convict you. Confession also includes confessing your inner truth—telling God about ALL your feelings surrounding the sin you have committed, or others have committed against you.

Repentance is simply a decision to turn around and go in the opposite direction, back to God, and to willfully change your mind about a thought, thinking pattern, belief, or behavior. Repentance is making a decision that says, "This is no longer acceptable, and I choose to no longer allow myself to think this way or act this way." Remember in faith, 1 John 1:9, "If we confess our sins, He is faithful and just to forgive us our sins and to cleanse us from all unrighteousness" (NKJV).

To wrap up this step it is always good to voice acceptance of God's forgiveness and thank Him for it. If you find you "feel" like you need to confess a sin repeatedly, you probably have not forgiven yourself, in which case, you have not allowed yourself to fully receive God's forgiveness. Simply say, "I choose to forgive myself and I fully receive your forgiveness, Lord. Thank you that you have cleansed me from all unrighteousness. I declare that I am forgiven, in Jesus' name."

Renounce and Break Fellowship
To renounce something is to completely reject something and make a formal declaration to give up on, abandon, cut off, and refuse to co-operate with something. For our purposes, we are renouncing the sinful habits or attitudes and possibly demons we have previously agreed or partnered with.

Ask for Mercy
It is only for mercy that we don't get what we really deserve. Considering the truth that we are partakers of a superior covenant with God, based on the mercy and grace of God, pray that God's mercy would touch and cover anything you've missed or aren't aware of.

Bind
To bind is to restrict by binding or wrapping it up, with chains for instance. Matthew 16:19 says that whatever we bind on earth will be bound in heaven. We, therefore, can declare in the earthly realm that harmful spirits are bound, and they will be bound in the spirit realm, restricting them from operating and using their power against us. This will make it easier for us to be free from them and will restrict manifestations. Remember to mean what you say! In other words, make sure your heart agrees with your words.

Cast Out

To cast a spirit out, simply say, "I command the spirit of (name it) to come out of me now, in Jesus' name." Speak this command out as many times as you are led by the Spirit. There may not always be a "feeling" associated with your newfound freedom, so "in faith" believe you are being set free. You may find yourself spontaneously doing things like yawning, coughing, or even burping, signifying the exit of that spirit. This is good; allow it to happen.

Every Curse Broken

Everything we co-operate with, which is not of God, gives curses an opportunity to rest on us and operate in our lives. Proverbs 26:2 says, "Like a flitting sparrow, like a flying swallow, So a curse without cause shall not alight" (NKJV). The opposite is also true. A curse with cause WILL alight.

Deuteronomy 28:1-14 outlines all the blessings that will come upon us for our obedience and Deuteronomy 28:16-68 outlines all the curses that will come upon us because of our disobedience and includes multiple physical ailments such as plague, fever, and inflammation. Curses have not been done away with; they are still real just as blessings are real. Deuteronomy 30:19 says:

> "I call heaven and earth as witnesses today against you, that I have set before you life and death, blessing and curse; therefore choose life, that both you and your descendants may live; that you may love the Lord your God, that you may obey His voice, and that you may cling to Him, for He is your life and the length of your days" (NKJV);

As you can see from this verse, for our descendants to live, we must choose life and blessings by loving the Lord, obeying His voice, and clinging to Him, but we know that we are not able to do that on our own. We "all have sinned and fall short of the glory of God" (Romans 3:23 NKJV). So how do we do that this side of the cross, under the New Covenant with Christ as our Redeemer? We choose life and blessings through confession and repentance and warfare prayer that boldly confesses our redemption and the breaking of EVERY curse that has come upon us. We can make this confession because according to Galatians 3:13-14, Jesus Christ has redeemed us from the curse of the law, having become a curse for us by dying on the cross.[52] If we don't confess and repent for sin and iniquity, we end up choosing death and curses BY DEFAULT, without even realizing it.

Beloved, curses are evil, and evil is STUBBORN. Let's not be passive in our praying. We must be bold, strong, and courageous to dis-empower every evil agenda trying to stand against us.

Let's make sure to use our sword—the Word of the Lord. Declare the truth of who you are and Whose you are. Declare Who God is on your behalf. If something is not working, worship the Lord and pray in tongues, then ask God how to proceed.

Ask Father to send Holy Spirit to Completely Fill You
After demons have left you, and curses are declared broken, it is important to ask Father for more of Holy Spirit so you are completely filled with Him, believing in faith, that Father will give you what you ask for.[53]

Let's begin!

---

[52] "Christ has redeemed us from the curse of the law, having become a curse for us (for it is written, "Cursed is everyone who hangs on a tree"), that the blessing of Abraham might come upon the Gentiles in Christ Jesus, that we might receive the promise of the Spirit through faith" (Galatians 3:13-14 NKJV).

[53] Luke 11:9-13

THE RELIGIOUS SPIRIT OR MINDSET

I believe the number one block to believers receiving from the Lord, whether it be healing or anything else, is the Pharisee or religious spirit/mindset. This spirit or mindset makes Christians believe they are saved because they are DOING all the right Christian things, and it blocks them from having a real relationship with God. It keeps people stuck in the natural realm going through the motions of church but unable or unwilling to be in the Spirit, connected to and communicating with Holy Spirit.

The religious spirit, in partnership with a few others, will keep people attached to the world, immersed in worldly knowledge, worldly understanding, worldly wisdom, and worldly logic structures. Second Timothy 3:5 describes a person affected by this demon or mindset, "They will ACT religious, but they will reject the power that could make them godly" (NLT, emphasis mine). Those influenced by a religious spirit are "actors" in the game called "church." They are preoccupied with outward appearances and avoid inward transformation and sanctification like the plague.

The religious spirit is the spirit that was on the Pharisees in the Bible. It kept them blind to many things, including the love and compassion of God, Who Jesus was, the new way God wanted to relate to them through mercy, grace, and compassion, without the sacrifice of animals,[54] and even their

---

[54] To the Pharisees Jesus said, "But go and learn what *this* means: 'I desire mercy and not sacrifice.' For I did not come to call the righteous, but sinners, to repentance" (Matthew 9:13 NKJV).

own sinfulness. It kept them locked into the old ways and unaccepting of God's new covenant.

Luke 12:1 says, "Beware of the leaven of the Pharisees, which is hypocrisy" (NKJV). Hypocrisy according to Wikipedia is "the practice of engaging in the same behavior or activity for which one criticizes another or the practice of claiming to have moral standards or beliefs to which one's own behavior does not conform."[55] Here's a parable Jesus told that illustrates it well:

> "Then Jesus told this story to some who had great confidence in their own righteousness and scorned everyone else: "Two men went to the Temple to pray. One was a Pharisee, and the other was a despised tax collector. The Pharisee stood by himself and prayed this prayer: 'I thank you, God, that I am not like other people—cheaters, sinners, adulterers. I'm certainly not like that tax collector! I fast twice a week, and I give you a tenth of my income.' But the tax collector stood at a distance and dared not even lift his eyes to heaven as he prayed. Instead, he beat his chest in sorrow, saying, 'O God, be merciful to me, for I am a sinner.' I tell you, this sinner, not the Pharisee, returned home justified before God. For those who exalt themselves will be humbled, and those who humble themselves will be exalted" (Luke 18:9-14 NLT).

Self-righteousness, pride, haughtiness, judgementalism and contentiousness are a few of the key characteristics of this spirit. The religious spirit or mindset puts heavy burdens on people, holds others to a standard that is impossible and does not allow mercy or grace to cut anyone any slack. This spirit does not discriminate against who it influences or connects to. It does not

---

[55] https://en.wikipedia.org/wiki/Hypocrisy

only affect church leaders as some might presume, but it can affect every Christian when given the opportunity.

The religious spirit is seen at work in the Bible every time the Pharisees tried to trap Jesus into an argument and ACCUSE him of going against the law/rules of the temple. Each time Jesus healed someone on the Sabbath, and the Pharisees were upset about breaking a rule, this spirit was exposed. They should have been rejoicing with the one who was set free, not bemoaning the timing of it.

Many of you, reading these words, are not full-blown Pharisees. IF a Pharisee had picked this book up at all, they likely would have already become offended and thrown it in the trash. They may have already told numerous people how heretical it is, accused me of being a false teacher, and left a bad review on Amazon. No, the ones that have read this far are not controlled by a Pharisee spirit, but perhaps may still be influenced, to some degree, by a "little Pharisee" inside. If you have grown up in the church at all, you may need to repent and renounce this mindset.

I remember my daughter as a little girl coming home and telling me about what she had been taught in Sunday School that day. To NO fault of her own, she informed me, you could tell if someone was a Christian by how they acted. In other words, she was being taught to. . . first, segregate people into Christians and non-Christians; second, to judge people; third, to base that judgement on outward things; and fourth, to look down on those who weren't like her. This was a religious spirit at work. I quickly corrected what she had learned and made sure she understood that being a Christian was about loving Jesus and there was no way any of us could know the state of anyone's heart (unless God showed us). Additionally, in NO WAY are we to judge or look down on anyone for perhaps not acting perfectly or exactly how we think they should. Lastly, Jesus loves each and

THE RELIGIOUS SPIRIT OR MINDSET

every person despite their actions or mistakes and does not hold their sin against them, so neither should we.

Of course, by the Holy Spirit, we are to discern spirits, discern what is happening, whether it's from God or not, and judge the words we hear and receive. When I listen to a sermon, I pay attention to the Holy Spirit and His witness in me. Does what I'm hearing line up with the Word of God? Is Holy Spirit telling me He's the author of what I'm hearing? Sometimes I hear a word and I pray on it; I ask God to give me confirmation.

It is also wisdom to discern who to spend time with and who's opinion or advise to listen to. Sometimes Holy Spirit will give you a sense that something is off about someone, but it's not so you can get all judgemental. Sometimes it's to warn you, to be careful about how much access you give them in your life, and sometimes it's to get you to pray for them.

One sure sign of the religious spirit is the rejection of any and almost all manifestations of the Holy Spirit. I used to think that if I was uncomfortable in an environment where there were manifestations, it wasn't of God. I have since learned that this is false. A sense of being uncomfortable around manifestations is usually caused by a spirit of religion and we need accurate discernment to know the difference. Unfortunately, though, a spirit of religion can cloud our discernment.

We visited Catch the Fire in Toronto in the early 90's when revival broke out and many supernatural manifestations were happening around us. I was uncomfortable because it was "out of the box" for me. I wasn't used to what was happening; I'd never seen such manifestations before, but I did not judge. I did not presume to know whether what was happening was of God or not. I was not so arrogant and self-righteous to think I had all the answers. I simply admitted that I didn't know and remained open to the possibility that it was indeed from God. I understood that I was (and still am) a work in progress and God was still teaching me and revealing Himself to me. (Now, more than twenty-five years later, such manifestations don't surprise me at all.)

Supernatural things happen when a supernatural God manifests His power. Sometimes God is communicating to us through the manifestation and sometimes it is simply our temporal flesh reacting to the presence and power of God. For example, the presence of God can be "weighty" or feel heavy on someone which can cause their flesh to not be able to stand up straight or to have to get on the floor.

Pastor John Arnott from Catch the Fire spoke at a conference I was at, and he gave an example of someone who crowed like a rooster under the anointing of Holy Spirit. Their first impression was "That's odd. What could that be?" At first thought, they didn't think it was God, but then they realized God was trying to tell them something through it. God was saying, in His not-so-obvious way, "Wake up! It's the dawn of a new day."

God does not speak in clear, obvious ways; He usually speaks in ways that require us, the listener, to pay close attention and to seek Holy Spirit for an interpretation. He speaks in mysteries so only those who are diligently seeking Him will hear. Proverbs 25:2 says, "It is God's privilege to conceal things and the king's privilege to discover them" (NLT). Matthew 13:10-12 says, "His disciples came and asked him, "Why do you use parables when you talk to the people? He replied, "You are permitted to understand the secrets of the Kingdom of Heaven, but others are not. To those who listen to my teaching, more understanding will be given, and they will have an abundance of knowledge. But for those who are not listening, even what little understanding they have will be taken away from them" (NLT).

There are times, however, when a person in a crowd of worshippers is not pure of heart and they will manifest what is not God, but the entire corporate move can still be holy despite this. If the corporate body is biblical and the leaders are not in gross unrepentant sin, a supernatural manifestation that seems to affect the whole body is going to be of God, regardless of our acceptance of it or comfort through it.

There was a time, many years ago, when I believe a spirit of religion caused me to manifest. It happened at a time when I felt very insecure and fearful of others judging me. I was part of a small group of women who met every week. The leader of the group had a spiritual burden on her heart for Israel and wanted all of us to join a group of intercessors, interceding and repenting for antisemitism. Unfortunately, I was not in a place where I sensed that burden at all. Not having that burden made me feel guilty. I wondered if there was something wrong with me and didn't know how I would participate in intercession without the Spirit moving me around that issue. I was concerned about appearances and what the others would think of me.

During intercession, I did manifest in a way that was typical of intercession, crouched on the floor in travail, however, I was very aware of thoughts in my head that didn't agree. In my mind, I didn't want the pastor to come near me. My thoughts were contradictory to what was happening in the Spirit, and I knew this wasn't normal. I spoke to the leader of the group afterward and we prayed it through together gaining understanding of how I opened the door to the enemy through my insecurities and concern about appearances. So, as you can see, this spirit of religion is sneaky and it is easy to be taken advantage of by it, especially when one has a wounded soul and/or grown up in a legalistic, religious environment at church or at home.

Perhaps you have discerned this spirit in operation in your life. Perhaps you have not. Since our purpose in this discussion is to be free, let's consider these scenarios and what OUR reactions might be if we were to experience them:

Scenario	Religious Response	Godly Response
Your congregation is petitioned for donations to the local crisis pregnancy center.	Annoyance and judgement: "They got themselves into that mess, let them get themselves out." Or feeling an OBLIGATION to donate every time and thinking, *they're always asking for money.*	• Compassion and prayer • Seeking the Holy Spirit for direction on whether to give. • Asking the Lord how much to give. • Following the lead of the Holy Spirit in faith and joy.
You learn that a group of praying women are hosting a table at the local psychic fair for prophetic evangelism.	Shocked and annoyed, thinking, *don't they know psychics are of the devil?* OR feeling OBLIGATED to join them, thinking, *well if they're going, I should too. I don't want them to think I'm any less spiritual than they are.*	• Understanding and supportive • Praying for Godly wisdom, protection, and words of knowledge to point people to Jesus. • Knowing that God's direction for your ministry may not look the same and that's okay.

Scenario	Religious Response	Godly Response
You see someone from your church angrily yelling at the grocery store clerk.	Inwardly you decide that they must not really be a Christian because Christians don't act that way. You resolve never to connect with them again.	• Understand that they must have had a stressful day and are in process like everyone else. • Pray for them. • If you know them, connect with them later. • Take them out for coffee to bless and encourage them.

How would you respond in these scenarios? Would you respond in a Godly way or a religious way?

We have a decision to make. Are we going to allow the Holy Spirit to search our heart? Or are we going to just skim over this material and not do the real work it entails? That is up to you, but you will only get out of this process what you put in.

One of the greatest indicators of a religious spirit is the annoyance that rises up as we are confronted with the possibility of sinful attitudes in our heart. Someone who is heavily influenced by a religious spirit, as I said before, is prideful and refuses to submit to inner transformation. A person who has a relationship with the Spirit doesn't mind allowing the Spirit to search their heart and expose what is there. They are in fact EAGER to do it as they want to be free and glorify God to the best of their ability.

Applying the steps previously mentioned, let's begin. Pray something like this:

"Lord, I thank you for Who you are. I honor you and glorify your name. You are the Alpha and Omega. You are the beginning and the end. You are the everlasting God. The One Who never slumbers nor sleeps and the One Who sees me and loves me just the way I am. (STEP 1: Confess and Repent) Lord I confess that I have been prideful—that I have thought myself better than others and righteous in my own efforts. I have been haughty and puffed up, thinking I had it all together, when I don't. I confess that I have judged (name the person); I have held their sin against them and thought poorly of them (repeat for every person this applies to). I confess that I have been critical toward (person or organization). I am sorry Lord. I repent and choose to turn back to you. I recognize that without you, I am nothing and it is only by your sacrifice that I am made holy. Forgive me Lord for my sin. I confess that I have believed lies—lies that have taught me to judge and condemn others by what they do. Forgive me God. I repent. (Continue to confess any other sin related to the spirit of religion. Do not skip over anything. Ask Holy Spirit to help you.) Thank you for your forgiveness, God. I release myself now and I choose to fully receive your complete forgiveness in Jesus' name. (STEP 2: Renounce) I don't want to ever operate in these ways again, so right now I renounce the spirit of religion and all association with it. I fully renounce and cut off from my life all pride, haughtiness, wrong judgements, self-righteousness, criticism, and (list all attitudes associated with the sins you just confessed). Lord, I ask for your mercy and grace to cover anything I've forgotten or am unaware of. (STEP 3: Bind) I bind the spirit of pride, haughtiness, self-righteousness, judgementalism, criticism and all demonic spirits related to my sin including (name any demon associated with the sin you have confessed and renounced) AND I bind the spirit of religion. I speak directly to every demon associated with religion—I bind you and declare your maneuvers against me to be powerless and ineffective now, in Jesus' name. I break your power and put a gag in your mouth NOW. You will not cause me harm or discomfort, in Jesus' name. (STEP 4: Cast out) I command the spirits of pride, haughtiness, self-righteousness, judgementalism, and criticism to come out of me now in Jesus' name (include any other spirit you may have bound earlier in the prayer). Finally, I command the spirit of religion to loose me now—come out NOW never to return in Jesus' name. LEAVE ME NOW! Come out in Jesus' name. (Repeat as many times as you are led by Holy Spirit. If no natural manifestation occurs, such as coughing, yawning, burping, etc., blow out of your mouth as an act of faith, believing you are being set free.) Father, thank you for delivering me. Thank you, Jesus, that all things are under your feet and since I am in you, all things are also under my feet. (STEP 5: Ask Father for more of Holy Spirit, to fill you afresh) Father, send your Spirit to fill me up completely. Baptize me afresh with your Spirit and power. Cause every void in me to be saturated with your presence. May there NOT be one place untouched and overtaken by you. Consume me completely, Lord. I am yours. In Jesus' name, Amen."

Anger and Forgiveness

Anger
Anger seems to be one thing that gets overlooked. I have not heard much teaching or direction on anger in the church. But I have learned, suppressed and pent-up anger can be very harmful to our heart, soul and even body. Anger is not something we want to "bank," save or hide away. Knowing how to process it, is vital to our well being. So, let's talk about it.

"Is anger wrong?" This seems to be an important question to consider. If we looked to Jesus for our answer, which is always a good strategy, we would consider John 2:13-17. In this scripture, we see Jesus overturning the tables of the money changers and driving out, with a whip made of cords, those doing business in the temple. Sounds like Jesus was angry, but the Bible describes it as zeal. '"Take these things away! Do not make My Father's house a house of merchandise!" Then His disciples remembered that it was written, "Zeal for Your house has eaten Me up"' (John 2:16b-17 NKJV). Merriam-Webster describes zeal as being "a strong feeling of interest and enthusiasm that makes someone very eager or determined to do something." Synonyms for zeal are "fervor, fire, passion."[56] In this passage, Jesus is taking a stand for righteousness and against injustice. Standing against injustice is the appropriate response for Jesus and for us. Injustice should make us angry but it's what we do with that anger that can cause us problems.

Here's another example of Jesus being angry:
"And He entered the synagogue again, and a man was there who had a withered hand. So they watched Him closely, whether He would heal him on the Sabbath, so

---

[56] https://www.merriam-webster.com/thesaurus/zeal

that they might accuse Him. And He said to the man who had the withered hand, "Step forward." Then He said to them, "Is it lawful on the Sabbath to do good or to do evil, to save life or to kill?" But they kept silent. And when He had looked around at them with anger, being grieved by the hardness of their hearts, He said to the man, "Stretch out your hand." And he stretched it out, and his hand was restored as whole as the other" (Mark 3:1-5 NKJV).

Jesus was angry at the hardness of the hearts of those around Him in the synagogue. He was angry that their desire to follow a law superseded their compassion and love for others, which in God's Kingdom is unjust. Justice in the heart of God is to see His children healed and made whole, every day of the week. "He has shown you, O man, what is good; And what does the Lord require of you But to do justly, To love mercy, And to walk humbly with your God" (Micah 6:8 NKJV)? Treating others justly is good. Hating injustice is also good. But how do we handle the anger that rises in us toward the injustice when it happens?

Ephesians 4:26 says, "And "don't sin by letting anger control you." Don't let the sun go down while you are still angry, for anger gives a foothold to the devil" (NLT). Be angry, but don't let it control you. Be angry, but don't hold onto it—not even past the sun going down. In other words, don't go to bed angry; process it, recognize it, express it appropriately, and choose to forgive every day.

I went to see a friend and pastor for a deliverance appointment, and the main thing he dealt with, was my pent-up anger. When it came out, even I was surprised. It turns out, we can bury it so deep, we don't even realize it's there anymore;

our hearts hide it and deceive us.[57] Unfortunately, unbeknownst to us, it can also control us. Everything we do and say, can have an underlying tone of anger, and it can color our perspective of everything. Our expectations can become distorted and bent toward negative outcomes because of anger.

I had thought, in error, that it wasn't appropriate for a Christian to express anger or even to be angry. This of course is not true, but it must be expressed in appropriate ways, calmly, and in wisdom. It turns out, if you don't let anger build up, it CAN be expressed calmly—without blowing your top. If we feel that someone is treating us unjustly, we must confront them in love (when safe) and make our heart known. We must be honest and not let it go unchecked. If that person is unwilling to change their ways, then it might be appropriate to put some distance between you and them—to put boundaries in place.

Lastly, ALWAYS go to God with anger. He is always eager to help us process what we are feeling. And He is not offended, mad or disappointed in us for being angry or even expressing that anger to Him with passion. Thank God, right! He can handle our emotions. Talk to God about your anger and be specific. Tell Him, who you're angry at and why. Tell Him all your grievances and He will speak to your heart. One exception, however, is if we are angry at God. I don't think it is wisdom to unleash angry words against God. That's not cool. And you might find out very quickly how uncool it really is. Being angry at God is sin and based on a misunderstanding of His character.

God is the God of the universe. He is ALMIGHTY God. Let's not lose sight of His supreme power, majesty, and complete awesomeness. If you are blaming God for unjust treatment by other people, you are misunderstanding God and forgetting that

---

[57] "The heart is deceitful above all things, And desperately wicked; Who can know it" (Jeremiah 17:9 NKJV)?

each person has free will to make their own choices. God does not control people like puppets. If you are blaming God for something else like a loss or natural disaster, I encourage you to take a step back and ask Holy Spirit to give you wisdom and understanding.

Holy Spirit is here on this earth, inside His followers. But the devil and his power are also alive and well on planet earth. First Peter 5:8-9 says, "Stay alert! Watch out for your great enemy, the devil. He prowls around like a roaring lion, looking for someone to devour. Stand firm against him, and be strong in your faith. Remember that your family of believers all over the world is going through the same kind of suffering you are" (NLT).

We cannot forget about the devil's influence around us. There are still so many unbelievers here, all empowering the devil through their sin. Even entire nations, actively involved in sin, empowering the devil. We see disaster and loss everywhere because of the consequences of their sin. Sometimes, unfortunately, the sin of others and the sin of nations affects us and causes *us* pain. Remember though, it is only because of the presence of God that we are not all entirely consumed by the devil. The power and presence of God hold him at bay; he is held back from annihilating us by the presence of Holy Spirit in the earth. Let's be thankful for that. Blaming God for something hurtful is very much going to block you from receiving the mercy and grace of God and being healed. It is a deception from the evil one.

Many precious people try to make sense of their suffering and can't. They don't understand why God seemingly did not intervene in their circumstances. *Why did I endure such abuse?* People wonder, *why did God not stop it?* Beloved, I believe, if He could have, He would have. But God cannot control the actions of a person who has free will and is likely under the influence of demons. He can, however, heal you of your wounds and restore you. He can and will heal your heart if you will REPENT for blaming Him and being angry at Him. (Forgiving your perpetrator is also an essential step, but we will get to that shortly.)

Four years ago, the reality of how many people blame God for the maladies in their lives gripped me and this prophetic word bubbled up:

"There's a stirring this morning. There's a voice rising that must be heard. There's a message and a word that is calling, beckoning, and longing to release its freedom. Intercession bubbles. Spirits groan.

The Lord would say to you, "Don't give in to deception. Don't believe the lies of the enemy. Beware, he prowls around like a roaring lion seeking whom he may devour. Don't be devoured by his lies. Have I (God) not said, "I am for your good, not for your destruction?" Have I not said, "I am NOT against you?" Have I not said, "You are mine and I am yours?" Have I not given ALL to rescue your barren soul and have I not said, "It is finished?" Have I not waited and longed to be known by you just as I know you? And I say to you, KNOW ME! Know ME. KNOW me."

My heart is gripped this morning with a message I must convey. I have seen it repeatedly and the same issue comes up continually before me as I minister to others. It sits in front of me like a flashing neon sign that CAN'T be ignored. It MUST be exposed.

I see beloved ones covered in ashes, the remains of a life and heart once lived but no more. I see beloved ones suffering and trudging through their days with nothing but grief and sickness, their lives completely destroyed by another. Lives crushed in the grip of a viscous spiral of sin, hurt, anger, blame, offense, bitterness, un-forgiveness and hate. It ends in death but where does it begin? Know this. KNOW where it begins, and you can avoid it all together.

Misunderstanding God. Not knowing God and blaming God. Well, He is sovereign, right? He is in control of everything, right? If He wanted to, He could stop that person in my life from hurting me, from sinning against me and knocking the wind right out of me, right? But He doesn't. He just sits by and watches. YES, OR NO? This is the question that DEMANDS an answer. Have you had this dialogue in your head? Is this what you believe? If it is, you my friend are spiraling.

This is where it begins. Your nightmare begins with how you respond to what the other is doing. It begins with a distorted belief about Who God is and Who He is FOR you. It begins with believing the lies the enemy is feeding your mind about God's stamp of approval on your hurtful circumstances.

Here's a news flash for you: You Christian, have an enemy and his name is Satan and Satan's number one goal is to drive a wedge between you and God, to cause you to become offended at Him. As soon as Satan gets you to agree with that, BOOM, you are off the rails! You are out of bounds, out of fellowship and you are free game for the devil. DON'T DO IT! Know your God!

Here in lies the tension: sovereignty and free will. Contrary to popular persuasion from the enemy, sovereignty and free will are not contradictory; they exist simultaneously, and both are true. God IS sovereign. He is God and there is no other. He is the One Who made you and the universe and put all the laws in place. He is the One that created order out of chaos. He is the One Who decided on the rhythm of life and decided that living things would reproduce after their own. He is the One that breathed His breath of life into us. He is also the One that decided at the beginning of time to place man over the earth—to appoint us to steward the earth and rule over it and He is the One Who is eternal and just and doesn't, in fact can't, go back on His Word, even when we mess up. He is the One that despite His power and authority, chose to give us authority on His earth and to work through man. He is the One Who sovereignly chose to limit Himself also by giving us free will, free choice to serve Him or not to serve Him, free choice in all of life, free will to choose our spouse and free will to love or not to love.

God did not want puppets or robots that He could control. He wanted family, ones that chose Him and chose to love Him. He wants relationship with us, authentic relationship with a heart connection. Does God attempt to intervene? Yes! Does God attempt to sway our hearts toward the right choice? Yes! Does He move by His Spirit and put love beyond our own ability in our heart? Yes, of course He does. He can because He's God but ultimately, we do have the final choice. By His sovereign will He gives us extra grace and the ability to say "no" to sinful things (1 Cor. 10:13). He does not allow us to be tempted beyond what we can bear, and He provides a way out for us, but we must choose that way out. We must resist the devil and choose what is right. Unfortunately, some of us fail at that. Sometimes the people in our lives choose the wrong way, even after God has pulled out all the stops, and they end up sinning against us. Sometimes the people in our lives hurt us beyond imagination and

GOD'S HEART GRIEVES. He sees and His heart aches. He sees our tears, broken hearts and broken lives and HE WEEPS for us.

Beloved, stop shaking your fists at God. It is only providing the devil with more ground to encroach upon. It is only serving to defeat you further. Realize that none of it is God's fault. Resist being offended at God and praise Him for Who He is. Thank Him for being faithful to you in all seasons. Know that God is good and His mercies for you are new every morning. Know that God's heart for you is for the restoration of ALL things and that He is walking with you, even carrying you through it all to the other side.

If you will do this and continue, despite what is happening around you, forgiving all who have hurt you, THEN, you will see restoration of joy, peace, hope and love and you will be victorious in Christ. God is your answer and your defender, NOT your enemy. YOU ARE extravagantly loved by the Creator of all. This is truth that we must bind ourselves to even amid pain and trying circumstances, even amid evil coming against us in its fullest form. Stand with God in truth. Submit to His Lordship, stay rooted and firmly planted in the truth of God's Word and resist the devil. Resist his evil manipulations of your mind. Resist being offended. Resist hate and he must flee. Simply put, God is love. If what's happening to you is not love, it's not God. God is love and God is good. . . ALL the time."

In an effort to know God, let's again consider what love is. Love is best described in the well-known passage, 1 Corinthians 13:4-7. Here's The Passion Translation:

"Love is large and incredibly patient. Love is gentle and consistently kind to all. It refuses to be jealous when blessing comes to someone else. Love does not brag about one's achievements nor inflate its own importance. Love does not traffic in shame and disrespect, nor selfishly seek its own honor. Love is not easily irritated or quick to take offense. Love joyfully celebrates honesty and finds no delight in what is wrong. Love is a safe place of shelter, for it never stops believing the best for others. Love never takes failure as defeat, for it never gives up" (TPT).

God is perfect love. We can expect God to relate to us with all patience, gentleness, kindness, never putting shame on us, truth, and joy—all while celebrating who we are. We can expect Him to relate to us with PERFECT love. We, as humans, fail at loving well every day; we are prone to impatience, jealousy and pride, but God is not. He never has an off day or a bad day where He struggles to control His emotions. He is even-keeled, steady, rock-solid.

Amidst all God's love however, there IS something that God WILL do that doesn't always FEEL good, but just because it doesn't feel good doesn't mean it's not love. Since we are God's CHILDREN, and God relates to us as a Father, God will discipline us.[58] From time to time, a GOOD parent will need to show "tough love" to their children, so they mature and head in the right direction. God does the same thing. To discipline a child is to love them well; discipline has the best interest of the child at heart.

"For our earthly fathers disciplined us for a few years, doing the best they knew how. But God's discipline is

---

[58] "My child, don't make light of the Lord's discipline, and don't give up when he corrects you. For the Lord disciplines those he loves, and he punishes each one he accepts as his child" (Hebrews 12:5b-6 NLT).

always good for us, so that we might share in his holiness. No discipline is enjoyable while it is happening—it's painful! But afterward there will be a peaceful harvest of right living for those who are trained in this way" (Hebrews 12:10-11 NLT).

God DOES NOT discipline or punish us for sin that has been confessed, turned away from and covered in the blood of Jesus, but He will discipline His children to re-direct them from something they are CURRENTLY doing, to protect them. For example, several years ago, I began a new job as a Compassion Caregiver to a senior. There were a few things about the arrangement that I quietly questioned in my heart. I was not a trained Personal Support Worker and I wondered if my employer was honest with the family about that. Also, my employer did not offer liability insurance. However, the job paid well so I chose to ignore my concerns and went ahead with it. When I applied for the job, I was just recovering from a cold. I assured my potential employer that I was not one to be sick like that often, which was true. I had a cold lasting more than 2 days, maybe once a year.

I began work and within a few days, I was sick with a cold again. And do you know, I continued in that cycle for almost 3 months—the whole time I was employed by this employer! It cycled between a head cold to a chest cold with only a few days in between where I felt normal. This was VERY strange!! Some days I wore a mask, others I used a lot of medication, kept my distance, and disinfected the kitchen where I worked. It was not good. I felt guilty the whole time because I didn't want to make my senior sick. Finally, I quit the job. I couldn't do it. My heart was too convicted. As soon as I quit, my health was restored completely, and the cold did not return. I had no special medical treatment to make it go away. God was trying to tell me something; He was trying to protect me from a bad situation, and I was out of His will. Working that job wasn't necessarily sinful, it just wasn't wisdom.

If a Christian continues in their own way (sometimes sinful but not always), ignoring the conviction and discipline of God, I believe He will allow more serious illness in their lives. He will do whatever is necessary to get through to them. He does this to re-direct and make us holy. Other ways He disciplines could involve losing something like a job, position, favor, ministry, or whatever has become too important to us.

Now is the best opportunity to respond to the conviction of the Lord, to admit all our anger to Him, repent for hanging on to anger and for blaming God for our suffering.

Forgiveness

In the Spring of 1990, my husband and I took a lovely vacation to Western Canada. We stayed at the amazing Chateau Lake Louise, visited Banff, Alberta and took many scenic hikes through the Rocky Mountains. We decided to begin to try to start a family with this marker trip. I expected to be expecting very soon after, but my expectations were dashed when even 15 months later, I STILL was not pregnant.

I had experienced much trauma as a young girl regarding pregnancy—watching my mother go through two painful miscarriages, receiving evil reports from my mom regarding her doctor, way too much information for my age and experiencing maternal neglect due to my mother's mental illness. All these emotionally traumatic events left marks on my soul that were still affecting me as I tried to conceive.

After some prayer counselling (more on that later), I conceived for the first time but quickly found myself in tears, grieving a miscarriage at eight weeks gestation. I held the phone to my ear as I solemnly explained to my parents that I had miscarried; dad's words of compassion were comforting but my mother's comments were far from it. "Well, you weren't really pregnant anyway." Jaw dropped, breath. . . stopped. I don't remember my response. All I remember is the blade cutting my heart, creating yet another wound.

After hanging up the phone, I sat with my prayer counselor friend, while I talked to her about all the ways my mother had hurt me. (We happened to be living with our friends at the time as our new house was being built.) She calmly but very directly asked me, "Do you hate your mother?" Her question shook me. It felt like time stood still as the conviction of Holy Spirit overtook me. The Lord pulled back the curtain of my heart and I was mortified by what was there. Hot tears streamed down my face as I whispered my confession, "yeah, I guess I do. Jesus! Forgive me!" *What kind of person was I?* I thought. The answer of course was, "A person with wounds of the soul who had been purchased by Jesus and invited to be renewed by grace," but for a moment I felt the shame of my sin. It was NOT my finest moment, but Holy Spirit did His work, the Lord forgave me, I forgave myself, and my mom for many things.

As it turned out, forgiving my mom, and releasing the hate that was in my heart, was the final doorway to my healing of childlessness. (For my full story, see my book "Barren No More.") My husband and I went on after that first miscarriage to have four children, including a set of twins. Perhaps I will have an opportunity to share more on that later.

Of course, your story won't be the same but there may be similar elements; it's not uncommon to have been hurt by a parent either due to neglect, abuse or hurtful words spoken. Family life can be VERY demanding and challenging—especially when one is still carrying emotional burdens from the past. My mother had been through so much as a child and did not have any opportunity for healing. People who are hurting on the inside can't love others well as they are still trying to cope with their own pain. They can't help but focus on themselves, trying to survive and they end up hurting others in the process. It is inevitable.

Forgiving others is a very important key to unlock healing. MANY, many people, if not all of us, have multiple opportunities to forgive others. We have all been hurt by someone. Romans 3:23 says, "For everyone has sinned; we all fall short of God's glorious standard." Sometimes, the infraction against us is so horrific, forgiveness feels impossible, and we have absolutely no desire to extend it. However, forgiving others is not an option according to God if we ourselves want to be forgiven. Mark 11:25 says, "But when you are praying, first forgive anyone you are holding a grudge against, so that your Father in heaven will forgive your sins, too" (NLT). This truth is further reiterated in the parable of the unmerciful servant found in Matthew 18:23-35.

You probably know it, but the parable of the unmerciful servant begins with a king forgiving a servant of a debt too large for him to ever repay. Of course, he was grateful, happy and relieved. However, that servant then went out and demanded payment of a much smaller debt from a fellow servant. When that servant couldn't pay, the forgiven servant threw him in prison. Other servants reported the incident to the king and the king confronted the forgiven servant saying, "You wicked servant! I forgave you all that debt because you begged me. Should you not also have had compassion on your fellow servant, just as I had pity on you" (Matthew 18:32-33 NKJV)? That servant, who refused to have mercy on others, was delivered to "the torturers" until he paid the original debt back. Matthew 18:35 says, "So My heavenly Father also will do to you if each of you, from his heart, does not forgive his brother his trespasses" (NKJV). This parable says it all. Forgiving others is required if we want to be forgiven. Refusing to forgive others will lead to us experiencing torture or torment somehow, either through mental or physical anguish.

How do we forgive others? Forgiving others is a choice and an act of the will. We do not wait to "feel" like forgiving someone; we just do it because we are required to. As we continue to make that choice, eventually, our feelings will soften and change, and we will find ourselves feeling compassion for our perpetrators. That may seem impossible now but trust me, it will happen when you lean into Christ to be empowered through grace. Remember what you yourself have been forgiven of and then ask Holy Spirit for the compassion you need to move forward in His will.

Remember also in the parable above, one servant owed a HUGE debt and the other owed a small debt. The King expected both to be treated equally. Very often this is true in life. We may have *seemingly* been forgiven a small debt, but we may be required to forgive, in many cases, a debt that SEEMS so much larger than our own. It's non-negotiable friend if you want to enjoy relationship and eternity with the King as well as a healthy body this side of heaven.

Prayer
First, we're going to sit down with a pen and paper and ask Holy Spirit to reveal to us every person we are angry with and need to forgive. Write their names down. Secondly, we are going to ask the Holy Spirit to show us why we are angry and how that person made us feel. Then in prayer, first, sanctify your imagination and then tell Holy Spirit about the experiences you listed above.

> "Lord Jesus, thank you for being with me. Thank you for showing me my heart and being patient with me. I confess to you God, that at times I have not honored you with my imagination; I have used it for ungodly

purposes, and I am sorry. Please forgive me. Thank you, Jesus, I receive your forgiveness and I declare your blood over my imagination, purifying it and setting it apart for Godly purposes. I ask you Holy Spirit to help me guard my imagination, so I don't slip into ungodly imaginings in the future. Right now, I sanctify my imagination for you Lord, and I bind all deception right now in Jesus' name. Lord, I ask you now to give me the desire to confess my anger and to forgive every person who has hurt me."

Now go through the list, one person and event at a time: "Lord, I confess that I am and have been angry at (say the person's name). I am sorry that I have held on to that anger for so long. Please forgive me. (Say the person's name) hurt me deeply when they (say what the person did). She/he made me feel (list every feeling you had due to the injustice)."

As you confess how they made you feel, imagine, with your eyes closed, putting those feelings into a bowl. When you are done confessing your feelings, imagine giving that bowl to Jesus. See Jesus in your mind's eye standing before you, taking the bowl from you, making sure to take notice what Jesus does with the bowl. I learned this exercise from Dr. Douglas E. Carr and I pray that you are able to engage with it. Each time I have done it, it has brought great healing to my heart. Repeat this exercise with each person and injustice on your list.

Now, pray to forgive each person for each event:
"I know Lord, that since you have forgiven me, I now need to forgive others. So right now, in the name of Jesus, I choose to forgive (name the person) for (name what they did). I choose to release them and their sin against me into your capable hands God and trust you to be their righteous judge and redeemer. I pray Lord

that they would come to know you and be healed of the pain in their heart that caused them to hurt me. Thank you, God, for your empowering to live by your Spirit in the realm of health and healing and to truly desire good things for myself, my family and (name the person) and their family. Fill me with your Spirit Lord, In Jesus' mighty name, Amen."

After praying this prayer, you may find the memory of what you have just voiced forgiveness for continues to come back to your mind. Each time it does, refuse to re-hash hurt emotions and negative thoughts about that person, but voice again, forgiveness toward them and pray for them. Pray for them more and more, allowing the Holy Spirit to elaborate your prayer according to His heart and the compassion for them in your heart will grow. Rehearse forgiveness toward them often until it becomes part of your heart and emotions.

IDOLATRY

Idolatry clogs up our spiritual gateways like nothing else and prevents us from receiving healing. Why? Because it doesn't reflect whole-hearted love for God nor complete trust in Him—in fact, it demonstrates the complete opposite. For Christians, idolatry is covert, disguised in deception and can be falsely clothed in good intentions. No genuine Christian knowingly engages in it, it's not obvious, we live in denial, and we don't actually understand what idolatry is.

First, any time we recognize, attribute spiritual power to, call on, worship or sacrifice to any other god or deity, other than the One true God of the Bible, Jehovah, we are guilty of idolatry. Idolatry many times, involves the worship of idols or graven images that have been crafted to represent a so-called "god." If you've ever been to Prague, Czech Republic, you may have seen an example of this. Found at the center of Prague's Zoo is a statue of Radegast, the (false) god of hospitality, fertility and crops;[59] you may even have seen "gifts" people have left there at the base of the statue as they have attempted to gain its favor.

Idolatry though is not just active in these obvious ways. It is more prevalent in a passive sense when we have EXTREME admiration, love, or reverence for something or someone to the point that they or it is more important to us than God. This is the type of idolatry that trips up many Christians without realizing it.

Idolatry happens to be the subject of the very first commandment God gives Moses in Exodus 20.

> "You shall have no other gods before Me. You shall not make for yourself a carved image—any likeness of

---

[59]https://www.waymarking.com/waymarks/WMMX16_Radegast_statue_Prague_Czech_Republic

anything that is in heaven above, or that is in the earth beneath, or that is in the water under the earth; you shall not bow down to them nor serve them. For I, the Lord your God, am a jealous God" (Exodus 20:3-5a).

What does it mean for God to be jealous? In short, it means He wants ALL of us and not just part. The longer answer involves recognizing that God has loved and continues to love us with everything. He has given us ALL He has. He loves us with an everlasting love, a love that never fails and a love without condition. He loves us so much He gave us His only Son for our redemption. God expects us to reciprocate that same love to Him, by loving Him first, with all our heart, mind, soul, and strength and by loving Him the most out of everything and everyone in our lives, including our children and family. God is not interested in sharing the throne of our heart with anyone or anything else.[60] We are in a love relationship with God (even to the point that we are called "The Bride of Christ") and when we give our attention, affection and adoration to things or people to the extent that it surpasses that for God, we are being unfaithful to Him. To God, it feels as though we are having an affair and it is dishonoring to Him.

We can identify obvious examples of idolatry in the Old Testament. For example, when the Israelites got tired of waiting for Moses to come down from the mountain and told Aaron they wanted to make a gold calf out of their jewelry. Moses had been gone for forty days and forty nights and they did not know what had happened to him, so they were anxious. They desperately needed God to lead them and help them but the only way they heard from God was through Moses; since Moses was MIA, they felt they needed to create their own god. (It was that very

---

[60] Kyle Idleman, *gods at War: The Battle for Your Heart that Will Define Your Life* (Louisville: City on a Hill Productions, 2012) DVD.

common trap we all seem to fall in from time to time—God is silent, or we can't hear God, or God takes too long to answer/act, so we take matters into our own hands.)

The Israelites fashioned a gold calf and they said, "This is your god, O Israel, that brought you out of the land of Egypt" (Ex.32:4b NKJV)! When Aaron saw the calf, he built an altar before it and the following day, they had a festival. They offered burnt offerings to the calf, brought it peace offerings, and ate and drank in merriness. Verse 7 of Exodus 32, God saw what they had done and urgently told Moses, "Go, get down! For your people whom you brought out of the land of Egypt have corrupted themselves" (NKJV). Reading further in Exodus 32, God becomes so angry at the Israelites for their rebellion and disloyalty, Moses had to plead with God not to destroy them.

We also see idolatry alive and well in the New Testament, especially at Caesarea Philippi where there were 7 sites and/or temples for the worship of pagan gods and where people sacrificed their children to the god of Pan.

In our world, currently, there is DEFINITELY still the worship of other deities and even Satan (Satanists) but among Christians, idolatry looks different. However, is still very much alive and well. There are well-meaning Christians who think they can worship nature and the stars in the practice of wicca, astrology and horoscopes. They think they can practice yoga (originating from Hinduism),[61] look to crystals for healing and certain charms on a charm bracelet for increased fertility, and other health benefits.

The truth is, there are only two spiritual powers that exist, God and Satan, good and bad, and there are only two spiritual

---

[61] This article explains the spiritual significance of each yoga pose and its connection to the false god of Hinduism, Shiva: https://www.livestrong.com/article/395082-spiritual-meanings-of-yoga-postures/

kingdoms, the Kingdom of Light and the Kingdom of Darkness. That means, if the God of Abraham, Isaac and Jacob, Jesus or Holy Spirit is not the spiritual One you are addressing, inviting, or interacting with, the spirit you are interacting with is very likely from Satan's kingdom—there is no other option. (One exception may be when you are interacting with an angel from the Lord, but this event would be part of the worship of Jesus/God, not be independent of it.) There are NO good spirits that are part of a neutral kingdom or spiritual space. Don't be deceived! Satan and his entourage can transform themselves into angels of light for the purpose of tricking you into playing their games.[62] And just because you're speaking or casting a positive "vibe" onto someone does not make it pure or good. Anytime we are attempting to control someone else's life, for good or bad, we are dabbling in witchcraft and witchcraft is of the devil.

I know that there will be some who don't want to give up their pagan practices, like expecting crystals to heal or a fertility charm to bless fertility because at times, they seem to work. Here's the problem though, as soon as you ascribe spiritual power to a physical object of any kind, you dishonor God and give demons an opportunity to attach to that object. Now the object DOES have spiritual power but it's of the bad kind. The demon attached to that object will appease you for a time and perhaps cause something good to happen in your life for the SOLE purpose of drawing you in to enslave you further. Over time, that demon will begin to wreak havoc in your life as you get deeper and deeper into bondage. Eventually you will experience great torment and strife. If I've just described you, you can be free from its grip through the steps already described

---

[62] "And no wonder, since Satan himself masquerades as an angel of light. So it is no great surprise if his servants also masquerade as servants of righteousness, but their end will correspond with their deeds" (2 Corinthians 11:14-15 AMP).

in this book, confession, repentance, renunciation etc., but also it is necessary to destroy any physical object you've turned into an idol. (If you are experiencing deep bondage, you may need help getting free.)

Perhaps this previous discussion doesn't apply to you. Perhaps you have been able to identify this type of idolatry already and you have stayed clear of it. That's great! But it doesn't mean you're not involved in idolatry some other way. As previously mentioned, idolatry can show up in our lives covertly when we admire, adore, love, regard, honor or pursue someone or something more than God.

I ministered to a woman once who struggled with deep depression and suicidal ideation. She had been through deliverance and received freedom from a spirit of heaviness, but she was not able to maintain her freedom. (This is a dangerous situation as the oppression that comes back can be way worse than the first.) I watched this precious woman go into a phone call free of depression and end the phone call bound again, so I asked her about it. She desperately wanted her daughter's forgiveness but was denied it. Through Holy Spirit, it was revealed to me that she was becoming bound by depression again because she held her daughter's forgiveness in a high place; it was higher and even more important to her than God's forgiveness. This is idolatry. We are forgiven when God forgives us and if our loved ones don't forgive us, frankly that is between them and God. Yes, it can be very sad when our loved ones refuse to forgive us and re-connect but it does not determine our standing before God. Have faith that the Lord is working on your behalf to soften your loved ones' heart toward you. Give them the space and time they need to recover and heal with the Lord.

Kyle Idleman and City on a Hill Productions has produced an excellent small group Bible Study DVD curriculum addressing this very issue called, "gods at War: The Battle for Your Heart that Will Define Your Life." The DVDs include powerful personal testimonies from people just like you and me. In the study, Kyle identifies gods of our culture that many of us worship without even realizing it, like pleasure, money, sex, power, and even love.

How do we identify idols in our heart—the gods that are warring within us for pre-eminence demanding our adoration and affections? It's not an easy task as Jeremiah 17:9 says, "The human heart is the most deceitful of all things, and desperately wicked. Who really knows how bad it is" (NLT)? We tend to live in denial, and you may have already assumed that nothing about this conversation applies to you either, but I would encourage you to dig a little deeper. Look beyond your initial assumptions and the surface of your heart. Be willing to allow Holy Spirit to draw the curtain back and reveal to you what's really there.

Kyle Idleman suggests some probing questions to help us identify idols. They are:

1. What has left you feeling the most disappointed?
2. What do you complain about?
3. What do you sacrifice your time and money for?
4. What do you worry about?
5. Where do you go when you are hurt and need comfort?
6. What makes you unreasonably mad?
7. What do you dream of?
8. Whose encouragement or approval means the most to you?[63]

In addition, consider these questions on the next page:

---

[63] Idleman, *gods at War: The Battle for Your Heart that Will Define Your Life*. DVD.

1. What do you allow to affect your self-worth? What makes you feel bad about yourself? What do you turn to, to help you feel good about yourself?

2. Is there a circumstance in your life that needs to be present for you to *feel* successful?

Also, fill in the blank:
"My life and happiness ride on this one thing:_____."
"I will never be completely happy until _____."

What if you don't get that promotion at work, that pay increase, or that four-bedroom house with the double garage? What if you never get the recognition you've worked hard for? What if you don't achieve the goals you've set out for yourself? Will you still be able to find joy in life or will your life be ruined?

After reflecting on these questions, can you now see if anything has become too dear to you? There could be various things you've identified. I would encourage you to make a mental note of them or write them down for reference later. In the upcoming paragraphs, we're going to dig a bit deeper and focus on a few things which are particularly prevalent as idols with women: romantic love and family relationships.

It is well known, we as humans, have an emotional need that is universal across races and cultures—that is the need for love. God created us that way. He is a relational God and He created us in His image. God created us for love and to be loved, but that love is supposed to come primarily from God Himself—through relationship with Him. A problem occurs when we don't have enough intimacy in our relationship with Him or enough spiritual discernment to experience it. We end up desperately searching for love in all the wrong places trying to fill the void. We look to other people, a spouse, children, pets and sometimes even material things. The elusiveness of perfect love in our lives drives us to do whatever it takes to get it and to LATCH onto things and people with all our might—TURNING THOSE THINGS AND PEOPLE, INTO IDOLS. Love is such a deep need in us that not experiencing it can make us utterly desperate.

When I was young, I longed to find that one man who I would marry—that one man who would love me and cherish me properly. I know now, that one man is Jesus, but when I was young, I didn't know Him. When I was young, I wrongly believed that once I found the right romantic relationship, all would be right with the world. I believed that once I married, I would finally have true love and happiness. Now I know, I was wrong. It turned out that expecting one man to meet all my needs, including my deepest emotional needs, was too high an expectation for a human being. It turned out that my husband was not and is not and never will be, God. Shocking, I know. It turns out some love, unconditional love that meets my deepest need, that loves through my worst mood and worst sin, comes only from God.

Now, there may be some women reading this who have trouble fully relating to the previous paragraph. There may be some women who might say, "Actually, I think my husband is pretty good at loving me unconditionally. He's quick to forgive and gives me grace when I need it," and that's awesome. I'm very happy for you. Some men have had an excellent role model in this area and have been taught well. Be careful though, beloved. Don't allow your relationship with your husband to become more important than your relationship with God. Be diligent to nurture your connection and intimacy with Jesus and be careful not to look to your husband for what only God can and should provide. Your husband is human, and he will make mistakes. Expecting your husband to be like God puts unreasonable pressure on him to be what he is not. There should not be ANY relationship that is more important to you than

God's—not your marriage, not your relationship with your mother, nor your relationship with your children, future or existing. God should always be first.

A friend of mine had an experience while visiting a church for a special meeting. The offering plate was being passed but she had no cash. Surprisingly she heard the Spirit tell her to put her "promise ring" in the plate. Yes! God told her to give up the very first ring her now husband had given her while dating. That one! She explained to me her shock and said to the Lord, "But Lord, he's my love!" Jesus was calling her to release that which she held dear and to come back to Him as her "first love." She did comply and do what God called her to do and I know she will be blessed for it. Perhaps there is a prophetic act God is calling you to do, to demonstrate to Him your enduring love and faithfulness?

One final area that needs to be considered is our children. We must release them back to the Lord so He can protect them. It is imperative that we realize that we cannot control everything in their lives, and it is beyond us to keep our children safe, 100% of the time. We must partner with God in this. We must have faith and peace in our heart that God is protecting them and working on their behalf. God cannot work with anything we insist on keeping in clenched fists. Let them go. They must be in the Great Potter's hands for Him to fashion and protect. "And yet, O Lord, you are our Father. We are the clay, and you are the potter. We all are formed by your hand" (Isaiah 64:8 NLT).

Prayer

> "Lord, I thank you for Who you are. I honor you and glorify your name. You are the Alpha and Omega. You are the beginning and the end. You are the everlasting God. The One Who never slumbers nor sleeps and the One Who sees me and loves me just the way I am. Lord, I confess that I have not put you first in my life.

I confess that... (confess all occult activity, looking to find out information about your future from psychics, tarot cards or tarot card readers, and horoscopes, spirit guides, attempting to converse with the dead, etc.)

I am sorry Lord that I have unknowingly looked to demonic powers for help and wisdom. I repent and I choose to forgive every person who introduced me to occult activity or encouraged me to connect with demons. I choose to forgive (name each person specifically) for (name how they led you into idolatry). (An example may be: "I choose to forgive Aunt May for taking me to that psychic or I choose to forgive Liz for sending me that YouTube video that introduced me to Tarot cards.") Lord, please forgive me and cut off from my life all influence demons have acquired through my participation with them. I renounce all demonic spirit guides, demon influences, psychic abilities, and divination in Jesus' name. I renounce idolatry and false idols. (If you have been worshipping specific false gods, renounce them by name.) I renounce every prayer I have uttered to false gods, and I renounce every false covenant I have made with them. I renounce putting my faith in them. Deliver me and wash me clean from their influence Lord.

I also confess that I have made things and/or people into idols; I have loved them too much and have held onto them too tightly. Specifically, Lord I have loved... (name all the things you have loved more than God) more than you and I am sorry. I confess that (example: the approval of man, my family, job, bank account etc.) has become too important to me and I have turned them into idols. I am sorry God for finding my worth in these things. I am sorry God for finding my success in these things. All I need is found in you so help me God to connect with that reality and experience your approval, acceptance, and love, for real. Open my spiritual senses to sense you and your presence with me. I let go of worldly things now and accept that you God are the most important person in my life, and you provide for me the most important things. I understand that your approval is the only approval that matters, so I let go of the need to be approved by man right now, in Jesus' name. Please forgive me God for idolatry and spiritual adultery. I repent and turn back to you completely. Cleanse me, Lord. Thank you that you are merciful and full of grace. Thank you that when we confess our sins to you, you are faithful and just to forgive us and cleanse us from all unrighteousness. I choose to forgive myself and I receive your forgiveness Lord in its fullness. I declare that I am forgiven of my sin.

I completely renounce idolatry and I turn away from it now, in Jesus' name. I bind all demons that have gained access to me through idolatry. I bind all deception, lying, trickery, and false voices and I bind idolatry now, in Jesus' name. I declare that my sin is now under the blood of Jesus' so every curse that has touched my life because of my sin is broken now and no longer has any right to operate. I cancel every curse coming from idolatry and I command the spirit of idolatry and all its cohorts to leave me now, in Jesus' name. Every legal right they have had over me is now gone and cancelled. Idolatry no longer has a hold on me. GO NOW, in Jesus' name! (If no physical manifestation occurs, blow out of your mouth in faith.)

I declare the blessing and favor of the Lord over my life. Goodness and mercy shall follow me all the days of life and I shall dwell in the house of the Lord, in freedom, forever. I will love the Lord my God with all my heart, mind, soul, and strength with His help and I will see the goodness of the Lord in the land of the living. The land of my life will be called blessed and fruitful in Jesus' name.

INIQUITY

Iniquity. This word tends to be misunderstood; many think it's just another word for sin, but it's not. Sin is something we do, think, say, or feel that is NOT aligned with righteousness and faith.[64] Iniquity is a pattern or bent of *character* that is passed down through the generations in your bloodline that threatens to cause or causes you to sin in a certain way. From Dr. Carr's book, *Breaking Patterns of Perversity*, he says iniquity can be define as, "A bent, twisting, perversity, distortion of character, or pattern of ungodly behavior/ perversity passing down ancestral lines."[65] He later goes on to say, "The English word "iniquity" comes from the Hebrew word "avon." Iniquity describes character flaws behind the action of sin."[66] Iniquity is a propensity to sin a certain way or a weakness. We may not have actively sinned according to that iniquity, but when considering Isaiah 64: 6-7, the distortion of character separates us from God nonetheless.

> "But we are all like an unclean thing, And all our righteousnesses are like filthy rags; We all fade as a leaf, And our INIQUITIES, like the wind, Have taken us away. And there is no one who calls on Your name, Who stirs himself up to take hold of You; For You have hidden Your face from us, And have consumed us because of our iniquities" (Isaiah 64:6-7 NKJV, emphasis mine).

---

[64] "But he who doubts is condemned if he eats, because he does not eat from faith; for whatever is not from faith is sin" (Romans 14:23 NKJV).

[65] Dr. Douglas E. Carr, *Patterns of Perversity: Freedom from Iniquity* (Sturgis: Doug Carr Freedom Ministry, 2022), xi. Print.

[66] Carr, *Patterns of Perversity*, 18. Print.

Why is it important to consider iniquity when contending for healing? Because iniquity that has not been confessed and cleansed in the blood of Jesus blocks us from receiving resurrection life and is passed down through the generations—three to four generations deep. Here are two passages from the Bible supporting this truth:

> "You shall not make for yourself a carved image—any likeness of anything that is in heaven above, or that is in the earth beneath, or that is in the water under the earth; you shall not bow down to them nor serve them. For I, the LORD your God, am a jealous God, visiting the iniquity of the fathers upon the children to the third and fourth generations of those who hate Me, but showing mercy to thousands, to those who love Me and keep My commandments" (Exodus 20:4-6 NKJV).

> "The LORD is longsuffering and abundant in mercy, forgiving iniquity and transgression; but He by no means clears the guilty, visiting the iniquity of the fathers on the children to the third and fourth generation" (Numbers 14:18 NKJV).

It is important to actively confess and repent for iniquity. The Israelites in Nehemiah 9 are an example to us:

> "Now on the twenty-fourth day of this month the children of Israel were assembled with fasting, in sackcloth, and with dust on their heads. Then those of Israelite lineage separated themselves from all foreigners; and they stood and confessed their sins and the INIQUITIES OF THEIR FATHERS" (Nehemiah 9:1-2 NKJV, emphasis added).

Just in case there are a few well-meaning readers who are thinking, *we're under grace now so it's not necessary*, consider the following: Jesus died for the sins of every person in the whole world, so does that mean that every single person in the world is just *automatically* saved? Without repentance? Without acknowledging their sin or their need for salvation? Without submission to God? Without knowing Jesus? No, it doesn't. Each person must accept the gift of salvation through REPENTANCE (which includes confession) and believing that Jesus died and rose again—by being born of the Spirit and by confessing with their mouth, "Jesus is Lord." Each person is required to enter salvation by taking these steps. It is this submission to God that *activates* the miracle of re-birth. Just as we submit to the principle of repenting for our own sin, so we also must submit to the principle of repenting for iniquity, to be free.

Do you remember we talked about the first Passover earlier? The Israelites were told to slaughter a spotless lamb and then to apply the blood of that lamb to their door frame, the gateway to their home, so that the spirit of death would pass them over. It wasn't enough that the blood was shed. It wasn't enough that the blood sat in a bucket at their door. No, they had to dip the hyssop branch into the blood and smear that blood over their door frame, at the top AND on both sides.

Jesus' blood was shed for us. But, in the same way, it isn't enough that it was just shed. It isn't enough that His blood spilt and dripped down His body. To ACITIVATE its power in OUR lives, Jesus' blood also needs to be applied to our doorframes symbolically, to OUR spiritual and inner gateways, so the spirit of death passes over us too (our inner "gateways" are the places of entrance into our body and soul). Confessing our sins and the iniquity of our fathers and mothers and speaking the blood of Jesus over our spirit, soul and body is just like taking that hyssop branch and smearing the blood where we need it most.

To understand iniquity better, let's have a look at an example in the lineage of Abraham. In Genesis 20:2 we see Abraham being fearful, deceitful, disrespectful, and selfish when he lies to king Abimelech about who Sarah is, in an effort to protect himself. (He told the king that Sarah was his sister because he was afraid the king would kill him to take Sarah as his wife.) As a result, king Abimelech believed it lawful to take Sarah as his concubine and did so. Not only did this cause great grief and embarrassment for Sarah, but it also almost cost king Abimelech his life and the lives of his whole household. Abraham was caught in his lie as God revealed the truth to Abimelech in a dream. King Abimelech confronted Abraham and returned Sarah to him. Later, in Genesis 26, Isaac, Abraham's son does EXACTLY the same thing to his wife, Rebekah. Then in the next generation, deception, lies, disrespect, and selfishness continue as Jacob steals Esau's blessing (Genesis 27). The propensity to deceive to get what one wants or because of fear, continues down the line, entangling them all in sin.

I'll never forget the day I lay, face down, on the carpet in my living room, repeating the phrase, "I submit to you God." I had found myself parenting badly and I "saw" my father in my actions. When I was young, he had trouble controlling his temper and now, so was I. I didn't like what I felt. And I didn't like how I was acting. I had already repented for acting out in anger, but I didn't seem to be able to stop. I felt caught in a vicious pattern, unable to break free. I had had enough, so I passionately pursued God, confessing the iniquity in my family line including fits of rage, poor anger management, yelling, violence, and even murder, and ended up "eating carpet." Not intentionally, of course. As I confronted the demons that wanted to hold me, Holy Spirit put me on my face, in submission to Him, to protect me and set me free. He knows what He's doing! Thank God. It was a real-life James 4:7 moment, "Therefore submit to God. Resist the devil and he will flee from you." Sometimes, submitting to God by specifically confessing iniquity is the key to deliverance and sometimes you've got to get on your face—quite literally.

Another moment came, as I homeschooled our daughter for the first time when she was only 6. This time however, I reminded myself of my mother. I had lost patience with Jessica as I tried to explain the lesson and again, I had come to a place of deep conviction by Holy Spirit. I was no longer able or wanted to make excuses for myself, so I prayed. As I prayed, asking the Lord to help me have more patience, a very sinister voice in my head told me, "But you don't know how to do anything else!" I knew that thought was not from God nor from myself. No, I knew this was directly from the devil and I wasn't going to agree with his lies. I called out the "father of lies," told him to shut his mouth, and confessed the truth Holy Spirit showed me. I confessed that God, my Father, was shifting everything and taking me on a wonderful journey where He would teach me everything I needed to know about being a good, patient mother and teacher. I saw with eyes of faith my heavenly Father filling my need for a righteous role model in the parenting department. Again, I had to confess the iniquity in my bloodline and forgive my mother to be released from the iniquitous pattern of yelling and speaking harsh words out of frustration. Praise God for His mercy and grace that sets us free from every bondage.

Iniquity is directly related to many diseases. You know how when you enrol as a patient with a new doctor, and you complete the questionnaire about your family's medical history? This is because some diseases run in families; they are genetic and carried along through the DNA. These diseases are held in place by iniquitous patterns that have not been dealt with nor cut off, through repentance, the blood of Jesus and the necessary adjustments in behavior.

What does that mean, "necessary adjustments in behavior?" Well, some iniquitous patterns are *reinforced* through our behavior. This means, we could pray and repent for the iniquity in our family but then continue to give it legal right to continue, through what we do. For example, deep rooted fear in the bloodline can influence behavior, so ask Holy Spirit to show you anything you are doing that is rooted in, or began in fear. This is not necessarily your fear but fear from previous generations so don't just use your carnal mind to decide what's from fear and what's not. Ask Holy Spirit! Keep in mind, your answer from Holy Spirit may not come right away but may come as you are going about your day, doing the things you normally do. He may just quietly whisper to you, "This is fear."

To illustrate, consider a woman who doesn't wear any makeup. There's nothing wrong with not wearing makeup unless the reason why is linked to fear or some other lie regarding her identity. Perhaps a young woman from a *previous* generation was severely chastised and called a "whore" by her father when she tried makeup for the first time and as a result, never wore makeup again because of the hurt in her heart and the fear of not being loved. This pattern was then passed on through the generations, keeping the iniquity of emotional abuse and self-loathing alive and well. A woman in this position might do well to ask Holy Spirit, "Why don't I like to wear makeup? What is at the root of that decision in my life? I don't like makeup. But why; is it fear? Is it because I believe I won't be loved or accepted if I do? Is it because I'm afraid of rejection or looking like a whore?"

Another example is superstition. There could be behaviors, habits, items, or traditions that have been modeled to you and passed on to you that are rooted in suspicion or superstition. I still remember as a youngster having a rabbit's foot key chain for luck, walking along the sidewalk being careful not to step on the cracks saying, "Step on a crack, break your mother's back," and seeing adults throw salt over their shoulder at the dinner table. Wanting or needing "good luck" is a sin as it doesn't reflect faith in God. Make sure to get rid of any item said to be a "good luck" charm, whether it was passed on through the generations or not.

I see in my mind's eye someone turning the deadbolt on their front door twice in a row, just to make sure it's locked properly. I don't understand why someone would do that, but I'm seeing it so it must be important to mention. I believe this kind of behavior could be considered "obsessive compulsive disorder" which of course includes other behaviors too, like washing hands compulsively because of the fear of germs, hoarding because of a fear of not having what is needed later or shame about being wasteful, compulsively cleaning household surfaces, and others. These behaviors will keep the iniquity of fear rooted in your blood despite what you pray.

What about the family tradition of opening Christmas presents on Christmas Eve? Why do some families do that? Is it just for fun? Or was there another reason for which that tradition was started in the first place? I remember hearing of a family whose ancestors had their home broken into overnight on Christmas Eve and all their gifts stolen. They woke up on Christmas morning to devastation. From that time on, they opened their gifts Christmas Eve instead of Christmas morning and that tradition was continued on through the next generations. In summary, the family BEGAN opening their presents on Christmas Eve because they were fearful of their gifts being stolen again and continuing in that behavior kept the entire family partnering with fear and trauma.

What about the tradition of eating fish every Friday as some Catholics do? Why do that? What happens if you don't? Is it motivated by fear? Is it biblical and rooted in faith? These are important questions for us as we untangle ourselves from ungodly generational behaviors and iniquity.

Iniquity has a very broad scope. It could be ANY bent, perversion or weakness of character that causes or attracts sinful behavior. Some common weaknesses resulting in negative patterns seen in families are fear, shame, lust, sexual perversion, abuse, rage, pride, addiction, greed, deceit, frustration, rejection, victimization, and idolatry.

Patterns in most of these areas are easy to detect. A pattern of lust and sexual perversion will manifest in obvious ways like addiction to pornography and/or sex, fornication, adultery, habitual masturbation, homosexuality, voyeurism, sexual abuse, molestation, rape, sodomy, sadomasochism, bestiality, pedophilia, and any other sexually deviant behavior. Also keep in mind that lust is not just about sex. Sometimes people lust after power, influence, money, and material things.

Rage obviously manifests as yelling, throwing things perhaps and the like. Addiction can manifest in many ways as well. Addiction to pornography/sex was already mentioned but people can be addicted to MANY things including food, sugar, caffeine, prescription drugs, legal and illegal drugs, smoking, alcohol, shopping, attention, social media, games etc.

Pride can manifest as arrogance, arguments, condescension, not accepting advice or help, unwilling to submit, unwilling to be taught or to be wrong, unwilling to see one's faults, boasting, bragging, anger, frustration, competitiveness, contentiousness, criticism, control, deception (hiding the truth), egocentrism, narcissism, entitlement, greed, and others.[67] Greed, deceit and frustration can easily be seen in

---

[67] Douglas Carr, *Free Indeed from Root Spirits* (Sturgis: Doug Carr Freedom Ministry, 2014), 142-143. Print.

people's behaviors when they lie, tell half-truths, keep secrets, steal, hoard, withhold from others, pinch pennies, freeload off of others, get angry, yell, throw things and perhaps verbally abuse others. Victimization and rejection perhaps are not so easy to identify, so let me explain these a bit further.

Victimization

Victimization manifests in our lives when we are victimized *repeatedly*. Sometimes we accept it as normal, and at times don't even realize we're being victimized. It operates in those who have been abused, by convincing them of lies associated with the abuse. These lies could include, *it's my fault, I deserved it, I'm not worth anything more, I'm unlovable,* or *I'm trash and will always be abused*. It can be identified when a PATTERN of abuse arises in one's life—they are abused as a young child, then they are abused by boyfriends/girlfriends, they marry someone who is abusive, they are treated badly by friends, and bosses and they may even abuse themselves at times with negative self-talk or worse.

A *spirit* of victimization acts like a magnet, attracting abusers to further victimize them and LABELS a person as a victim. Ever felt like you had a "kick me" sign on your back,[68] or a "use and abuse" me sign? Well, it's not a sign, but a spirit that has labeled you as a victim willing to participate.

A spirit of victimization is affecting our life if we are experiencing repeated abuse or victimization. Mentally we can be convinced that we are above it, but if the manifestation of it is still happening, our spiritual health is not lined up to what we believe in our head and deliverance will give us a new level of freedom. Occasionally someone affected by this spirit will accept it as part of who they are, but not always.

---

[68] Carr, *Patterns of Perversity*, 43. Print.

To be free from victimization: if as an adult we've allowed abuse in our lives and we've not enforced appropriate healthy boundaries, we first need to repent and forgive our perpetrators. Of course, a child is NEVER responsible for the abuse they suffer but *as adults* ARE responsible for continued abuse, they have tolerated. Please know I don't mean to sound uncompassionate here.ABuse is evil! Believe me, I know. A child who has been raised in abuse is confused about what love looks like and can very often not even identify abuse in their life as an adult. God understands too and He is full of compassion. Repentance is not about blame and pointing fingers. Repentance is simply about changing our mind about something; coming to the understanding that something is wrong and turning away from it.

Ask Holy Spirit to remind you when the very FIRST instance of abuse occurred, what happened and who was involved. Also ask Holy Spirit what lies you believed about the abuse. Make notes for reference in prayer. Then, focussing on the event Holy Spirit revealed, tell Him about it, what happened, what it did to your heart and how it made you feel. This is a necessary step in acknowledging the event and releasing it all to Jesus, including every hurt emotion and feeling. Ask Holy Spirit to heal you and show you where He was in the room at the time of the abuse. According to the Word, the presence of God is with us ALL the time; He never leaves us nor forsakes us, so He was there! You just weren't aware of it at the time. Ask Holy Spirit to make you aware of His presence in that event, now.

You may ask, "Well if He was there, why didn't He stop it?" Beloved, sometimes people will ignore God and follow the evil inclinations of their heart instead. God is sovereign but He sovereignly chose to limit Himself when He gave us free will. We all have the capacity to make a decision apart from God and His influence. Believe and understand that God did not endorse or author your abuser's actions.

Next, forgive the abuser. I know this is difficult! Remember though, forgiving your abuser is not letting him/her off the hook; it is getting the devil's hook out of you. Your abuser is still responsible and accountable to God for what he/she has done.

Next, RENOUNCE the lies, if any, that you believed about the abuse (example: It was your fault, you asked for it, it was normal, you had to allow someone to abuse you to keep them happy or to be loved etc.), renounce the spirit of abuse and the spirit of victimization, bind them in Jesus' name, and forcefully COMMAND the spirits to get out

Lastly, ask Father God to send the Holy Spirit to fill you afresh and as a follow through, ask God to help you identify any abuse that is CURRENTLY happening in your life. If there is anything, you will need to confront it, call it out and refuse to continue to allow it or co-operate with it anymore. This may require you to make a plan first though! Don't put yourself in a vulnerable situation where you don't have a roof over your head. Use wisdom and ask God to show you your next steps.

Rejection
Rejection operates similarly. A hurtful rejection happens, and the one being rejected believes lies about it and themselves that sound like, *I deserved it, it's my fault, I'm ugly, I'm unlovable, I'm unlikeable, I'm a reject, I never fit in, something's wrong with me*, etc. A pattern of rejection then shows up in their life as the spirit of rejection labels them "a reject" attracting even more rejection. The spirit of rejection will even cause us to reject others as a self-preservation coping mechanism; we will reject others before they have a chance to reject us.

The process to be free is the same. Ask Holy Spirit to show you where the pattern of rejection began and pray it through.

Forgive all those who have rejected you. Renounce rejection and renounce all the lies connected to it. Cast that spirit out and be filled with Holy Spirit.

It is imperative that we understand and believe the truth about ourselves. We are not rejects and we are not rejected! God the Father sent His One and Only Son to die for us, just so we could be back in relationship with Him—so we could be adopted as His. We are the beloved of God! We are CHOSEN, pre-destined, and highly favored in His sight and that is ALL that matters. If another person has not valued us, it is not because there is anything wrong with us but because they did not see our worth or their own internal wounds caused them to want to tear us down. If we get hung up on people rejecting us, then we are putting a greater value on the opinions of people than on the opinion of God. Don't do that! It's a trap. It will get us entangled with idolatry which will just be another thing that will make us sick.

Idolatry

As we've discussed already, idolatry is the worship of other gods, looking to other (false) deities for healing or spiritual power or it can simply be placing a higher value on something else above God.

It can manifest in many ways. On the more obvious side of things, our ancestors may have:

- looked to the stars for guidance (astrology)
- worshipped nature
- looked to crystals for healing
- participated in rituals or witchcraft
- been superstitious
- believed in horoscopes
- were psychic or went to psychics

- read Tarot cards
- believed in the power of other gods (examples might be: the goddess of fertility (isis), the god of weather (zeus) or the goddess of volcanos, fire and lightening (Hawaiian goddess of pele))
- used dreamcatchers or other things to try and ward off evil spirits
- made sacrifices to other gods

On a tamer note, idolatry can be loving or valuing others or things more than God and pursuing those things more passionately than pursuing God. Some common things that people tend to hold too dear are money, power, career, sex, romantic love, opinions of people, acceptance by others, material possessions, spouses, children, and sometimes other family members. Take an inventory and ask Holy Spirit to help you identify ways your ancestors may have been involved in idolatry.

Before praying to be free of iniquity, take a *complete* inventory now of ALL iniquity you believe you and your ancestors have been entangled by. Think back about your parents, siblings, and grandparents. Make a list of things you think may apply to your family. Look for patterns in multiple people and generations. Ask the Holy Spirit to help you. Then begin praying something like this:

> "Lord, I thank you for Who you are. I honor you and glorify your name. You are the Alpha and Omega. You are the beginning and the end. You are the everlasting God. The One Who never slumbers nor sleeps and the One Who sees me and loves me just the way I am.

Lord, I confess to you that my family has not obeyed your commands, we have not kept your laws nor honoured you with our lives. *As a family*, we have been involved in things that have broken your heart. We have worshipped other gods—worldly things and worldly success, (name other things that your ancestors may have valued higher than God, like money, status, power, false religion, creation). I confess to you, on behalf of my family, the iniquity of (name all iniquity Holy Spirit revealed to you earlier) and I repent. Lord God, I am sorry, and I ask for your forgiveness. God, I thank you that you are a merciful God and a God Who is patient and longsuffering. I turn from the iniquity of my ancestors now and I receive your forgiveness in my life and the lives of my family and all future generations. I now choose to forgive my ancestors for their sin and iniquity and for the negative effects that have come upon my life and the lives of my children. In the name of Jesus, because we are forgiven, I renounce and cut off from my life and the lives of my children, even since the womb, the sins and iniquity of my ancestors, every consequence of them, every demonic spirit empowered by them, and every curse associated with them. I bind every demon (name them individually if you can) in my bloodline, and I command the spirit of (insert name) and (insert name) [again, call them out individually] to leave my bloodline now in Jesus' Mighty Name. I declare that every curse is broken by the sacrifice and blood of Jesus and that my bloodline is now cleansed and set free from every evil intent and assignment. Thank you, Jesus that you became a curse for us and have nullified every curse previously operating in our lives. We receive you Lord as our new family and bloodline and welcome your blood to flow through our veins. Holy Spirit come and fill me afresh and fill me completely; don't leave any spot untouched by your presence. I welcome you Holy Spirit and give you control. In Jesus' Name. Amen.

Words and Power

There are many scriptures that talk about the power of the tongue and words:

> Proverbs 18:21 says, "The tongue can bring death or life; those who love to talk will reap the consequences" (NLT).
>
> Proverbs 13:3 says, "Those who control their tongue will have a long life; opening your mouth can ruin everything" (NLT).
>
> Proverbs 15:4 says, "Gentle words are a tree of life; a deceitful tongue crushes the spirit" (NLT).
>
> Psalm 34:12-13, "Does anyone want to live a life that is long and prosperous? Then keep your tongue from speaking evil and your lips from telling lies (NLT)!

And then we have James 3 which teaches us that the tongue can do incredible damage, completely direct our lives like a rudder on a ship and even set a whole forest ablaze with one little word. Yikes! We best be careful how we speak!

King David confirms that the tongue is very often used by evil to cause much damage:

> Psalm 64:2-3, "Hide me from the plots of this evil mob, from this gang of wrongdoers. They sharpen their tongues like swords and aim their bitter words like arrows" (NLT).
>
> Psalm 140:1-3, "O Lord, rescue me from evil people. Protect me from those who are violent, those who plot evil in their hearts and stir up trouble all day long. Their tongues sting like a snake; the venom of a viper drips from their lips" (NLT).

Have you ever been hurt by words? That old childish saying, "Sticks and stones may break my bones, but words will never hurt me," is one big fat lie. Words can hurt MORE than breaking bones and the damage can last a lifetime. Words have power!

The New King James Version of Proverbs 18:21 says, "Death and life are in the POWER of the tongue," (emphasis added). Very often words and phrases spoken to us, over us or about us, from long ago still haunt us today. But God can set us free from those words and set our life back on track according to His will!

There was a time when I was young; I had been disobedient somehow, or too much to handle, so my mother sent me to my room. Unbeknownst to her I had snuck down the hallway and planted myself just outside the kitchen as she spoke to my grandmother on the telephone. She complained to her mom about her life and said words about me she shouldn't have. Those words stuck with me deep on the inside, but I blocked the memory from my mind. It wasn't until I had given birth to Jessica, my first-born, that the memory began to stir and press for attention.

I began to feel emotionally upset and triggered but I wasn't sure about what or why, so I contacted a good friend who was a prayer counsellor. I asked her to meet with me for ministry and she agreed. We met and as soon as we sat down to pray, the memory surfaced. I shared it with my friend, and she began to minister healing prayer. Within minutes, the grace, power, and compassion of God washed over me and a vision from Holy Spirit began playing on the screen of my imagination.

> I was a little girl amidst a crowd of other children, waiting for the arrival of a special guest who was coming to greet us and bless us. There was a barricade that kept us back, but there wasn't enough room for everyone along the front where we were sure to be greeted.

It was crowded—six, seven children deep, all pushing and vying for a position where they could be greeted and received. Not surprisingly, I was at the back not able to make my way forward, feeling rejected and unseen. We all waited as the excitement grew and voices got louder. *He won't greet me; He probably won't even notice me*, I thought, as I allowed the others to push and jostle me back.

Suddenly, there He was! He had arrived. He began coming down the line greeting and smiling at the children in the front. I watched Him, longing to be included. Again, *He won't greet me*, I thought, *I'll just be left out again*, but suddenly, everything changed.

In the blink of an eye, supernaturally, my position changed, and I found myself propelled right to the front—right before our guest, Jesus. Clothed in bright white, He took my hands in His and fixed His eyes on mine. I became lost in His gaze and everyone else disappeared. His fiery blue eyes pierced right into mine—right into my soul, cutting away lies and eradicating everything warring against the truth.

"Barbara, I love you," He said. Time slowed and His Words hung in the air with fresh breath and new life. Once again, slower this time, "B-a-r-b-a-r-a, I love you." A few moments passed as I tried to take it all in; His eyes locked on mine, communicating past human limitations. As love overtook me, eyes wet with salty tears, I thought astonished, *He said my name! He just said my name. How does He know my name? I never told Him my name.*

Over the next few moments, the truth of my value in His eyes, enlightened my heart. He greeted me. He knows me. He sees me. He loves me. I am His. It was all I needed. One encounter with Jesus and the Word transformed me from the inside out. Forgiveness flowed and healing came.

Words. They can hurt or they can heal. They can build up or they can tear down. But Words spoken by God Himself right into our heart, are in a league all their own; they are sure to mend the most broken places and heal the worst pain.

If you have been hurt by words spoken by others, I would encourage you to forgive that person and pray something like this:

"Lord, thank you for Who you are. Thank you that you are for me and not against me. Thank you that you see all and hear all and you redeem all. Lord, there have been words that have been spoken to me and over me that have literally haunted my mind and life. You know. You saw it when it happened, but I confess it to you now. [Name of person] told me that, [repeat what the person said], and I believed them. Their words pierced my heart God and I need your healing. I renounce the words, [repeat what the person said], and I come out of agreement with them now. I know they were not of you, God, so I repent for believing them and receiving them, and in the authority of Jesus, I break their power over me now. I say those words are now powerless, and I command them to fall to the ground, in Jesus' name. Forgive me God for believing lies. Thank you, Lord. I now choose to forgive [say the person's name] for speaking lies to me and over me and making me feel [confess how those words made you feel]. I choose to release her/him into your hands as their judge God and I ask you Lord not to hold it against them. Have mercy on their soul. Thank you, God, for your faithfulness to me and them. In Jesus' mighty name, amen."

Have you ever spoken words about yourself that tear you down—perhaps words that sound like, "I can't believe I did that. I'm so stupid," or "I'm such a loser. I can't ever seem to get ahead." If you find yourself saying things like this, renounce them as soon as you realize what you've done. Say, "I renounce that in Jesus' name. And I repent for tearing myself down with my words." We have enough enemies to contend with, without having to contend with ourselves!

There are two further scenarios I'd like to address when it comes to words that hurt. One scenario happens when a prophetic person gives us a "word" they think is prophetic, but it's a negative word and the other is when we respond to negative circumstances by wanting to control and we end up saying things like, "I'm NEVER going to do that," or "be that," or "I'm always going to…" This last scenario leads us into making vows to ourselves, which leads us into bondage.

Negative Prophetic Words
Back in chapter 4, we talked about how God created everything through words. God said, "Let there be light'; and there was light" (Genesis 1:3). All He did was say it and it was. God's Word is powerful! His Words create and will always accomplish what they were sent for. Modern-day Prophets or people operating in the prophetic gifting also may utter powerful words that are legitimately from God's heart and mind, blessing us greatly. However, occasionally a prophetic person may miss it and speak something prophetically of a negative nature that ends up empowering negative outcomes. It's very unfortunate, but it does happen. To guard against being blindsided or becoming sick because of it, let's talk about it.

All words spoken over us for PERSONAL prophesy are supposed to be for the purpose of encouragement, edification, and comfort.[69] The word should therefore be of a positive nature and should NEVER include the foretelling of negative things like accidents, calamity, misfortune, or disasters. A prophetic person is to seek the Lord for HIS will and heart for the person they are speaking with. In light of this, everything they perceive should come from a place of peace, love, and healing.

If a prophetic person perceives that there is a challenging circumstance coming our way or discerns the enemy is trying to mess with us somehow, they should seek the Lord for His REDEMPTIVE word that cancels the enemy's plans and deliver God's word to us and ONLY that word. The LAST thing we need is for a prophetic person to prophesy the devil's plans into existence.

If we are given a prophetic word that foretells an accident, illness, or bad event, DON'T receive it, no matter who the person is. Even if that person is seen as reputable AND even if they follow it up with something positive, don't receive it. If it happens in a corporate setting, don't make a scene, and embarrass them, simply renounce, and cancel their words on your own in prayer later. Simply say, "I renounce the lie that... [repeat the negative word]" An example may be if someone prophesies that you're about to go bankrupt, but God will restore you later. In this case, I would pray, "I renounce the lie that I'm about to go bankrupt." You could also pray, "I know Lord that it is not your will for me to go bankrupt nor to be stolen from; I know that your mercies are new every morning and it is your heart for me to prosper in all things. If there is anything I am doing that would give the enemy a legal right to cause me to

---

[69] "But the one who prophesies speaks to people for their strengthening, encouraging and comfort" (1 Corinthians 14:3 NIV).

go bankrupt, show me God and I will repent immediately." *In a private setting*, if someone says to you, "You're about to go bankrupt, but God will restore you after," you could say, "I'm sorry, I don't receive that. I don't believe it is God's plan or will for me to go bankrupt; based on Jeremiah 29:11, His plans for me are good and for my benefit and prosperity.

Always test the word that you are given from a person who claims to speak anointed words from God. Ask yourself, *does it line up with God's Word, does it reflect God's heart and character?* If it doesn't, renounce it, and always forgive the person who spoke the misguided word. No one is perfect and growing in prophecy is a journey that can begin with more blunders than we want. So let's be gracious.

Personal Vows and Promises to Self
Sometimes when we go through abuse, trauma, or unfair circumstances when we are young, we make vows (spoken or inner) to ourselves to try and control our lives and avoid pain. A vow is simply a promise made to oneself with deep conviction to "never" or "always" do or be something and may involve a bitter judgement against another person who has caused us pain. It is an attempt to protect ourselves from being hurt, either because we've been hurt already, or we've witnessed others being hurt.

When my husband and I were trying to start a family and couldn't, I realized that I had made three vows regarding having children and they were holding me hostage. Firstly, because of trauma in childhood including watching my own mother go through two miscarriages, being told very graphic information I didn't need to hear and accumulating ridiculous amounts of fear around doctors and hospitals, I made a vow when I was an adolescent to NEVER have children. Secondly, shortly after moving into our first home after getting married, I didn't like the neighborhood we lived in (we had some neighbors involved in sketchy business), so I made a vow not to have children while living there. I did not want to raise my children in that neighborhood. Thirdly, I made a vow not to have children while driving the car we drove as it was very unreliable. It had left us stranded on the highway a few times and I certainly didn't want to have a baby on board in that situation. I was not successful at conceiving and birthing our first-born until all these vows were either met or broken in prayer. Jessica was born 13 months after moving into a new house and 9-10 months after buying a new to us car. All three vows were sin because they were all an attempt to control, but in addition, the first vow was made because of fear, the second was made because of judgements against our neighbors and the third was made because I knew it wasn't wisdom to drive an unreliable car with an infant. Instead of making a vow, we should have just listened to wisdom and gotten the new car!

Once we make commitments to ourselves, we step out of God's plan and into our own. We decide God is not trustworthy and we take things into our own hands. When we do this, we lock Holy Spirit out of those aspects of our life and because of our obstinate independence, end up giving the devil an opportunity instead. Unfortunately, the devil is not going to waste an opportunity.

In my situation, the devil was preventing me from conceiving, and he also caused me to miscarry, but the devil could also cause sickness because of vows. I would encourage you to ask Holy Spirit to remind you of any time you may have stubbornly and emphatically said, "I'm NEVER going to [blankety blank]!"

Were you abused in any way as a child? Abuse can cause us to decide to NEVER be like our parents or to NEVER treat our own children the same way. This sounds reasonable as it would be good not to parent the same way, however, every vow to self always comes from an independent spirit that does not trust

God and this vow usually includes a bitter judgement against our parents. Now we have two sin issues operating in us giving the devil a foothold.

Scripture is clear that we are to honor our father and mother, even when they don't do the best job. Understanding that our parents did the best they could with what they had and knew is key to having our heart in the right place. Exodus 20:12 says, "Honor your father and your mother, that your days may be long upon the land which the LORD your God is giving you" (NKJV). Scripture is also clear that we are not to judge others (look down on someone in condemnation):

> "You may think you can condemn such people, but you are just as bad, and you have no excuse! When you say they are wicked and should be punished, you are condemning yourself, for you who judge others do these very same things" (Romans 2:1 NLT).

> "Do not judge others, and you will not be judged. For you will be treated as you treat others. The standard you use in judging is the standard by which you will be judged" (Matthew 7:1-2 NLT).

In his book, *Shadow Boxing*, Dr. Henry Malone gives a real-life example of someone who was held hostage by her inner vow and bitter judgement against her father:

> "A grandmother once came to me seeking help. With tears in her eyes, she confessed that she was abused as a child and that she abused her three children. She was troubled by watching her adult children physically abuse her grandchildren. Often, she found herself abusing them, too. "I can't take it any longer. You must help me," she begged.

> I asked her to share about her childhood abuse. She was the third of six children. Whenever one child did

something wrong, her father punished all six of them."[70]

Dr. Malone goes on to describe the horrific abuse the children suffered but I will spare you the details. He continues:

"When she was ten years old, she made an inner vow. She promised herself that "if I ever have any children, I will never do to them what Daddy does to us." While she didn't punish them in the exact same way, she beat her children with whatever was at hand... Quickly I saw that the vow she had made had imprisoned her and set her on a track that she could not get off simply because she had judged her father. When she repented of her inner vow and asked God to forgive her for judging her father, freedom came. We broke the vow and its results ceased."[71]

Recognizing our mistakes, repenting, asking the Lord for forgiveness, and breaking our vows will also lead us into freedom and we can do that now. Pray:

"Lord, I confess that I have tried to control my life, that I have attempted to protect myself in my own strength by making a vow and I have also looked down on and judged (the person's name) for his/her behavior toward me. I choose to forgive (person's name) for hurting me and/or mistreating me. Father God, I now repent for being bitter, for making bitter judgements against (name the person), for wanting to be in control of everything, for pushing you out of my life, for not trusting you and not submitting to you and your authority. I repent for thinking that I could do a better

---

[70] Dr. Henry Malone, *Shadow Boxing* (Lewisville: Vision Life Publications, 1999), 78. Print.
[71] Malone, *Shadow Boxing*, 78. Print.

job than you of keeping myself safe. I repent for relying on my own strength instead of you. Lord, I ask for your forgiveness. I now renounce the vow that I will (repeat the vow). I cancel those words in Jesus' name and I now break my agreement with them. I command them to fall to the ground and I decree them powerless over my life. Father, I bring every part of myself and my life back under your authority, care, and protection and I choose to trust you with my life. I ask you again God to be Lord over EVERY part of my life. I choose to forgive myself for making this vow and I now break and cut off every curse that has come from my disobedience and self-protection. I break the power of every evil force that was released to carry out these curses over me, my family, my destiny, and my future. I thank you Lord that my family and I are covered in the blood of your Son, Jesus, and that He has redeemed us from every curse by becoming a curse for us. Thank you, Lord, that when we confess our sin to you, you are faithful and just to forgive and cleanse us from all unrighteousness. I receive your forgiveness and cleansing, and I give you praise. Fill me afresh, Lord, with your Holy Spirit to overflowing and baptize me again in your power. In Jesus' most powerful name, Amen."

Body Perspective

When I was young, I hated my hair, my teeth, overbite, and prominent chin; unfortunately, orthodontics was never an option for me, and I could never figure out how to manage my curly, frizzy hair (hair straighteners didn't exist when I was young). I now have long hair for the first time in my life and am grateful for its fullness in middle age, but my teeth, overbite, and chin remain the same. None the less, I have learned to see myself through my Father's eyes and love myself the way I am.

I am sure most every person reading this has had similar thoughts about themselves. Maybe it wasn't your hair, but your nose or perhaps your high forehead. We have all had critical things to think and say about our looks and body, haven't we? Unfortunately, this does not honor God nor His creation (us).

Additionally, as we are aging, our body may fail us somehow—perhaps getting weaker, softer, and not as flexible. Being diligent to continue to move and stretch becomes vital to everyday life. This can be annoying and difficult to cope with at times. Inside we're still young, but we can't act young anymore. We may not feel we have the energy to keep up with the grandkids, exercise, or maintain our homes and yards as we want. I used to do a "WOG" in the morning—an intermittent walk/jog route that I really enjoyed, but I haven't been able to do that for several years now as my joints cannot tolerate it.

Is there something your body refuses to do now that you're older? Perhaps you used to enjoy roller coasters, but now you can't handle them. Perhaps you used to enjoy water skiing but now it's a thing of the past. We're not sick really, just aged. How does this make you feel? Are you angry about it? Are you angry at your body for getting old? Releasing and repenting for these attitudes, plus gaining a new perspective of our body so we can celebrate and bless it, will help us come into healing.

God created us. He created our inner parts and our outer parts. Psalm 139 says He formed us in our mother's womb knitting us together and there are so many amazing things about our body that only a Creator could think of and design. He is a master builder, intricately wiring us and connecting all our systems together.

Genesis chapter one gives us the account of God creating everything, including us. In an overview, Genesis one tells us that God created man in His own image and likeness. Genesis chapter two gives us a closer look at the creation of man, specifically the creation of our body. I don't know about you, but because of my upbringing, I've always thought of the body as an inferior creation to the spirit, but this is wrong thinking. We need to elevate our thinking and understanding with regard to the human body; God did not create our body as they are now. God created our body before the fall, in Glory with perfect intentions.

Genesis 2:7 says, "Then the LORD God formed the man from the dust of the ground. He breathed the breath of life into the man's nostrils, and the man became a living person" (NLT). As Patricia King so perfectly points out in her "Women of Influence" online course, the "dust" of the earth which God used to form man was not dust as we know it today. Dust is not a desirable thing now; we continually try to eliminate it from our homes but before the forbidden fruit was eaten, the earth was the Garden of Eden, and it was full of Glory. In fact, the "dust" of the earth were Glory particles infused with the very presence of God. The human body was a thing of beauty, shimmering and shining with Glory, perfectly made, and expertly functioning.

I mentioned before, but see fit to reiterate now, that we are primarily spiritual beings, we have a soul, and we live in a body of which all have been magnificently created by God. All three parts of who we are, are integrated and connected. No one part functions on its own. We were created in the image of God, Who also is three parts in one. Just like God, our three parts are in agreement, in unity and harmony one with the other. Proverbs 17:22 says, "A cheerful heart is good medicine, but a crushed spirit dries up the bones" (NIV). The condition of the heart (inner man) and the spirit affect the body and the bones.

I used to think of the spirit as a light living in a person's belly, kind of like an orb; I'm not sure where that came from, but it's not an accurate picture. The truth is, the spirit gives life to the body; it's impossible for a human body to live without the spirit inside.[72] A more accurate picture of how the spirit and soul are integrated into a body is to see each and every cell infused with both. Indeed, the field of epigenetics is beginning to discover that human DNA carry emotional and soulish data like "tags" turning genes on or off which in turn affects a person's physical well being. Hence, each and every cell has a soul and a spiritual component, not just physical.

Patricia King explains in her "Women of Influence" online course, if our soul and spirit were able to step out of our body and appear separately, they would look the same as our body in appearance. Our soul and our spirit are not blobs in the center of our bellies, they are expressions and exact replicas of who we are; they function differently but they appear the same.

Why is this important? Well, at the moment of salvation, the Holy Spirit comes to make His dwelling—His abiding place—inside of us. He actually comes and makes His home in us, but not in some obscure, unknown place in our belly, but in EVERY CELL of our body! The Holy Spirit is not confined! His presence is alive in every cell and His power can be invited to operate throughout our entire being, even *possessing* our organs,

---

[72] "For just as the body without the spirit is dead, so also faith without works is dead" (James 2:26 NASB).

muscles, tendons, and any body part not behaving as it should. Praise God! Renewing our mind—hearing the revelation of Holy Spirit is the gateway to faith and healing.

Once again, in Luke 13:10-16, a "daughter of Abraham" was bent over for eighteen years because of a bad spirit or demon in her body. If a demon, которая is a spirit, can cause this kind of physical problem, how much MORE can the HOLY SPIRIT possess your body and cause it to function according to His perfect will?

> "Don't you realize that your BODY is the temple of the Holy Spirit, who lives in you and was given to you by God? You do not belong to yourself, for God bought you with a high price. So you must honor God with your body" (1 Corinthians 6:19-20 NLT, emphasis mine).

Even more truth can be pulled out of this scripture. It says, we were bought at a high price, but which part of us? ALL OF US! Each part of who we are, spirit, soul, AND body, was purchased and now belongs to Jesus. Our body has become His body. Considering this, how much more should we love, appreciate, and bless our body with our words and actions, taking care of it properly? How much more should we guard against sin—especially sexual sin which defiles the body? How much MORE do you think Jesus wants it functioning properly, being free of sickness and disease?

Allowing all this good revelation to sink deep into our heart and mind, let's also make sure we are aligning ourselves with righteousness. You may want to:

1. Confess and repent for hating or disliking your body.
2. Repent for not celebrating your body.
3. Confess, repent, and renounce any curses (negative words) *spoken* over your body (eg. "I hate my…," "I'm sick and tired of…," "I'm fat," "I'm ugly," etc.).

4. Confess, repent, and renounce any negative *thoughts* and *beliefs* about your body.
5. Confess and repent for all sexual sin.
6. Confess and repent for any other sin you've committed against your body (e.g., overeating, alcohol abuse, drug abuse, eating too much junk food, treating your body like a trash can, whatever HS convicts you of, *perhaps* even unnecessary surgeries or surgeries you've had without first asking God for His opinion and direction).
7. Confess and repent for all anger you've held against your body.
8. Confess and repent for any judgements you've made against your body.
9. Forgive your body for aging and not functioning as it should.
10. Repent for dishonoring your body.
11. Repent for overworking your body and not knowing when to allow yourself to rest.
12. Repent for not keeping the sabbath—one day every week to rest and focus on the Lord.
13. Forgive yourself for all the above.
14. Release to God, by speaking it out loud, any sin that was committed against your body by someone else. Tell God about it and confess to Him your feelings (not because they are bad or sinful but to get them out of your body). Forgive anyone who has committed sin against your body.
15. Ask God to give you a new love for your body.
16. See your body from God's perspective.
17. Break curses over your body.
18. Cast out a spirit of infirmity.

19. Remove trauma from your cells by praying, "I pull out trauma from every cell of my body right now, in Jesus' name."

20. Speak love and blessing over your body—even specific body parts. "I speak blessing over my body. I speak over my teeth in Jesus' name, and I thank God for them and how they function, allowing me to eat good food. I declare health over them and proper alignment in Jesus' name. I say they are blessed of the Lord and in their rightful place, in Jesus' name."

21. Anoint your body with oil.

22. Dedicate your body to Jesus.

23. Treat your body with respect and honor going forward by taking proper care of it. Eat properly, allow yourself to rest appropriately, get enough sleep, perhaps work less, exercise, move, don't stay sedentary, shower, groom yourself appropriately, and even wear nice clothing. If you don't care about what your clothes look like, have you ever really thought about why? Perhaps you've convinced yourself that it's about not being vain, but I would challenge you to think again. Wearing baggy, ratty clothing could be an outward sign of how you really feel about yourself. Allow Holy Spirit to examine your heart friend and get on the same page with Him. Honor yourself by wearing descent clothing.

Following through with the previous suggestions will help you come into alignment with God and bring about divine health. Remember to believe what you pray to activate faith.

Facts verses Truth

As a believer, your job when praying regarding the healing of your body is to declare the truth of what already is, not ask God to heal you and not moan and complain about the facts. Your job is to STAND in faith. Jesus has already provided for your healing;

in the spirit realm, you are already healed. Your healing simply needs to be pulled into the earth realm through faith. We can, however, still admit the facts. We must be truthful about everything.

Let me explain. The fact may be that you have pain somewhere in your body. I am not suggesting you deny the facts. Let's look at Abraham. Abraham had a promise from God that an heir would come from his own flesh, but he was way past the years of physically being able to bear children, as was Sarah. The only way he was going to have a biological child was through a miracle. Listen to Romans 4:19-21:

> "Without weakening in his faith, he (Abraham) *faced the fact* that his body was as good as dead—since he was about a hundred years old—and that Sarah's womb was also dead. Yet he did not waver through unbelief regarding the promise of God, but was strengthened in his faith and gave glory to God, being fully persuaded that God had power to do what he had promised" (NIV, brackets and emphasis added).

Abraham was able to face the facts but still be strengthened in his faith and be fully persuaded of what God was able and willing to do. We also can be strengthened in our faith and be fully persuaded of what God has already provided for, regardless of what we see and feel in the natural realm.

The fact is: a fact and the truth according to God are two very different things. The facts about our circumstances are volatile, temporary, always changing and can totally turn around in an instant according to our faith. The facts come from a worldly, natural perspective of our situation. The truth, on the other hand, is eternal and comes from a heavenly perspective. The truth is constant and does not change. The truth is God's view of a situation and comes straight from His Word.

Potentially, our confession of the facts and truth could sound something like this:

"The fact is I'm in pain, but the truth is, Jesus bore all my pains when He was beaten and crucified and has carried them all away, far from me never to return. Jesus has already paid for my healing and has purchased me as His very own possession. I belong to Christ and nothing apart from Christ can reside or stay in my body. I am His. My body is His body. Jesus Christ bore upon Himself all pain, infirmity, sickness, disease, and adverse conditions that may want to attach themselves to me, but I do not give them permission. I renounce all permission I may have unknowingly given them in the past. Complete healing and wholeness is available to me right now and in Jesus' name, I receive it now. I take it from the heavenlies, and I apply it to my earthly body right now. I take it because it belongs to me and I thank God for it. I praise God and give Him the glory that the natural facts must submit to the supernatural truth of God right now, in Jesus' name. I speak to my (name the body part or organ causing trouble) and I say, "Be healed in Jesus' name." The Lord rebukes every malady. The Lord rebuke (name problems specifically). The Lord rebukes sickness and disease and I cut my agreement with them now in Jesus' name. Thank you, Lord! Every argument in my mind that has set itself up against the knowledge of God, I now pull down with force, in Jesus' name. Every lie of the devil, I renounce and rebuke in Jesus' name. If I have somehow agreed that *I deserve this illness*, I repent for believing it and I renounce that lie, in Jesus' name. (If there are other lies that the Holy Spirit brings to mind, renounce them.) Thank you for cleansing me of all lies and all unrighteousness, Lord. I know that I will see your goodness and your complete faithfulness in my life, despite my shortcomings because that is just Who you are. Your mercies are new every morning and I receive them now. In Jesus' name, amen."

Repressed Emotions

There's a quote from the 2008 movie Fireproof that I will never forget: "Don't just follow your heart 'cause your heart can be deceived. You've got to LEAD your heart."

"Follow your heart;" we hear that a lot in the world, don't we? On the surface we think it's good advice but what it's really saying is follow your feelings. Feelings of the heart can be fickle, changing frequently according to moods, not generally grounded, or rooted in truth—very much of the flesh and not the Spirit.

What happens when we don't *feel* like going to work? We still go to work, don't we? If we followed our feelings every time, we'd soon be fired. Jeremiah 17:9 tells us, the heart is full of deceit. It would be best to LEAD our heart in partnership with Holy Spirit in truth and holiness.

Having said all that, let's not assume that our feelings are not important. Let's not think that our feelings should be ignored or stuffed into tiny boxes and stored away in the closets of our heart. Our hearts need to be healed by acknowledging and being truthful about our feelings. Too often we have been taught not to express our feelings and resulting emotions. Maybe we've been told, "don't be a cry baby," "get over it," "you're so sensitive," and been shamed for the feelings we have had. Perhaps we've buried our emotions to survive or perhaps we've wanted to appear to others as a "good" Christian or as someone who has it all together. Healing comes when we strip away the masks and admit what we truly feel to Jesus in prayer. When we are willing, Holy Spirit is so gracious to help us identify the feelings that need to be released.

Back in chapter 5, I mentioned the miser from Proverbs 23:6-7; he is a good example of someone who does not walk in the truth of his heart or in integrity. Instead, he pretends, he says the *right* thing even though it's not the honest thing. What he says does not line up with his heart. "'Eat and drink,' he says to you, but his heart is not with you" (Proverbs 23:7 NIV). The miser hides how he really feels.

God want us to walk in truth and He wants us to be truthful about the deep things of our heart. Integrity means to be honest, and the Bible has much to say about it. Proverbs 10:9-10 says, "He who walks in integrity walks securely, But he who perverts his ways will be found out" (NASB). Psalm 119:1 says, "Joyful are people of integrity, who follow the instructions of the LORD" (NLT). Proverbs 2:7 says, "He grants a treasure of common sense to the honest. He is a shield to those who walk with integrity" (NLT). Proverbs 11:5 says, "The godly are directed by honesty; the wicked fall beneath their load of sin" (NLT). Most striking of all is Psalm 32:1-5:

> "Oh, what joy for those whose disobedience is forgiven, whose sin is put out of sight! Yes, what joy for those whose record the LORD has cleared of guilt, whose lives are lived in complete honesty! When I refused to confess my sin, my body wasted away, and I groaned all day long. Day and night your hand of discipline was heavy on me. My strength evaporated like water in the summer heat. Finally, I confessed all my sins to you and stopped trying to hide my guilt. I said to myself, "I will confess my rebellion to the LORD." And you forgave me! All my guilt is gone" (NLT).

"Are all our feelings sin though?" you may ask. No, not all, of course, but many of the NEGATIVE ones? Yes. You're not going to like this, but many of the negative feelings we have are based on worship of self. (Ouch! That's a serious truth bomb, right there. I hope you're wearing your steel toed boots!)

Hmm… you may be pondering, *what does she mean by that?* Well, frustration, I think is a good example. If I'm frustrated, I am frustrated because something is not going MY way or going how I expect, want, or need—something is more challenging than it needs to be and is testing my patience. Another example is jealousy. If I'm jealous, I feel as though someone else has more favor than ME. Thirdly, if my feelings are hurt, angry, bitter, or even hateful toward someone, it's usually because someone has done something to ME that I don't like; it could be something that has simply inconvenienced me, made me look bad, feel bad or it could be worse. But the point is, it's ALL about me and hanging on to those emotions is harmful to ourselves. There are times when anger is not sinful necessarily, but again, we've already talked about the need to confess our anger to God in a timely manner to avoid it becoming sin and giving the devil a foothold.

A good example of a negative emotion not being sin is sadness. Many times, we are sad because others have gone through tough things or injustice of some sort and being and empathetic toward others is a good thing.

Have you ever wondered how Jesus coped emotionally with all the betrayal, rejection, humiliation, and sheer abuse He suffered? How did Jesus not become offended and how did He not have wounded feelings and emotions? If anyone has the right to have hurt feelings, it was Jesus. The answer is: He WASN'T focused on Himself; his focus was always on others. This is in NO WAY meant to cause anyone shame. We are human! It is only to reiterate the need to get our feelings OUT by confessing them to the Lord.

All the negative feelings and emotions we try to bury, make us sick. So, it's time to get a feelings jar started or a feelings journal and use it to confess our feelings to Jesus. At the end of every day, ask yourself, "How did I feel today and why?" and write it down. Tell Jesus about it while you're at it and give it to Him. Taking this inventory is so very helpful at not holding onto and storing emotional baggage. The Lord wants truth and honesty to rule our heart. Let's not hide or wear masks pretending to be okay. Let's get real friends. Let's release to the Lord everything He purchased including our feelings and emotions.

Have you ever tried to justify your anger and offense to the Lord? I have and it didn't go very well. Why? Well, because whatever we've suffered, Jesus has suffered more. Yes, the Lord is compassionate and longsuffering—absolutely! He understands and He allows us to grieve our losses and sufferings, but there is a time when He will say, "Okay, beloved, it's time to come out of that cave. I need you to rise up in my Spirit and be my witness on the earth."

I know. Many have suffered unimaginable things and that may be you, but Jesus suffered it ALL. The good news is "we do not have a High Priest who is unable to sympathize *and* understand our weaknesses *and* temptations (and sufferings), but One who has been tempted [knowing exactly how it feels to be human] in every respect as *we are, yet* without [committing any] sin" (Hebrews 4:15 AMP, round brackets mine). When we are willing, in the power of Holy Spirit, to shift our focus from ourselves back to Jesus, we will realize our suffering doesn't compare to His. Jesus said in this world we would have trouble,[73] but take heart, "I have overcome the world" (John 16:33 NKJV). In other words, "Be encouraged! I have overcome everything the

---

[73] Jesus was not talking about sickness or disease as "trouble" in this verse. He was talking about being hated by the world—about suffering persecution, and injustice (eg. rejection, abandonment, abuse, and loss perhaps of loved ones, resources, jobs, opportunities, friends, etc).

world has thrown at you, and you are invited to join me in that same victory by focusing on me and not yourselves—by worshipping me and finding your identity in me" (paraphrased). If your sufferings and grief are keeping you in a pit of despair, your focus is off. Focus on the risen Christ—the Christ Who has overcome it all and will punish the devil for what he has done to you.

Jesus was incredible. He was human, yet He had such a close relationship with His Father, He was able to derive all His worth and value from Him. *In no way did He ever look to another human being for validation.* Did you hear that? Read it again. In NO WAY did Jesus ever look to another human being for validation or love. He was completely secure in Who He was as God's Son. We should and can be the same. But, if we're honest, we're not there yet. We are still a work in progress, in the process of renewing our mind in many ways, but most importantly about who we are to and in Christ.

If we too can get to the place where we so believe in the love of God for us and we completely trust in His acceptance of us just the way we are, we wouldn't need validation from anywhere or anyone else, and we wouldn't care if someone didn't like us or said something mean to us or about us. Our heart would be secure. We would be unoffendable.

First John 4:15-16 says, "If anyone acknowledges that Jesus is the Son of God, God lives in them and they in God. And so we know and RELY ON THE LOVE GOD HAS FOR US. God is love. Whoever LIVES IN LOVE lives in God, and God in them" (NIV, emphasis added). Do you RELY on God's love? Do you live in or *constantly* abide in the love of God? Hmm... Yeah, I fall short of that too. But if we were to RELY on God's love, and if we were to LIVE in God's love, we wouldn't NEED to get love from anyone else, would we? The phrases that we sing in a popular chorus, "Christ is enough for me," and "Everything I need is in You," would be true of us. We would know that we know, we are loved all the time and we would be able to express that love to others *despite* how they act toward us. How incredible that would be.

If we were secure in the love of God, knowing our true status as sons and daughters, we wouldn't *need* anyone else. This isn't to say we shouldn't be in relationship with anyone else, it just means our self-worth would not ride on relationship with others. We were made to love others. We were made for relationships, but not to *get* anything, only to give. We were made to be a blessing, to love others well, and to represent Jesus on the earth through that love.

May it be our goal to have all our needs met in Jesus Christ and not rely on anyone else to meet those needs. Only in our security with Christ can we truly be immune to the emotions that bind us. May we have an undisputable revelation of the love of God in its fullness and trust it to be everything we need and more, causing us to be completely free from offense in every form. Bring us deeper into your love, Lord, and into fellowship with you. Help us to let the feelings from the past go and bring us higher into your love and truth.

Spend some time in prayer and let God know how you have been feeling. Be specific and allow Holy Spirit to minister His love to you.

Injustice

We've talked a bit about injustice and the righteous anger that can come up in us when we witness it. However, right now, I want to quickly mention injustice in a slightly different context. Injustice can be a blockage to our healing when we are the ones who are perpetrating it. If that doesn't sound like it applies to you, please don't skip over this section. Injustice can be *very* subtle and sneaky, so please read through and allow Holy Spirit to speak to you.

When we are ill and seeking the Lord diligently for answers, it is common and helpful to fast. We can fast food completely (so long as we are physically able to do this), or fast certain foods, but either way it is a great way to pull on God to satisfy every appetite, craving, and hunger with His love, His Word, and His voice. Deuteronomy 8:3 says, "...man shall not live by bread alone; but man lives by every *word* that proceeds from the mouth of the Lord" (NKJV).

Food in general, particularly sweets and "comfort" foods tend to dull our spiritual senses—they put cotton in our spiritual ears so to speak. Restricting access to these comfort measures forces us to find our comfort in God and helps us to hear the Spirit's voice distinctly and receive the revelation we need. *Hunger* helps us to hear God. Satisfying that hunger with earthly things causes us to no longer be hungry, thus we don't seek to be filled with His Word. When we fast, however, we should take Isaiah 58 into consideration to make sure it is as effective as it could possibly be.

Isaiah 58 is an amazing passage of scripture calling us to "fast" the right way—the way that God has chosen. It's not just about restricting food but re-aligning ourselves to God's ways. Isaiah 58 speaks for itself so here it is:

> "Cry aloud, spare not; Lift up your voice like a trumpet; Tell My people their transgression, And the house of Jacob their sins. Yet they seek Me daily, And delight to know My ways, As a nation that did righteousness, And did not forsake the ordinance of their God. They ask of Me the ordinances of justice; They take delight in approaching God. 'Why have we fasted,' they say, 'and You have not seen? Why have we afflicted our souls, and You take no notice?' "In fact, in the day of your fast you find pleasure, And exploit all your laborers. Indeed you fast for strife and debate, And to strike with the fist of wickedness. You will not fast as you do this day, To make your voice heard on high. Is it a fast that I have chosen, A day for a man to afflict his soul? Is it to bow down his head like a bulrush, And to spread out sackcloth and ashes? Would you call this a fast, And an acceptable day to the LORD? Is this not the fast that I have chosen: To loose the bonds of wickedness, To undo the heavy burdens, To let the oppressed go free, And that you break every yoke? Is it not to share your bread with the hungry, And that you bring to your house the poor who are cast out; When you see the naked, that you cover him, And not hide yourself from your own flesh? Then your light shall break forth like the morning, YOUR HEALING SHALL SPRING FORTH SPEEDILY, And your righteousness shall go before you; The glory of the LORD shall be your rear guard. Then you shall call, and the LORD will answer; You shall cry, and He will say, 'Here I am.' "If you take away the yoke from your midst, The pointing of the finger, and speaking wickedness, If you extend your soul to the hungry And

satisfy the afflicted soul, Then your light shall dawn in the darkness, And your darkness shall be as noonday. The Lord will guide you continually, And satisfy your soul in drought, AND STRENGTHEN YOUR BONES; You shall be like a watered garden, And like a spring of water, whose waters do not fail. Those from among you Shall build the old waste places; You shall raise up the foundations of many generations; And you shall be called the Repairer of the Breach, The Restorer of Streets to Dwell In. "If you turn away your foot from the Sabbath, From doing your pleasure on My holy day, And call the Sabbath a delight, The holy day of the LORD honorable, And shall honor Him, not doing your own ways, Nor finding your own pleasure, Nor speaking your own words, Then you shall delight yourself in the Lord; And I will cause you to ride on the high hills of the earth, And feed you will the heritage of Jacob your father. The mouth of the Lord has spoken" (NKJV, emphasis added).

SHAME AND SELF-HATE/REJECTION

We've already touched on body image, but now we're going to touch on the rejection of self and self-hate partnered with shame. Perhaps it's not your body you're unhappy with, but your soul. Perhaps you're disappointed in yourself for some reason or a past injustice has left you feeling unlovable, dirty, or tainted. I'm sorry friend if you find yourself in this situation.

Healing follows cleansing. When a wound is cleansed, then it can heal. Cleansing equates with applying the blood of Jesus over your wound and pursuing holiness, through prayer, spending time in the secret place with God, and reading the Word. Pursuing holiness is a process where we allow God to lead us and make the necessary adjustments in our heart, sometimes, one step at a time, empowered by the Holy Spirit. Perhaps you have felt overwhelmed by this book; it would not be surprising—it's A LOT to cover and confront all at once. Perhaps it would be best for some to digest one chapter at a time and take it slower; it is completely acceptable if you do. Perhaps, this is a book that you need to re-visit time and time again.

Many believers, I think, when pursuing holiness, will focus on what they do and don't do—how they behave, but good behavior is the *fruit* of holiness, not holiness itself. Holiness is more about loving God, believing God, agreeing with God about EVERYTHING, believing who you are in Christ, and aligning our heart with truth. Perhaps one of the main areas people struggle with is seeing themselves through the eyes of Christ and loving themselves as Christ loves them. To the extreme, some people are stuck in life or are sick because they have agreed with self-rejection and even self-hate. Somewhere amidst that, shame lives and operates kind of like glue, keeping them there, unable to get free. Only you can determine where you are on the scale of shame and rejection of self.

Here's the thing: Christ saw enough worth in you to die for you. Christ values you even above His own life. So, when we reject or hate ourselves, we're not agreeing with God. When we have believed and allowed shame to take hold of us, believed and accepted rejection and received the negative report from others, we are NOT believing God—we have not aligned ourselves with God's Word, but we have aligned ourselves with the enemy of our souls.

Yes, we needed redemption. We needed to be saved from our sin and decrepit state, so we accepted God's forgiveness AND we also let ourselves off the hook at the same time. In order to live forgiven, we must allow ourselves to receive the fullness of God's grace and mercy. Let God be God and call the shots. Let God determine our worth and our status as FORGIVEN AND CLEANSED, no matter what.

Shame may have come on us in a few different scenarios:

- From things we've done and regret.
- From experiences of being caught in the act, perhaps by a parent (possibly embarrassing situations).
- From words spoken over us like: "Shame on you!" or "You should be ashamed of yourself!"
- Sin that others have committed against us.

In order to illustrate my point of how God can heal us of shame, I'm going to be completely vulnerable with you. I wasn't saved until I was twenty-two years old, so my teen years were lived as a sinner. Thank God, He has forgiven it all. Anyhow, when I was sixteen, my father saw my boyfriend and I touching each other's bodies as we were watching television in the basement TV room. I didn't know or hear him come down the stairs. It wasn't until my father confronted me later when he

SHAME AND SELF-HATE/REJECTON

advised me to "use discretion" that I realized what had happened. At the time, I was so embarrassed and ashamed by what he saw. I was devastated, but time went on and it soon faded away and I forgot about it (or so I thought).

Fast forward about thirty-six years. One night, out of nowhere, I had a dream: an unnamed man and I were in the act sexually. In the dream I was hesitant to be in the situation, but didn't resist necessarily, when suddenly, Father God came around the corner and entered the scene. Suddenly, everything and everyone else disappeared, and Father God and I embraced. I completely *melted* into His arms becoming one with Him and felt with such intensity the absolute perfect love He had for me. There was absolutely no shame in His demeanor, countenance, or heart for what He walked in on, only complete and perfect love.

When I awoke, it still felt so real. I asked the Lord what it was about, and He gently reminded me of the experience I had with my earthly father that was filled with shame. I had forgotten about it; but it was still buried in my soul. God showed me that He graciously allowed the dream to *re-form* my experience with a Father walking in on or witnessing me in a sinful act and as a result, transformed my past memory and expectation for the future. I hadn't thought about that experience in a long time, but God knew it was an open door for the enemy, so He sovereignly took care of it. Father God completely undid and removed the shame over that situation. My mind has now been renewed as to what I can expect when Father God knows and sees me not being perfect. I can rest and be assured that there is no shame in it at all. I can expect only love, mercy, and compassion at its best. Praise God!

I pray this has ministered to you and helped you to see that you too can be relieved of shame. Shame is not of God. Shame is from the devil and meant to keep you in torment, outside of the love of God. If you let Him, Father God will communicate to you in similar ways to set you free. Ask God to heal you and to take from your soul all shame and regret. Enter the fullness of forgiveness and mercy as you boldly and courageously choose to trust Father with your deepest secrets.

Go into the secret place with God and imagine yourself before Him. In your hands is a bowl into which you can place every shameful experience and every regret. Imagine yourself giving Father the bowl and "see" in your mind's eye what He does with it. If you will focus and allow your Godly imagination to be controlled by the Spirit, God will communicate to you through images on the screen of your imagination. I can tell you what God thinks of you, but it is so much more powerful when it comes directly from Him.

Trust Him beloved. He will meet you where you are and He knows exactly what you need.

The Orphan Spirit or Mindset

On August 8, 1975, Prophet Bob Jones died temporarily and had a significant spiritual encounter with the Lord where the Lord asked the saints an important question. Jesus asked, "Did you learn to love?" In this death experience, the answer to this question determined the rewards that each saint received as they were embraced by Jesus and entered heaven.[74] Bob Jones was sent back to us that day with a new mandate, but He has since gone again to Glory, for good. Bob Jones' testimony gives us great clarity on where we fall short and reminds us of Jesus' mandate: love others and do it well. Are you surprised by the suggestion that we may need to learn, all over again, how to do that?

Before the fall, love was not a problem; it came naturally. We were made from love, out of love, and to love. Unfortunately, one bite of the forbidden fruit changed everything. Love became elusive and loving others well became impossible as we focused on ourselves. Consequences of the fall rippled on down the generations touching our lives from childhood, causing strife in families and marriages. Perhaps you know exactly what I'm talking about. Perhaps images and memories are bubbling up as you relate to love gone wrong or love never expressed in any form or fashion. While it's true, most parents do the best they know how, for many, it has not been enough, and they have grown up feeling more like an orphan than a son or daughter.

I'll never forget my mother coming out of the funeral home after her mother's memorial service. I quickly exited through the

---

[74] https://www.youtube.com/watch?v=FrDtDTAD184&t=1213s

back door to escape the stuffy, depressing atmosphere and my mom followed soon after. I turned to look at her and she said with a childlike voice, "My mother never loved me." My heart sank as I realized that apart from any intervention from the Lord, we learn to love by how we were loved. I had never felt tremendously loved by my own mother and now she was confessing the same about hers. This was a moment of clarity for me; lack of love is a cycle—a cycle with no end until someone sees it, intentionally forges a connection with love Himself, Jesus Christ, is healed of their own lack of love by fully embracing their identity as a son or daughter of God and is empowered and taught by the Holy Spirit to love like Jesus.

Forging a relationship with Jesus, Holy Spirit, and the Father puts us in a spiritual position to be loved perfectly as a son or daughter of God; Galatians 3:26 says, "For you are all children of God through faith in Christ Jesus" (NLT). But how much of your new spiritual condition gets passed on through to your soul and physical experience? Are you able to walk with the Lord, in the cool of the day through the garden, as Adam and Eve did, in the Spirit? Are you able to communicate with the Lord? Do you hear His voice? Do you trust Him to meet all your needs according to His riches in Glory? Have you stopped striving and toiling to meet your own needs?

Restoring our relationship and experiencing it is a process. The time we have spent living apart from Father God and sometimes the experiences we've had with our earthly fathers have trained us to continue living independently, like an orphan, looking after ourselves. It takes healing, a paradigm shift in our thinking, a de-programming and renewing of the mind to really be able to believe and trust God to be a good and perfect Father. We don't even know what that is or what it looks like, as none of us has ever had one. All our earthly fathers (even the good ones) and all of us too, have fallen short of the glory of God, somehow.

So how do we know if we're still behaving and living as an orphan despite our new identity in Christ? Well, asking Holy Spirit is a good start, however, considering how an orphan lives also helps. An orphan lives independently and relies on oneself. They struggle for what they need, and they earn everything by the sweat of their brow. They work like dogs and strive to be accepted. They hoard and save things because they don't know when they will need that thing they never use. They eat fast fearing they won't get enough, and they stash food in their pockets for later, just in case. They are jealous of others, lack peace, lack a sense of security and belonging and they don't feel loved. Orphans don't feel protected, they don't trust, fears plague their mind, and they desperately search for safety in things and human relationships, going from one person to the next.

Does any of the above sound familiar to you? Do you have a witness in your spirit? If so, don't worry. We are going to be free of the orphan spirit today.

In order to understand Father God's acceptance, let's consider the parable of the prodigal son, in Luke 15:11-32. The story paraphrased goes something like this:

The youngest son severely insults his father and severs ties with him and his family by asking for his inheritance early. He basically says to his father, "You're dead to me." He then leaves to go out on his own and squanders all his money on wild living. Eventually, he runs out of money, lives in a pigsty for a time and finally when he has nothing to eat, decides that he will swallow his pride and go home. He plans on asking his father for forgiveness so that perhaps he can work as a hired hand on the family farm—at least then he would be able to eat. The son begins his journey home and even while he is still a long way off, his father who has been watching for him, sees him in the distance. His dignified Jewish father, ditches his dignity, pulls his robe up above his knees, and RUNS to meet him—no hesitation, despite what the son has done.

The son says to his father, "Father, I have sinned against heaven and against you. I am no longer worthy to be called your son" (Luke 15:21 NIV). But here's the part I want to highlight: His father's reaction is not one of anger, rejection, or disappointment, but excitement, love, forgiveness, and total acceptance.

> "But the father said to his servants, 'Quick! Bring the best robe and put it on him. Put a ring on his finger and sandals on his feet. Bring the fattened calf and kill it. Let's have a feast and celebrate. For this son of mine was dead and is alive again; he was lost and is found" (Luke 15:22-24 NIV).

Wow! What a reception! It didn't go at all like the son expected. He expected to be a servant, but instead he was totally restored as a son, with all the benefits, including a new portion of inheritance. The son received everything the father gave him with no resistance or false pride or insistence on earning anything back. There was no probation period and no consequences to endure.

This is how our heavenly Father treats us when we come back to Him, and this is what true sonship looks like. Every time someone returns home, Father runs to meet them, throws open His arms, has a big party, rejoices and celebrates, while restoring everything that was given up by them voluntarily through their disobedience, all without question or explanation. What an amazing, gracious Father we have!

Holy Spirit is ready and willing to take you on a healing adventure, to change your experience and heal your emotions.

Many people don't want to rehash the past, but if you don't allow Holy Spirit to take you there, the wounds will remain and fester, possibly infecting your whole life. It begins by simply opening your heart to Daddy God, admitting to Him what has hurt you and asking Him to heal your heart. Healthy emotions and healthy expectations will be restored when you continue in prayer and forgive your earthly dad and mom. We must forgive, to break any curses resulting from a lack of love and orphan mentality. Hopefully you're well on your way there by now after covering the previous chapters.

Some of you have been told and trained to *suck it up*, *shake it off*, *get over it*, and *don't be a cry baby*. You've gone to dad or mom in need of compassion and consolation and all you received was chastisement. You needed a hug, and you got a rebuke. Is that you? Are you afraid to be rejected by Father when you admit that your heart is hurting? Do you need to be strong? Push it down? Does that voice play on repeat in your head? Does it stir something in your heart? If so, I'm sorry you were treated that way. It was wrong and it was not a healthy way to handle your pain and brokenness. You will need to forgive those who treated you that way.

There is a place that we need to be that is totally secure in the love of the Father. There is a place of total acceptance, where we can walk with Him and talk with Him every moment of every day if we choose to trust Him to be everything He has promised. Most importantly, we must remain in that place even when things around us tell us something different; when our physical circumstances don't line up, we must be unwavering in who we are to Him and in Him. We must know that we know, He fights for us, and He is good all the time—without question and without doubt.

Let's throw off the reasoning of our natural mind and the lies that get our emotions all stirred up and stand solid on a foundation of truth. Let's take every thought captive and make it obedient to Christ—arrest the fear and throw it out. Rest, my friend, in His unfailing love for you. Rest in His arms of grace and mercy. Hear Him sing over you with joy and rejoice over you with gladness. You belong to Him, and He only has your very best interest at heart. He longs to release to you His very best gifts.

Before we get to a final prayer to break the orphan mindset, there are two specific issues I want to target. They are as follows:
- Not being wanted by our earthly parents.
- Being mistreated or neglected by our earthly fathers.

Not Being Wanted
You could be carrying a stigma of not being wanted if:
- Your conception was not planned, expected, or wanted.
- Your parents or a relative clearly favored a sibling over you.
- You were told you were an "accident" or even a "mistake."
- Your parents complained about the financial burden of meeting your needs.
- You were conceived out of wedlock.
- You were adopted.
- You were conceived in rape.
- Your mother tried to abort you.
- Your mother thought about aborting you.
- Your mother tried to intentionally cause her body to miscarry.
- Your mother was abused physically with the intent of causing her to miscarry.

If any of these previous scenarios describes you, you may have felt like you have a "looser" sign on your back or a "kick me" sign. You may struggle with a sense of feeling inferior or not good enough. These are false identities we must confront and renounce.

It is important to come out from under the false identity of not being wanted. You may say, "But I wasn't wanted! I was given up for adoption." Indeed, it may be true—it may be a fact that you were adopted, but not being wanted is not true of who you really are. Your earthly parents may not have planned you, but it really doesn't matter. Your earthly parents are not the Creators—God is. God is the One Who creates. He simply uses our bodies to get the job done. Psalm 139:13-18 says:

> "You formed my innermost being, shaping my delicate inside and my intricate outside, and wove them all together in my mother's womb. I thank you, God, for making me so mysteriously complex! Everything you do is marvellously breathtaking. It simply amazes me to think about it! How thoroughly you know me, Lord! You even formed every bone in my body when you created me in the secret place, carefully, skillfully shaping me from nothing to something. You saw who you created me to be before I became me! Before I'd ever seen the light of day, the number of days you planned for me were already recorded in your book. Every single moment you are thinking of me! How precious and wonderful to consider that you cherish me constantly in your every thought! O God, your desires toward me are more than the grains of sand on every shore! When I awake each morning, you're still with me" (TPT).

You were VERY much wanted by your heavenly Father! In fact, according to Ephesians 1:4-6, you were chosen by God before the creation of the world to be holy and blameless in his sight and you were predestined to be adopted as His child through Jesus. So why are we putting more importance on being wanted by earthly parents than being wanted and even CHOSEN by God? Isn't that what we're doing if we choose to stay in a mindset of not being wanted? I encourage you today, right now, to come out of that mindset and reject the lie the enemy wants to hold you in.

Please forgive your earthly parents for not affirming you and loving you appropriately by communicating to you your intrinsic value. Pray like this:

> "I choose to forgive my earthly father and mother for not loving me well and not communicating to me my worth and value. Right now, I come out of agreement with the lie that I was not wanted. I renounce that lie and I confess that I was wanted and planned by my Heavenly Father Who knit me together in my mother's womb and chose me to be His before the foundation of the world. I choose to value God's acceptance of me over the acceptance of the world and my earthly parents and I choose to value God's love for me over the love that is in the world. I confess that God has wonderful plans for my life—plans to prosper me and not to harm me—plans to give me a hope and a future. In Jesus' name, amen."

Mistreatment or Neglect from Earthly Fathers
Our experiences with our earthly father can skew our beliefs about and trust in God, our heavenly Father, as we project our hurt feelings and experiences on all fathers. Our expectations for the future are very often set according to our experiences in the past.

I remember a time when I was young. My father was angry about my mother spending more money on me for something I needed. In his eyes, I didn't need it, but in reality. . . I did. I was hurt by his reluctance to provide for me, and I was fearful when he was mad. I'm sure he was overwhelmed by the expenses of a family of five, but as a ten-year-old, that went right over my head. I projected that experience onto God, and it caused me to see God as stingy, angry about providing for me, and reluctant to do so, though the TRUTH about God is the complete opposite. Philippians 4:19 says, "And this same God who takes care of me will supply all your needs from his glorious riches, which have been given to us in Christ Jesus" (NLT). Second Corinthians 9:8 says, "And God will generously provide all you need. Then you will always have everything you need and plenty left over to share with others" (NLT).

There's a beautiful song on YouTube by Misty Edwards called, "All Men Are Broken" that will soak your soul in love and truth as you listen. She is an incredibly anointed minister of prophetic song. Go find it and receive truth and healing into your heart. Let yourself feel what you need to feel and tell God about it. Then forgive your father, release him to God and receive Father God deeper than you ever have before. Father God wants to re-father you and redeem the time you spent in despair, depression, and grief over the lack of love in your father connection or the lack of having any father figure at all. You are deeply loved, and Papa God is turning it all around for you. You'll see. He'll touch every place that needs to be healed.

And in the name of Jesus, I cancel the curse of fatherlessness over you NOW! I decree that you have the greatest and best Father in the whole world, and you have never been without Him by your side. Every moment and every memory you have where you missed your father, Father God is now stepping into and filling that gap, rearranging, and redeeming it all, causing love to replace fear, attachment to replace detachment and belonging to replace estrangement.

Finally, pray this to renounce the orphan spirit and mindset:

"I thank you God for being my perfect loving, Father.
Open my eyes to see Who you really are on my behalf.

Help me to understand that I am not alone, and I never have been without you. I choose to forgive my father for being (absent, unloving, angry, unavailable, disinterested, disconnected, stingy, abusive etc.) I choose to release him to you God to be his judge and I ask God that you would have mercy on him, just as you have had mercy on me. I repent for being super independent, detached emotionally from you God, distant, not seeing you as my help and not relying on you as my Father. I now renounce and reject the orphan mentality, thinking that I don't belong, or that I must look after myself because no one else will. I bind the orphan mentality and spirit and I command it to go from my life now, in Jesus' name. I accept you God as my heavenly Father and I look to you for my help, my confidence, my sense of belonging, my provision, and my worth. Fill me up Lord with your Holy Spirit that I may pour out to others around me. In Jesus' name, amen."

FALSE RELIGIONS AND SECRET SOCIETIES

Our involvement with false religion, cults, and secret societies sets us up for demonic influence and invites demons of error, deception, confusion, and antichrist to attempt to control us; it is therefore necessary to discover what exactly are false religions, cults, and secret societies, to determine if we have been involved in them.

Merriam-Webster defines a cult as "a religion regarded as unorthodox or spurious."[75] Spurious means "of falsified or erroneously attributed origin—forged," and "of a deceitful nature or quality."[76]

In *Kingdom of the Cults*, Walter Martin agrees that a cult is any religious group which differs significantly from the norm of our culture, which is vague, but defines it with a little more clarity by writing:

> "...a cult might also be defined as a group of people gathered about a specific person or person's misinterpretation of the Bible. For example, Jehovah's Witnesses are, for the most part, followers of the interpretations of Charles T. Russell and J.F. Rutherford. . . Jehovah's Witnesses today still look to the Watchtower organization and its Governing Body to understand the Bible. In fact, Jehovah's Witnesses are taught that they *cannot* understand the Bible without the organization explaining it to them."[77]

---

[75] https://www.merriam-webster.com/dictionary/cult
[76] https://www.merriam-webster.com/dictionary/spurious
[77] Walter Martin, *The Kingdom of the Cults* (Minneapolis: Bethany House Publishers, 1965, 1977, 1985, 1997), 17. Print.

John the Apostle wrote first John as a letter to many of the churches in his time; His purpose was to reassure Christians there in their beliefs and to counter the false teachings circulating at the time that denied the identity of Jesus Christ as the Son of God.

> "Dear friends, do not believe everyone who claims to speak by the Spirit. You must test them to see if the spirit they have comes from God. For there are many false prophets in the world. This is how we know if they have the Spirit of God: If a person claiming to be a prophet acknowledges that Jesus Christ came in a real body, that person has the Spirit of God" (1 John 4:1-2 NLT).

> Jesus Himself said in Matthew 7:15-21:
> "Beware of false prophets who come disguised as harmless sheep but are really vicious wolves. You can identify them by their fruit, that is, by the way they act. Can you pick grapes from thornbushes, or figs from thistles? A good tree produces good fruit, and a bad tree produces bad fruit. A good tree can't produce bad fruit, and a bad tree can't produce good fruit. So every tree that does not produce good fruit is chopped down and thrown into the fire. Yes, just as you can identify a tree by its fruit, so you can identify people by their actions" (NLT).

I believe another scripture that helps us identify false teaching is found in 1 John 1:8-10:

> "If we claim we have no sin, we are only fooling ourselves and not living in the truth. But if we confess our sins to him, he is faithful and just to forgive us our sins and to cleanse us from all wickedness. If we claim

we have not sinned, we are calling God a liar and showing that his word has no place in our hearts" (NLT).

As well, 2 Timothy 3:16:

"All Scripture is inspired by God and is useful to teach us what is true and to make us realize what is wrong in our lives. It corrects us when we are wrong and teaches us to do what is right" (NLT).

In summary, we can identify a false religions or cults by the following characteristics:

- They gather around another person's teachings rather than the teachings directly from the Bible; people are even told they are not able to interpret the Bible on their own and must rely on the teachings of the organization to understand the scriptures.

- They dispute and don't recognize the true identity of Jesus Christ as divine—the only begotten Son of God, sent by The Father. As a result, they do not "worship" Jesus. They may like Jesus, trust His teachings, respect Him, but they do not worship Him as divine and are therefore misguided. (Remember Matthew 16:13-17, "When Jesus came to the region of Caesarea Philippi, he asked his disciples, "Who do people say the Son of Man is?" They replied, "Some say John the Baptist; others say Elijah; and still others, Jeremiah or one of the prophets." "But what about you?" he asked. "Who do you say I am?" Simon Peter answered, "You are the Messiah, the Son of the living God." Jesus replied, "Blessed are you, Simon son of Jonah, for this was not revealed to you by flesh and blood, but by my Father in heaven" (NIV).)

- Their leader(s) and/or founder(s) have consistent bad fruit in their lives displayed in their actions and/or words due to a lack of character and true divine direction.
- They may claim to be sinless and therefore, do NOT need forgiveness.
- Lastly, they may not see the Bible as the infallible "Word of God" in its entirety; they want to "cherry-pick" scriptures according to which ones align with their beliefs.

It is important to note in this discussion that we are speaking of groups of religious leaders and adherents who teach a *different* gospel from the true Gospel presented in scripture, involving the distortion of *core* Christian beliefs and the person and work of Jesus. Christians don't always agree on "peripheral issues" but that does not, by any means, give us reason to accuse such as being false teachers/prophets/apostles etc. For any Christian or denomination to believe they already have the FULL revelation of scripture now—that they are 100% right and everyone else is wrong—is heresy in itself and rooted in pride; we are all still learning and hearing from the Spirit the revelation of the mysteries of God.[78] Remember Jesus said in John 16:12, "There is so much more I want to tell you, but you can't bear it now" (NLT).

2 Peter 2:1-2 says:
"But there were also false prophets in Israel, just as there will be false teachers among you. They will cleverly teach destructive heresies and even deny the Master who bought them. In this way, they will bring

---

[78] "It is the glory of God to conceal a matter, But the glory of kings is to search out a matter" (Proverbs 25:2 NKJV). (Also: 1 Cor. 4:1, Luke 8:10, Daniel 2:47)

sudden destruction on themselves. Many will follow their evil teaching and shameful immorality. And because of these teachers, the way of truth will be slandered. In their greed they will make up clever lies to get hold of your money. But God condemned them long ago, and their destruction will not be delayed" (NLT).

Notice in the above passage, false teaching involves destructive heresies, denial of the Master (Jesus), shameful immorality, slandering of truth, and greed. Let's discern rightly the way of truth. Let's be careful who we slap slanderous labels on and be sure not to touch God's anointed ministers and teachers. Just because we don't agree with someone on every point, does not make them a false teacher.

Have you ever been involved in a false religion or cult that teaches false doctrine? Some religions that are considered cults from a Christian perspective are: Jehovah's Witness, Scientology, Christian Science, Unity, Witness Lee, The Way International, Unification Church, Mormonism, Church of the Living Word, Children of God, Swedenborgians, Worldwide Church of God, Unitarianism, Masons, and New Age.[79] Other religions teaching doctrine contrary to Christian beliefs, that may or may not be classified as "cults" are: Zen Buddhism, Hare Krishna, Baha'ism, Rosicrucian, Science of the Mind, Science of Creative Intelligence, Hinduism (Yoga), Transcendental Meditation, Eckankar, Roy Masters, Silva Mind Control, Father Divine, Theosophical Society, Islam, and Black Muslim.[80] If you have been involved in any of the aforementioned, don't despair, freedom is just a prayer away:

---

[79] Neil T. Anderson, *Helping Others Find Freedom in Christ: Connecting People to God Through Discipleship Counseling* (Ventura: Regal Books: A Division of Gospel Light, 1995), 279. Print.

[80] Anderson, *Helping Others Find Freedom in Christ*, 279. Print.

"Lord, I confess that I have been involved in (name the false religion) but I now know that (name false religion) doesn't honor you because it doesn't teach truth. God, I repent, and I ask you to forgive me for my participation in this false religion and for believing its lies. I choose to forgive myself and every person who led me into it, every person who encouraged me in it, taught me and participated with me. In Jesus' name, I now renounce the lie that (repeat the lie that you were taught and believed). (Repeat this last sentence until you have renounced all the lies the Holy Spirit brings to your remembrance.) I ask you God, to cut off from my life every effect of these lies, in Jesus' name. I renounce (name the religion) and every spirit associated with it. I renounce every lying spirit, the spirit of antichrist, deception, error, confusion, and witchcraft in Jesus' name, and I command them to leave me now. Thank you, God, for your forgiveness and grace in my life and I recognize you Lord, as supreme. I give you complete control. I say that every curse empowered through false teaching is now broken off my life and I am free in Christ to experience His love, joy, peace, and blessings, in Jesus' name. Amen"

Secret Societies

Another area we must consider are secret societies like Freemasonry (also considered a cult by many), Eastern Star (women's division of Freemasonry), Job's Daughter, Shriners, The Orange Order (Orangemen), Knights of Columbus, and all fraternities/sororities. There is always a spiritual element to secret societies that will distort truth and the worship of God. Through initiation ceremonies and oaths, participants are always, very subtly and deceptively led to worship false gods, the organization, and the leaders of it. Participants being initiated into the organization are usually required to take oaths of secrecy. Some societies require them to promise secrecy and lead participants to curse specific parts of their own bodies, including internal organs and reproductive organs as well as those of their family members, should they fail to comply. It sounds crazy and it's hard to believe, but these oaths are always on the "downlow" and are never talked about or admitted to. If a participant were ever asked about it, they would always deny it. No one would openly admit to this type of confession or oath taking, but it absolutely does happen. You may not have been involved in Freemasonry yourself, but your ancestors may have been, in which case, it is still very important to pray release from their demonic influence as the curses resulting from Freemasonry pass through the generations to at least four generations deep.

There is an excellent teaching by Linda Heidler from a conference that was held in February of 2015 at Apostle Chuck Pierce's church, Glory of Zion, called, "Reversing the Effects of Freemasonry." Go to YouTube to view the full teaching so that you are informed; the link is https://www.youtube.com/watch?v=8Z-D8bY6rS8 (go ahead and advance the video past the worship segment if you so desire). This link may only be available for a time; hopefully you can catch it. Here is the prayer she prays at the end of the video to lead you into freedom from Freemasonry and ALL its affects:

> "Lord, I come to you in the authority of Jesus, and I renounce all involvement with witchcraft and Freemasonry in my family right now and I stand before you God as one who wants my soul, mind, will, emotions, strength, and body, totally submitted and committed to you. I stand before you God, as your daughter/son—as one who has been bought by your blood, who has been set apart for you and by you. Lord,

where my true identity in you was exchanged for a false identity, or where I allowed a false identity to be imposed on me and where my true authority in you was stolen and replaced by false authority, I repent of it and renounce it now and I say, "give it back!" Right now, I take back my God-given identity that He created for me, and I take back the God-given authority that He has invested in me as His child and co-heir. Lord, where I have relinquished my God-given value or where it was stripped away from me, where I have been subjected to a value system that required me to perform and word hard in order to prove my worth or to feel like I was worth anything at all, I renounce it and I break away from that system right now; that is not the truth of God. I do not agree with it anymore. I reject the belief that I have to work, strive or prove my worth in order to be loved and I declare that my worth comes from God, and I am worthy of love simply because He made me. I take back my God-given, unique, intrinsic value and worth right now in Jesus' name. I throw out that slipshod slipper and I put on what God has given me. I declare that my feet are shod with the shoes of the gospel of peace and that I am prepared to share that peace wherever I go. I declare that I am sure footed, and that God has given me hinds' feet—feet that are able to walk in high places without intimidation or fear—feet that are swift, agile, and nimble in order to navigate any terrain and escape any trap. I declare that I am able to leap and run into my destiny with God and when I see the vision, I am going to run for it and not be worried about being tripped up by any slipshod slipper. Right now, I pull off that hoodwink and I take back my mind, my eyes, my ears, and my mouth. I now open my eyes, ears, and mouth and I declare that I am free to think, see, hear, and speak the way God wants me to. My spiritual senses are completely open to discern what God wants me to discern. I grab hold of my access to the mind of Christ and the wisdom of God, and I am going to expect and allow God to transform and conform my mind to the mind of Christ without hindrance. I am ripping off this noose from around my neck that has caused me to be in bondage and under the control of a freemason spirit; I am not going to be led around by any false worship system or spirit anymore. I declare that my heart and soul are now free to follow the leading of Holy Spirit and that ugly spirit that opposes and hates Holy Spirit is not going to have any influence or control over me anymore. I take away that dagger from my chest and I decide right now that I will no longer guard my emotions or be fearful of expressing myself. I choose to release my emotions and I declare that I am going to know the joy of the Lord and the joy of my salvation. I am going to know the compassion of Jesus; I'm going to know the love of God like I've never known it before. Where I have been blocked from knowing the love that God has for me, I'm not going to be blocked anymore. I am going to freely receive the love of God. I repent and renounce the words spoken by my family member before me, when they said they were "seeking the light of Freemasonry." Right now, I pull that dark cover off of my spirit and I take back my spirit that was made to commune with my Heavenly Father, to commune with Holy Spirit—that was made to receive revelation from Him. I take back my spirit and declare that it is free to commune with God and receive from Him and I ask you, Lord, for new levels of communion and revelation. Right now, I renounce and break all of the oaths and vows and curses spoken against my body, and I take back the health that you pre-ordained and purchased for me, God. I take back the strength in my body that you want me to have. Your Word says that your Spirit living inside of me quickens my mortal body and causes me to be in health. Lord, I know that my body is important to you as it is your temple, so I refuse to have my body infested with sickness, disease, weakness, or infirmity. I take back what you have given to me and what is rightfully mine, in Jesus' name.

I declare that I have repented of all participation in the ceremonies of Freemasonry. I have renounced the spiritual transactions that took place in those ceremonies. I have reclaimed my God given identity, worth, and destiny. I have reclaimed my soul, mind, emotions, will, and senses. I have reclaimed my physical body. I have reclaimed my spirit. I have broken all covenant agreements with the false religious system of Freemasonry.

I now submit myself, body, soul, and spirit to the living God, the God of Israel, Maker of heaven and earth. I fully enter into covenant with Him. I now position myself in active resistance to the devil. According to the Word of God: Submit to God, resist the devil, and he must flee (James 4:7)! I claim my right to every blessing of God in place of the curses that have been affecting my life. The Word of God says that the blessing of God will overtake me. Healing, prosperity, favor, protection, power, wisdom, and all the blessings of God are now free to come on me and my children. I am unhindered by any connection to false worship. I now freely enter into a new level of worship of the true and living God and of Jesus, His only Son with all my heart, soul, mind, and strength. I WILL go to new realms of worship in the Spirit and will join with angels in worshipping You, Lord. I will fulfill the destiny for which I was created. I will storm the gates of hell and prevail. Hallelujah! Amen."[81]

I would also add:

"I choose to forgive every ancestor who participated in Freemasonry or any other secret society; I forgive them for every curse and oath they spoke against me, my body, and my children and their bodies. I forgive them for activating curses against us and I forgive every person who deceived them, leading them into the secret society, and leading them while in it. I choose to forgive every person who led their initiation ceremony and I pray also for their families as well—that they would be set free from Freemasonry too, in Jesus' name. Amen"

---

[81] Linda Heidler, *Reversing the Effects of Freemasonry*, YouTube. https://www.youtube.com/watch?v=8Z-D8bY6rS8.

Final Thoughts

Thanks for sticking with me friend; I know it might have been a challenging journey. I deeply respect your willingness to allow Holy Spirit to lead you through some tough terrain.

Eternal life is a gift. Romans 6:23 says, "For the wages of sin is death, but the gift of God is eternal life in Christ Jesus our Lord" (NIV). It is not something that can be earned or bought; it is free, and it is from the Lord. Imagine for a moment that it's a gift, wrapped in shiny silver paper with a beautiful ribbon and bow. In order for that gift to be yours, you must accept, receive it and take into your hands. Once it's yours, you have a choice; once it's in your hands, you can admire the pretty wrapping, and display it on a shelf, but if you don't open it, you will never know what all is in the gift.

Many Christians don't open the gift. They receive it but they don't open it and see all the contents of the gift—all that it means for them. They think the gift is going to heaven when you leave this earth, but what they don't know or believe is it's so much more than that.

Second Corinthians 8:9 says, "You know the generous grace of our Lord Jesus Christ. Though he was rich, yet for your sakes he became poor, so that by his poverty he could make you rich" (NLT). In this passage, Paul is encouraging the Corinthians to be generous in their giving but at the same time he illustrates for us a miracle that occurred at the cross—the miracle of exchange. Paul highlights the exchange of our poverty for His riches and many other verses in the Bible tell us of other things that Jesus has exchanged with us. We have received His righteousness in exchange for our guilt and sin. We have received His health in exchange for our sickness. We have received His life in exchange for our death. We have received His spiritually alive divine nature for our fallen one—and we could go on. The key to an exchange though is the release of the old. We could not receive true life if we weren't willing to give up our old life, which in reality is death, and we wouldn't be able to receive freedom if we didn't give up our bondage.

Have you ever heard the analogy of the eagle that was raised in a cage? The eagle had the wings and the ability to fly and to soar at great heights, but since it was raised in a cage, it was used to being in the cage. Even though the door was open, it didn't venture out; it stayed in captivity even when it had the option to be free.

Do we sometimes get used to our captivity? Are we sometimes like that eagle that won't pursue or choose freedom? I think sometimes we are. I think our mindsets and wounded soul condition become familiar, like old slippers that we've worn forever, that have molded to our feet; they "feel" right, and they "feel" comfortable even though the foam on the bottom has worn out and flattened completely. New slippers would probably be more comfortable, but we prefer the old ones that have become familiar—the ones we have become attached to. "I don't need to change. I'm fine," we say to ourselves as we obstinately refuse refining. "There's nothing wrong with this cage. I have food. I have air. I'm surviving just fine the way I am." Although this may true, surviving is not what we are meant to do. We are meant to thrive! We are meant to soar! Yes, it takes some work. It takes some grit, but it is better to reach for the high call of God on our life than to just sit in complacency. God calls us higher.

I pray you are willing to reach for the higher places in God to experience His goodness and healing. I pray that you will run the good race and fulfill your destiny in Christ. May the mercy and goodness of God be made manifest before you, behind you, beside you, and all around you. May His healing come upon you powerfully and lift you up into a revelation of heaven on earth. And I pray that at the end of your life, when you are received into Glory, you will hear, "Well done, good and faithful servant" and that you will be received with shouts and cheers from all the saints.

All glory to God for His magnificent, amazing, power which He has made available to us, His children—those who trust in Him completely, fully, and eternally. Thanks for allowing me to speak into your life.

Blessings upon blessings be yours in Christ Jesus! Amen.

APPENDIX A
Roadmap to Healing Digestive Issues

The Lord showed me that a spirit of terror lodges itself in the digestive tract and digestive problems can result. First, we want to get the spirit of terror out, so it doesn't continue to cause harm, then plead the blood of Jesus over and through our digestive tract for healing. In order to get terror out, we also need to deal with what caused the terror. The Lord showed me that in many cases it is abuse. So, this document will give you direction on how to deal with abuse, fear, and terror so you can plead the blood and be healed.

You may be tempted just to pray "in your head," but the following steps need to be prayed "out loud." Your spoken words have power; your thoughts don't have the same power. If you need privacy, get in your car, and go somewhere, where no one can hear you. You don't have to be loud. If you're not used to praying out loud, practice talking out loud to God first. Talk to Him like He is a person sitting in front of you or next to you. Tell Him about your day. If it feels weird, tell Him it feels weird and ask Him to help you. Push past the weirdness. Close your eyes and "see" God's throne, or Jesus, in your mind's eye and talk to Him. There aren't any mistakes when talking to God. There's no rules. He loves you and wants to hear the sound of your voice. For example, just say, "God, I'm told I need to talk to you out loud. I'm not sure how to do that cause I've never done it before. It feels weird. But I want to be healed, so please help me feel more comfortable. Help me to push through this."

Sometimes in church, especially in the Catholic denomination, people are taught they have to address God a certain way or speak a certain way, but that is not true. God is just an amazing, loving, accepting Father who wants us to talk to

Him and He wants to talk to us too. I used to think that if I was uncomfortable then it wasn't good, but that is not right thinking; our flesh will try and keep us from connecting with God in the Spirit and it will feel uncomfortable to our flesh. Romans 8:7 tells us that our carnal mind is at enmity [actively opposed or hostile] with God. Romans 8:13 says, "For if you live according to the flesh, you will die; but if by the Spirit you put to death the misdeeds of the body, you will live." Beloved, put to death your need for comfort in your flesh and be obedient to the call of God to govern [move in the authority God has given you] your life, through the spoken word in prayer and declaration.

Below I present to you 15 steps to healing and deliverance from abuse, terror, and digestive problems. Please read through ALL the steps, making sure to agree with everything written with a full understanding of what you are praying, BEFORE beginning (a full prayer is re-capped at the end).

1. Make a declaration in prayer of your surrender to Jesus and your trust in God for deliverance and protection. For example, you might pray something like: "I confess that you Jesus, are my Lord and Saviour and I commit myself to you. I accept that you are my mediator and intercessor before Father God. Lord God, fill me with your Spirit and resurrection power; in faith I believe that you are working on my behalf and protecting me." Make sure to connect with God and discern His presence and heart through the Spirit. Prayer should be a two-way conversation with God when you, at the very least, sense His heart (you know when He is convicting you and trying to draw something out of you and when He is pleased, and you've said enough).

2. If you have committed any sin of abuse against anyone else, repent and confess it to God, then ask Him for forgiveness. Since we are not always aware of our own

APPENDIX A

behaviors and how they affect people, ask God to reveal if you are guilty of this sin in any way. Make a declaration that you receive His forgiveness according to 1 John 1:9, "If we confess our sins, he is faithful and just and will forgive us our sins and purify us from all unrighteousness" (NIV). You might pray something like this: "Lord God, search my heart and show me my guilt. I want to be clean before you. Is there anyone whom I have abused?" Then begin your confession: "Lord God, I confess that I have abused (person's name) when I (name action specifically). I acted out against her/him/them, and I hurt her/him/them grievously. I am deeply sorry, and I repent. Lord God, please forgive me." Discern the Spirit in this place friend. It is possible that God will want you to apologize to the person you hurt and ask for their forgiveness, but NOT always. You must discern His heart. You may also need to forgive yourself to sense His release. Pray something like this: "I choose to forgive myself for my actions and for hurting others in this way and I choose to release myself. I choose also to receive your forgiveness Lord in its fullness and completeness. I choose to allow your forgiveness to set me free and I now exercise my faith and declare that I AM forgiven." If after you have prayed this and you still feel convicted that you should apologize to the person directly, do it.

Okay, so now that we have gotten that out of the way, we can move on to your inner healing from the abuse committed against you.

3. Ask Holy Spirit to remind you when you may have experienced extreme fear and terror. Perhaps you know of a time, but Holy Spirit may reveal more to you. Holy Spirit has shown me that it is very often abuse, so ask Him to help you identify any abuse that you have suffered and face it.

Terror may have also found a way in by watching horror movies or participating in Hallowe'en. If this is the case, simply repent for these actions, allowing yourself to be entertained by fear and for "having fun" and partnering with demons. Follow the same pattern from above: confess, repent, say you're sorry, ask for forgiveness, forgive yourself, and receive God's forgiveness. Pray something like this: "Lord God, I ask you now to reveal to me every time I experienced terror (have a pen and paper handy just in case you want to write things down). Please show me each time I willingly let terror in and every time I had terror imposed on me by someone else." Now address each instance Holy Spirit revealed to you separately.

4. If you were abused, in Prayer, tell God what happened—specifically. Address the abuse you suffered by different people separately. Pray through one at a time. DO NOT SKIP THIS PART assuming God knows what happened; you need to confess it out of your mouth and get it out of your body and mind. God saw it. He was there. And He wept. He grieves along with you. It is important to understand that God cannot control what everybody does, so if someone hurt you, it is not God's fault. We all have free will; we all have the ability to choose what we want to do or don't want to do. God will try to sway people's hearts to His ways. He will try to intervene, but sometimes the evil desires in people's hearts prevail. Philippians 2:13 tells us that it is God in us Who causes us to want what He wants and to act according to His good purposes, but this applies to those Who have the Holy Spirit living in them only and even then, we do still have free will, so if our hearts aren't pure, if we haven't done the work to "work out our salvation," even a Christian can make a bad choice. What does it mean to "work out our salvation?" It means to

APPENDIX A

participate in our own healing by inviting Holy Spirit to search our hearts and show us what we need to do to live holy lives and to be healed. What are those things that we need to give to Jesus? Those hurts. Those wounds and those moments of loss, fear, disappointment, and trauma. It means to allow God to transform our hearts, desires, thoughts, and actions and conform them to His desires, thoughts, and actions so that we begin to be more and more like Him. Eventually our "knee jerk" reactions won't be driven by fear or self-preservation anymore, but by the Spirit.

5. Tell God how the abuser made you feel—every single feeling you can identify, speak it out and tell God about it. Make sure to include fear and terror. Allow yourself to feel what you feel. If you can't seem to do this, you will need to identify why you won't allow yourself to feel. I might venture a guess that it has to do with learning at a very young age that it wasn't safe to feel or to express your feelings. Or that in order to survive, you had to ignore your feelings—to push them down, just to get by and carry on with life. Perhaps there is so much pain there, that you think you can't possibly survive feeling what you feel. But I assure you, God won't allow you to break completely. If you're afraid to feel what you feel, tell God about it. Ask Him to help you. Give your fear to God and trust Him to open the "faucet" of your emotions just enough to bring healing gradually, bit by bit. Hold your hands out in front of you and imagine that it is a bowl. Close your eyes and as you speak out every feeling that you feel, in your mind's eye, "see" yourself putting those emotions into the bowl. This is an exercise to identify your feelings (rather than stuffing them) and to get them out of your body; toxic emotions will cause illness in your physical body. After you

POSITION YOURSELF FOR HEALING

put all your emotions and feelings into the bowl, in your mind's eye, see Jesus standing before you and give the bowl to Jesus. If you can't see Jesus in your mind's eye, take a minute to think about what He might look like, and draw a picture in your mind's eye of Him. If you can, in your mind's eye, notice what Jesus does with the bowl after you give it to Him. Jesus will use these pictures in your mind to communicate with you.

6. Confess your need for healing; ask God to heal your heart and apply the blood of Jesus over your heart

7. Ask God to show you where He was at the time of the trauma. With your eyes closed, He may give you pictures on your mind to show you where He actually was in the Spirit. The Holy Spirit showed me a moment of trauma when I was a baby. When in prayer, I had a picture in my mind of me as an infant, in a cradle, crying uncontrollably and no one was coming. The prayer partner with me asked Jesus to show me where He was in the room. Instantly the image in my mind changed and I saw Jesus standing over me, right beside the cradle and I saw Him put His hand on me to comfort me. I also saw my crying, completely stop. In that moment, the trauma that I felt, went away, and my memory and emotions were completely healed. The principle here is, Jesus embodies perfect love, and the scriptures say, "Perfect love drives out fear" (1 John 4:18). So, when Jesus shows up, perfect love shows up and fear is driven away bringing peace to traumatic situations.

8. Ask God whatever questions you need to ask. Examples might be: "Where were you God?" "Did you forget about me?" "Why did this happen?" Nothing is off limits here; God can handle your pain, doubt and even anger. If you are

APPENDIX A

angry at God, you need to confess that. If you are blaming God, you also need to confess that and ask for forgiveness.

9. Forgive the ones who hurt you. Understand that Jesus died for everyone, even the ones that hurt us. This means that the sin that person committed against you is forgiven by God the moment they confess and repent to Him. Understand that their sin is not any less forgivable than your own. We cannot expect mercy for ourselves, but then expect others to get what they deserve. Mercy is for everyone. Bring your heart into agreement and speak out, "I choose to forgive (name) for (what they did) and for making me feel (how you felt because of their actions against you)." If you need to, say it a few times, until you REALY mean it. If you're not sure you really mean it, tell God. Tell Him, "I want to do this" or "help me to want to do this." Then say it again, until you can get it out and mean it. Ask God to help you see that person's heart and what they have been through, possibly giving you some understanding as to why they would act the way they did. This may help you to feel some compassion for them so you can forgive.

10. Confess ancestral sin and ask for forgiveness. Abuse runs in families; it is something that is passed down through the generations, so we will need to confess abuse on behalf of our ancestors. It doesn't hurt to "over-confess" or to confess something that may not have happened. Don't let family loyalty get in the way of this. You are not dishonouring your parents by confessing a sin they may have committed. You're not talking to anyone else but God about it and God already knows. But don't think that if God already knows, you don't have to confess it. We do. God wants us to agree with Him and confess it all.

11. Make a declaration out loud that you receive and accept God's forgiveness for your family and yourself and thank Him for it.

12. Make positive declarations from the Word about Who you are in Christ. An example may be: "I thank you God that you have redeemed me and paid the price for my sin, that because my life is now hidden in Christ, I am the righteousness of God. I thank you God that your blood covers me and makes me whole. I thank you God that in you I am a brand-new creation; the old me is completely gone and the new me has come. I thank you God that I am your child, and you are a good, good Father. Thank you that you don't forget about me, but your eye is on me, and you see everything about me, and you still love me completely, just the way I am. Even when I don't do things perfectly because I am still a work in progress, you still love me and see me as righteous. Thank you that everything that concerns me, concerns you, and you take up my cause and you fight for me. You defend me and protect me. Thank you, God, that because your Spirit lives in me, I can't help but do what's right. Thank you that your Spirit in me, guides me, and directs every step I take. Thank you that I am no longer enslaved to sin, but I am free to be like you and I am free to do what's right. Thank you, God, that I am now a co-heir with Christ, and I share in Jesus' inheritance with all the saints (those who accept you). Thank you, God, that I am a saint, not because of what I've done but because of what Jesus has done for me. Thank you that in you, I am the light of the world. I have much to offer those around me. I am full of creative solutions for the world's problems. Thank you that in you, I am chosen and appointed by Christ to bear much fruit for the kingdom; fruit that lasts. Thank you that I am set apart as holy and I

APPENDIX A

am a sent one, sent to others to be a blessing to them. I thank you Jesus that you have given me all authority over the enemy, and nothing shall by any means hurt me." See scriptures: Matthew 5:13-14, John 1:12, John 15:1&5, John 15:15&16, Romans 6:18, Romans 6:22, Romans 8:14&15, Gal. 3:26,28 & 4:6-7, Romans 8:17, 1 Cor. 3:16 & 6:17&19 & 12:27, Eph. 5:20, 2 Cor. 5:17-19 and more about who we become when our lives are "in Christ." To understand what it means to be "in Christ" I have always thought of a brand-new Barbie doll in the box (it's simple and kind of weird but it's a good visual). The box is Christ, and I am inside of Him. Of course, He is an invisible barrier between me and the world but is still there and VERY much real. My life now exists in Christ only, protected and shielded by Him. Interestingly enough though, He is also in me. So, we become like one of those Dutch, doll sets where the dolls are nested inside one another. On the outside is Christ, then me, then Christ again which is perfect because then He protects me on the outside and on the inside.

To achieve complete healing, we need to continue to deliverance from bad spirits. When a wound is deep and/or a sin against you has been repetitive or has been repeated by generations before you (ancestors have committed the same sin against others, it is a pattern of sin in your family), a demon can attach itself to the perpetrator and be passed on to you through the sin, or through the bloodline of the family and influence behaviors; even when you don't want to do something, you find yourself doing it and are unable to stop (alcoholism or addiction of any kind and abuse are good examples). This is when the next steps should be walked through, but I would suggest having some prayer support (another person) with you physically.

13. Renounce and bind spirits/demons that might be attached to what happened. For instance, fear is a spirit (2 Timothy

1:7 says, "For God has not given us a spirit of fear, but of power and of love and of a sound mind" [some versions say self-control].) (Note: we're not talking about the "fear of the Lord;" that is different.) So, I would pray out loud, "I renounce the spirit of (abuse, fear and terror) and I bind them now, in Jesus' name." You can adapt this to whatever other spirit may be attached; for instance, if the abuse was sexual, I would also renounce and bind a spirit of lust, perversion and perhaps incest, if applicable, but you will also need to confess your own sins of lust, perversion, etc. first. Make sure you are bringing your heart into agreement with what you are praying and not just saying empty words and I say to pray "out loud" because bad spirits cannot read your mind; they cannot hear you renounce them or bind them unless you say it out loud and it is imperative that they hear your declaration against them. This is to let them know and God know that your time of co-operating with them or putting up with them or allowing them to influence you (knowingly or unknowingly) is over. You are exercising your free will to cut off any fellowship with bad spirits.

Matthew 16:19 says, "And I will give you the keys of the kingdom of heaven, and whatever you bind on earth will be bound in heaven, and whatever you loose on earth will be loosed in heaven" (NKJV). To explain this verse a bit, think about earth as the natural realm that we can see, and think about heaven as the invisible atmosphere all around us. Heaven is not a place up high in the sky; it exists in the invisible realm, an alternate reality, right where we are now. The verse could be paraphrased, "whatever you bind in the visible realm will also be bound in the invisible realm." The spirits live and operate from the invisible

APPENDIX A

realm but are bound by the sound of our voice in the visible realm.

To bind something means for example to wrap it up in duct tape or heavy chains so it can't move or operate and/or to put a gag in its mouth so it can't speak anymore. When you bind a spirit, you cut off its power and influence over you. Look at Mark 3:27. The context is talking about Satan being divided against himself. Verse 26 says, "And if Satan has risen up against himself, and is divided, he cannot stand, but has an end" (Mark 3:26 NKJV). Verse 27 gives us a clue about binding spirits. It says, "No one can enter a strong man's house and plunder his goods, unless he first binds the strong man. And then he will plunder his house" (Mark 3:27 NKJV). (Note: In demonology, a "strong man" is a demon leading a team of related demons. Demons are organized in a hierarchy just as angels are. See Ephesians 6:12.)

In the next step we will ask God to deliver us from bad spirits, and we will tell them to "go," but if we want God to plunder our house (clean out our souls and deliver us from bad spirits) without drama, we should first bind them. This is nothing to be afraid of; God has given all believers authority over bad spirits. Because of God's Spirit in us, they are like ants to us. Luke 10:19 says, (Jesus is speaking) "Behold, I give you the authority to trample on serpents and scorpions, and over ALL the power of the enemy, and NOTHING shall by any means hurt you" (NKJV, emphasis mine).

14. Ask Jesus to completely deliver you from the spirits that you have renounced in the previous step. Tell it to "go" out loud. Pray: "I confess that you Jesus, are my Lord and Saviour and I commit myself to you. I accept that you are

my mediator and intercessor before Father God. Lord God, fill me with your Spirit and resurrection power; in faith I believe that you are working on my behalf and protecting me. I ask you now Lord Jesus that you would deliver me from the spirit of abuse, fear, and terror. I completely renounce all forms of abuse, and I renounce all fear and terror in Jesus' name. I bind the spirit of abuse, fear, and terror now in Jesus' name and forbid any action against me. I bind and break their power now and I command the spirits of abuse, fear, and terror to leave me NOW, in Jesus' name, Go! Now! In Jesus' name (if you feel to repeat that last part, do it. If you feel to renounce, bind and cast out specific fear spirits, like the fear of abuse or the fear of backlash, do it.)." Say it like you mean it and believe **in** faith... KNOW (don't doubt) that you have authority over it. Tell it to "Go!" as many times as you want. Don't worry or fret about it. Believe in faith, God is on your side, and He is working it out. This is not happening in your power but in God's. You may cough or you may yawn—this can be a physical manifestation of something spiritual leaving your body, but it doesn't necessarily have to happen or always happen. Simply remain in faith that what you are asking God to do and what you are taking authority over, is going.

Look at the miracle in Matthew 8:5-13. A centurion comes to Jesus in need of healing for his servant who is at home paralyzed. Jesus offers to go to his house, but the centurion basically says, "no, that's not necessary. I know you have authority over this illness, and I understand authority. I tell my servant to do something, and he does it. Just say the word Jesus, right here, right now and my servant will be healed" (paraphrased). We have the same authority over spirits AND over the sicknesses and illnesses they cause.

15. Ask Holy Spirit to fill you completely so all the "gaps" left are filled with Him.

16. Plead and declare the blood of Jesus over every part of your digestive tract, mouth, esophagus, esophageal sphincter, stomach, small intestine, large intestine, colon, kidneys, bladder, bowel, etc. for complete healing. Rather than asking for healing, DECLARE it to be so with authority. Healing comes everywhere the blood of Jesus touches. By His stripes (and the blood shed from them), we are healed. Spend time telling Jesus, God, and Holy Spirit how much you love them and appreciate them and sing His praises.

APPENDIX B

Healing Scriptures

Psalm 23
Exodus 15:26
Exodus 23:24-26
Romans 10:17
Isaiah 55:6-12
2 Samuel 22
Psalm 103:1-4
Psalm 91
Psalm 121
Psalm 107:19-20
Psalm 34:19
Psalm 118:14-17
Isaiah 53:1-6
Matthew 13:10-15
Mark 11:22-25
Matthew 8:14-17
Isaiah 54:4-10, 13-17
Isaiah 57:18-19
1 Peter 2:21-25
Proverbs 4:20-27
Proverbs 3:5-8
Proverbs 12:28
Proverbs 16:24
Mark 5:25-34
Mark 9:23
Romans 8:31-39
Psalm 41:1-3

1 Corinthians 1:30
2 Corinthians 5:21
Matthew 5:17-18
John 14:27
John 16:33
1 John 4:1-4
John 10:7-10
John 6:63
1 John 5:1-5
1 John 5:18
Colossians 2:9-10
Colossians 2:13-15
Galatians 3:13-14
Romans 8:1-2
Romans 8:11-15
Romans 5:17
Romans 6:10-14
2 Corinthians 5:17
Colossians 1:13-14
Colossians 1:21-22
James 4:7-10
James 1:17-25
John 14:12-14
Romans 12:1-2
Matthew 16:13-19
Revelation 12:11

ABOUT THE AUTHOR

Barbara is an author, spiritual mentor, and pastor at heart, who has been passionately pursuing Jesus and the Kingdom of God for more than 30 years. With the Lord moving powerfully in her, she has experienced victory over barrenness, physical issues, and emotional strongholds that have threatened to control her life and is now imparting the same to others. Her passion is to share the love and power of God to heal from the inside out, through prayer and deliverance with all who will receive.

With a solid foundation on the Bible, the infallible Word of God and established fruit in her life, Barbara moves in the gifts of healing, discerning of spirits and prophecy for the encouragement of all and for the equipping of the Saints.

Barbara is aligned with a group of Apostolic leaders in Southwestern, Ontario, Patricia King's Women in Ministry Network, Apostle Barbara J. Yoder's Global Legacy Partners Network and is studying under Apostle Dr. Douglas E. Carr for credentials in deliverance ministry.

Barbara's other books are available on Amazon and www.destined.international:

1. *Key to Fertility: Re-Writing Your Stories for Success in Conceiving and Birthing Babies*
2. *Barren No More: Prayer Strategy for Every Believer Experiencing Fertility Challenges*
3. *Sweet Sorrow - Releasing Your Son to His Bride: What Every Mother Needs to Know*
4. *Slaying the Giant of Self-Publishing*

Barbara is the founder of Destined International Kingdom Ministries. Go to www.destined.international to read her blog, purchase her other books, and watch for upcoming opportunities to connect. Barbara is also the founder and Creative Director at ROOTED Publishing. Go to www.rootedpublishing.com to read her blog about writing and hire her to help you publish your next book.

Suggested Reading:

Victory Over the Darkness by Neil T. Anderson
Prayers that Rout Demons by John Eckhardt

BIBLIOGRAPHY

Anderson, Neil T. *Helping Others Find Freedom in Christ*. Ventura, California: Regal Books, 1995.

Anderson, Neil T. *Victory Over the Darkness*. Bloomington, Minnesota: Bethany House, 2014.

Bevere, John. *The Holy Spirit – An Introduction*. Palmer Lake, Colorado: Messenger International, 2013.

Carr, Dr. Douglas E. *Free Indeed from Root Spirits*. Sturgis, Michigan: Doug Carr Freedom Ministry, 2014.

Carr, Dr. Douglas E. *Patterns of Perversity: Freedom from Iniquity*. Sturgis, Michigan: Doug Carr Freedom Ministry, 2022.

Dedmon, Kevin. The Ultimate Treasure Hunt. Shippensburg, Pennsylvania: Destiny Image Publishers, 2007.

Idleman, Kyle. *gods At War: The Battle for Your Heart That Will Define Your Life*. Louisville, Kentucky: City on a Hill Productions, 2012. DVD.

Malone, Dr. Henry. *Shadow Boxing*. Lewisville, Texas: Vision Life, 1999.

Martin, Walter. *The Kingdom of the Cults.* Minneapolis, Minnesota: Bethany House Publishers, 1965, 1977, 1985, 1997.

Pierce, Chuck D. *God's Now Time for Your Life*. Ventura, California: Regal Books, 2005.

Sheets, Dutch. *Authority in Prayer: Praying with Power and Purpose*. Minneapolis, Minnesota: Bethany House, 2006.

Sheets, Dutch. *Intercessory Prayer*. Ventura, California: Regal Books, 1996.

Ward Heflin, Ruth. *Glory: Experiencing the Atmosphere of Heaven*. Hagerstown, Maryland: McDougal Publishing, 1990, 2000.

Wilson, Darren. *Father of Lights*. WP Films, 2012. DVD.

www.ingramcontent.com/pod-product-compliance
Lightning Source LLC
Chambersburg PA
CBHW070650120526
44590CB00013BA/894